How to Be Human*

*Though an Economist

How to Be Human*

Deirdre McCloskey

*Though an Economist

Ann Arbor

The University of Michigan Press

2003   2002   2001   2000   4   3   2   1

A CIP catalog record for this book is available from the British Library.

Library of Congress Cataloging-in-Publication Data

McCloskey, Deirdre N.
    How to be human—though an economist / Deirdre McCloskey.
        p. cm.
    Includes bibliographical references and index.
    ISBN 0-472-09744-X (acid-free paper) — ISBN 0-472-06744-3 (pbk. :
acid-free paper)
        1. Economics—Philosophy.   I. Title.
HB72 .M33   2000
330.1—dc21   00-009465

Preface

The implied reader of these little pieces is an economist, or at least someone who cares about economics, open to stretching its somber rules. She is someone who views economics as a good thing but is uneasy about its present state. The reception I got when the pieces were first published during the 1990s in journals and newspapers suggests that many economists are not really, as we Episcopalians call ourselves, the Frozen Chosen. Maybe I can persuade a few of the frozen to move closer to the fire.

The implied writer is a little sassy. Many of the pieces come from my regular column in the *Eastern Economic Journal* (1992–99), others from similar occasions in which my opinion, for its little worth, was being solicited for a wider audience—occasional columns in *Scientific American,* for example, or the *Times Higher Education Supplement* or the *Chicago Tribune.* They are, so to speak, editorials in the Newspaper of the Field, a newspaper which more than Ph.D.'s in economics read.

Light reading. I don't want to give anyone a headache. I want you to be amused. I try not to bore my friends.

But I ask you to realize that, sassy or not, I am serious and that the Dismal Science is in trouble. "I would not willingly Laugh," said Addison, the first voice in English of a bourgeois virtue, "but in order to Instruct." My instruction? That economists can bring themselves back to scientific and humanistic values and be human scientists, if they will only try.

Contents

Rule 1
Be Who You Are,
Even if an Economist

Some News That Will at Least Not Bore You

The piece appeared in the fall of 1995 as one of my columns in the
Eastern Economic Journal, *edited at the time by Hal Hochman. Hal*
tells me he hesitated before publishing it—not long, for he's a prince.
Jenifer Gamber, who has edited all my Eastern *pieces, is the princess.*
It was reprinted a few months later in the magazine for literary
intellectuals called Lingua Franca. *A friend of mine in English at*
UCLA, Kate Hayles, told me that at the time she thought it was a
spoof. (It's that way in English departments, postmodern irony upon
irony; in fact, the same issue of the magazine contained what became
a notorious spoof of postmodernism itself.) Said Kate to a graduate
student, "If Don McCloskey has changed his gender, I'll turn in my
Ph.D." To which the graduate student replied, "Can I have it?" A
shorter version appeared in July 1996 in Harper's *under the headline*
"Economist Drops a Bomb."

Michel Montaigne, the inventor of the personal essay, wrote in 1580 that,
regardless of what his official subject might be, "it is myself that I portray." The same could be said of the most "objective" of the economist's

scholarly productions. You write a paper filled with math and statistics about the labor market, but if anyone is going to read and use it you have to portray yourself skillfully—as someone worth listening to, someone who knows her stuff. You tell about yourself in many rhetorical ways. Bob Solow, the most graceful writer in our field, indicates with every other sentence: "I have command of a classic prose style, and here I am applying it to the dismal science. What a gas. Let's not get too pompous about this stuff."

That's my excuse for making a highly personal revelation here. We may be economists, but we are also human beings, and the two have something to do with each other (believe me, they do). Let's not get too pompous about this stuff. It's a fact that there is not a single openly (out, avowed) homosexual among the leaders of the economics profession. This is strange, one of those rare cases in which Student's-*t* is applicable. Whatever you think of the Kinsey percentage of men or women with homosexual experiences (the old 10 percent figure) or the more recent, lower figures, there must be hundreds upon hundreds of gays and lesbians in our field. Yet no prominent male economist of my acquaintance will answer to the question "Are you married?" with, "No, but my boyfriend and I have been together quite a while." Such a statement would bring the talk over a beer after a seminar to an embarrassed halt.

Straight people and some homosexuals will reply: "What does it matter? It doesn't effect how you take a first derivative," which is true. But the silence oppresses even when it does not intend to (and often enough it does intend to). Homosexuality is not about sex. It is about love and family. The "don't ask, don't tell" policy that straights want to impose on homosexuals ("Jeez, don't talk about your *sex* life!") means that gays and lesbians can't mention who they love in the way that straight people do every day (exercise: spend a day trying never to imply your affectional preference; you'll find it impossible). If every single example of a family in the new home economics is taken from a vision of the heterosexual couple with 1.3 children, someone is being left out. If the sight of two men holding hands in the hallway outside the Econ Department brings snickers to the lips of colleagues, someone is being stuffed back into a closet, the door slammed.

So is my "revelation" that I am gay? No. Unfortunately, it's rarer. I wish I had as large a community to relate to. The gay community is not out in economics, but post-Stonewall it is out in the world and widely respected. (That Western art would barely exist without the gay contribution and women's literature would be impoverished without the lesbian contribution and philosophy would never have gotten started without Socrates and his young men has always seemed to me to be a strong argument for respect, though not the core one, which is economic: people engaged in Pareto optimal exchanges among themselves should be respected and left alone, laissez-faire).

No, I am not gay. I am cross-gendered, and at age 53, having been a good soldier for over four decades, I am doing something about it. Not to startle you, but I am becoming a woman economist.

That's not precise. You can't in essence "become" a 100 percent woman or man if you don't start right. XY chromosomes cannot be changed into XX. More important, no one is in essence a woman without having had a girlhood and other female experiences and similarly for men and boys (it turns out, surprisingly, that there are about as many female to male gender crossers as male to female: I have met a San Francisco policeman who some years ago was a San Francisco policewoman). But we do not function in science or life with essences or 100 percents. If we did, it would be impossible for anyone to become a New Yorker who had not been born there or to become an economist who did not grow up with it (Bob Gordon and Larry Summers come to mind as growing up with it). To the poor extent I can manage it—everything I can think of costs about as much as a Mercedes, and at that price I'm buying—I'm going to become a tall and ugly but indubitably female economist. I go full-time in late November 1995. My legal name is already changed to Deirdre (DEER-druh; it's supposed to mean "wanderer" in Old Irish; *Donald* means "world ruler").

Why would anyone do such a thing? The "why" question has the usual answer we give in economics: stop asking it, since you might as well ask people why they like chocolate ice cream. Asking why suggests that you want to question the chocolate choice. That's the politics in the economist's otherwise indefensible lack of curiosity about psychology. For a couple of decades homosexuals have been exempted from the why question and its implication that there may be a policy to stop it. (Just say no. Resist sin. Try electroshock therapy. Go to jail. Get murdered.) "Understanding" isn't the issue here; toleration is. We're not talking about a fixed point theorem (or in my own case a non–fixed point theorem); we're talking about sympathy or moral sentiment (I take the phrase from Adam Smith and think women will see the point quicker than men.) People do not become women, whether the usual way or the way I intend, chiefly because of some benefit, no more than people become New Yorkers or economists chiefly because of some benefit. Cost and benefit is relevant but not very. I have realized that I have always felt more naturally a woman than a man, despite my inconvenient plumbing and my normally macho behavior. Trying it out carefully, under medical supervision (your local medical monopoly, I mean), with much advice, I am stunned by how well it fits me.

It isn't about sex, if you mean sexual pleasure or the sexual object. It's about identity, the subject. Nor is it about love, affectional preference. It's not about who you love but who you are. I've come to realize that economics is weak in thinking about subjects and identity. We're good at budget constraints, poor at accounts of who we are. That lack of psychological curiosity.

I'm not ashamed of changing into a woman. For one thing I have never regarded being a woman as shameful. For another the gender boundaries of our society should not be any more uncrossable than international boundaries or disciplinary boundaries. I was talking to myself the other day (I do that a lot: hmm) and declared: "It's odd that *more* people don't do this. After all, our ancestors changed nationality on a massive scale, and that's as fundamental as gender." When I realized what I was saying I laughed and replied: You don't get it, do you Deirdre? Most people don't *want* to change their gender! "Hmm. Oh. I hadn't thought of that. Odd."

Nor, as you can see, am I willing to try to hide it, moving to Spokane anonymously and becoming a secretary in a grain elevator. One can hardly hide a new gender from old acquaintances, and if I want to continue the mad career of D. N. McCloskey as teacher and writer I have to come out. Unsatisfactory as it is—you will always know me as Formerly Don—it's the best I can do with the rest of my life. Montaigne also said, "The greatest thing in the world is to know how to be one's own." Right.

Any among you who is inclined to view this as an ethical question has my respect. Economists do not pay enough heed to ethical questions, hiding behind the idiot's philosophy of normative/positive. But anyone who wants to be consistent and takes *ethical* to mean "following strictly the law of Deuteronomy 22:5, 'The woman shall not wear that which pertains unto a man, neither shall a man put on a woman's garment; for all that do so are abominations unto the Lord thy God'" had better be a strictly practicing orthodox Jew. Six verses later the Lord God says: "Thou shalt not wear a garment of divers sorts, as of woolen and linen together. Thou shalt make thee fringes upon the four quarters of thy vesture, wherewith thou coverest thyself," among 613 such specifications. If you believe with Jerry Falwell that quoting the Bible (in his case misquoting it: I suppose the guy doesn't even know Hebrew) settles ethical questions once and for all, I suggest you get serious and join the orthodox in Brooklyn.

If you believe, to take the opposite political pole, that it's a feminist issue, you also have my respect. But if you are "uncomfortable" with my choice, because in choosing to be a woman you think without inquiry that I am pursuing some notion of womanhood oppressive to born women, I have a lot to say to you. I'd ask, for one thing, who are you, dear, to be uncomfortable with another human being's harmless choice? Should I be uncomfortable with your New Yorkness, which you have also chosen, right down to your little black dress? As an economist who uses a utilitarian or laissez-faire line of reason in your science are you being consistent in attacking another's choice? If those questions don't make you uncomfortable with your talk about being uncomfortable, I'd go on to point out that I note your conventionally feminine gestures. You are complaining about me adopting "feminine" gestures and clothing and the like from safely within your own feminine gestures and clothing and the like. (If you can't see that you sit like a woman in our culture at least you can see that you dress like one.) I don't get to do it because I wasn't born into it, right? Where's the essentialism, the assignment of social roles to women by birth—is it in my life or in your argument? And if *those* questions don't give you pause, I'd turn to noting that I have no plan to adopt 1950s stereotypically feminine behavior, pillbox hats and white gloves and the home life of "Leave It to Beaver." I plan to be a strong woman, like many I know in economics, like Barbara or Marty or Elyce or Robin, and to use my position to advance the cause of women in the field. One thing we women need to do is to stop crippling each other by being uncomfortable with each other's lives, from mommy track to butch dyke. The men don't do it, I can tell you from the inside.

One real ethical question, beyond an inconsistent fundamentalism or an inconsistent (that is, second-wave) feminism, is how it affects other people. I love my wife of 30 years and my two grown children, for whom this has been hard, very hard: they thought they knew Donald. I can only say that I also thought I knew Donald and was equally startled when I figured out he was in fact Deirdre (so to speak: I'm not saying this literally; I've been thinking about this since I was age 11; but I didn't feel "like a woman in a man's body"). What they and I and you need is what is lacking in an economic science that studies *The Wealth of Nations* but ignores *The Theory of Moral Sentiments:* love.

My university, my community, my friends in economics and elsewhere, have been wonderfully loving. Saint Paul wrote that love does not vaunteth itself, is not puffed up: love is genial and amused, much as Adam Smith was in his life, a character we economists lost with Jeremy Bentham and his humorless ways. But I find that even most economists do not really follow the loveless and utilitarian model of their science.

I do not regret having been a man and in seminars, often enough, a tough-guy SOB (well, come to think of it, I do regret some of that, and so should all you guys). But I must say I vastly prefer being a woman (on grounds of identity, not utility: hair and pantyhose alone would drive any rational Maxine U back to being Max). I am going to try not to bring over too many of my nastier male habits to the new role. The way women economists of my acquaintance have reacted has been wonderful, and I'm starting to grasp what's special about female friendships.

It makes you wonder whether an economics that ignores love and friendship might be a little nuts. I'm going to be interested to see how all this alters my thinking about economics.

Or I could have asked Claudia Goldin or Francine Blau or Nancy Folbre. That would have been simpler.

It Helps to Be a Don
if You're Going to Be
a Deirdre

An editor at the (London) Times Higher Education Supplement *(August 23, 1996, during my year first year as Deirdre) made up the brilliant title. In British English, you know,* don *means "college teacher."*

If you are going to change your gender, it would be smart to get into academic life first. This is especially so, I think, in Britain, whose record on protection of gender-crossers is the worst in the non-Islamic world (and Turkey's is better).

I know quite a few people in academic life who have "transitioned," as the jargon has it, without much trouble. An academic librarian in Australia, a geophysicist at McGill, a chemist at Tennessee, a sociologist at Berkeley, a historian at Washington, a biochemist at Stanford, an administrator at Oxford. No problem. I have searched them out for reassurance that it can be done. But their stories need not have been so good. I know a math professor in a small college in Arkansas who has been mercilessly persecuted by her administration. What does seem to be true is that the more sophisticated the place the smoother the road. Hardly surprising.

My experience has been excellent, at the University of Iowa and as a visiting professor this year at Erasmus University of Rotterdam. At Iowa, back when I was very uncertain that things would work, I came out to the dean of my business school, Gary Fethke. He is like me a free-market economist. We have known each other a long time. His response, after sitting for a moment in slack-jawed amazement, was a stand-up comic routine: "Oh, thank God! I thought you were going to confess to converting to *socialism*." (Relieved laughter: he was going to react as a friend.) "This is great for our affirmative action program: one fewer man, one more woman." (More laughter.) "And wait a minute! I can cut your salary now to two-thirds of the male level!" (Not so funny). And then seriously: "That's a strange thing to do. How can I help?" And he did. The administration at Iowa, right up to the governor of the state, took the view that it was a private decision with no relevance to my employment—except that I might want to get involved some in women's studies and gender studies, as in fact I do and have.

At Erasmus the reaction was even more relaxed. My friend Arjo Klamer, the professor at Erasmus who was arranging for my visit there, reckoned a couple of months before I arrived that he had better tell the administration that the "Donald" they were hiring was in fact "Deirdre." He went to the rector.

Klamer: Remember that Donald McCloskey coming in January for the
    Tinbergen chair? Well, it will be Deirdre, not Donald.
Rector: Fine. I understand. Why are you telling me this?
*Klamer [thinking the rector could not possibly have understood; perhaps
    he did not know that* Deirdre *is a woman's name]:* I mean that "he"
    is coming as "she." She is changing her gender.
Rector: Yes, I understand. To repeat: Why are you telling me this?

I could have arrived in Rotterdam as a palomino horse, and the only question would have been does the horse have the same curriculum vitae? Can the horse lecture? Fine. Why are you telling me this?

Nothing's perfect (though the Dutch reaction approaches it). My male colleagues are, I think, uneasy. After all, it's their tribe I am deserting. I am still waiting for some of my British ex-pals to say hello now that I am here in the Netherlands across the Channel. I have been surprised by who has taken me up and who has let me down, the surprises of any big change in life. Arjo and Joel and Richard and Gary: wow. Bob and Doug and Jeremy and David: ouch. The women have been welcoming, especially after I took the step of having the operation. After that they knew for sure there was no male leer behind the scene.

I hear of doubts. (The messengers are all men, by the way: it puts them one up to be in the know.) I am told that some radical feminists say I cannot be a real woman. As a libertarian feminist, I cannot understand this. Either essentialism is true, and all we women are ruined; or it is not, in which case a womanly life is socially constructable. I cannot be a 100 percent woman, ever. Even setting chromosomes aside, I cannot have had a woman's life history. I lived 53 years as a male. But we libertarian feminists point out that society does not run on 100 percent. I can live the rest of my life as a 90 percent woman, which puts me within the range of genetic women anyway in superficials like height and hair length.

I hear about a few snickers from some of my male colleagues, especially in economics. How sad for them. Poor boys. But I see no sign, this early, of professional costs. Eventually I expect to pay the cost of being a woman in economics—or else of not being a woman, if you see what I mean; the effects presumably are somewhat the same. But even this odd profession of economics, not the most socially progressive, seems to have taken the change with aplomb. (Historians have had even less trouble, an argument for a historical education.) I was terrified in January 1996 as I went into the executive committee of the American Economic Association. But I needn't have worried. Al and Anne and Stanley adjusted instantly, and were even careful to call me "Deirdre" and "she." In an hour or so the other women and I were exchanging significant glances about the misbehavior of the men.

I cannot know from my own experience what the long run will bring. It helps to be mobile, of course, as it helps to be old and tenured and published and so forth. I do not think my path would have been so easy if I had been an assistant professor. Many gender-crossers come to their realization late, as I did. Biologically, such delay is a poor idea, giving decades of testosterone poisoning to offset. But in emotional and financial ways it proves to be an advantage to have had a man's career.

So take my advice. If you are the 1 in 3,000 who wishes to change your gender, get out of the navy, resign from the local council planning agency, give up your nice position on the assembly line in Coventry, and get yourself a professorship at the local university. Or move to Holland.

A Libertarian Abroad

I lived for the first full year as Deirdre as the Tinbergen Visiting Professor of Economics, Philosophy, and Art and Cultural Studies at Erasmus University of Rotterdam. Wet, cold, tolerant Holland. I wrote a parting column in 1996 for the student newspaper, Quod Novum *(What's New).*

Erasmus has been a lovely place to spend a year. Except for the weather. At year's end I was struggling across the ice one morning toward a man spreading ice-cutting salt. As I got closer, slipping in my heels, he reached out his hand to help me and addressed me in English so: "Professor McCloskey, may I help?" What is lovely is that even the groundskeepers at Erasmus (1) know English well and (2) know about the gender-crossing professor from America and (3) think nothing of it, wishing merely to help.

My colleagues and students and *Rotterdamse* friends have been the same, treating me as a woman colleague or teacher or friend without interference or disapproval or even a second glance. It is a case of "modern" as against "ancient" freedom. Ancient freedom is the right to belong, to be part of what the Erasmus economist Arjo Klamer calls the Citadel. By contrast, modern freedom—a peculiarly eighteenth-century invention—is the right *not* to belong, as in the Caravan freedom of America. In backward villages even in the Netherlands or in ancient Athens you couldn't opt out of the normal ways. In urban Holland, the Randstad, since the 1960s, especially in its universities, you can. I know.

But there's a paradox. In the modern world you are in some ways left alone, able not to belong, to a degree unthinkable in the ancient world. Yet nearly 50 percent of American national income is spent by "we" instead of "I," and the share is even bigger in Holland. A century ago in both countries the figure was more like 10 percent. We moderns are free, but to an unprecedented extent we are children of Father State, which does our buying for us.

Now I don't like this. I am a liberal in the old sense, a "libertarian," even an anarchist. I think the modern state is grotesquely too large. Most of its income, you ought to realize, does not go to the poor. It mainly gives jobs to university graduates, who shuffle paper and boss the rest of the community, with a police force and army to back them up. Plato could not have done better by way of giving jobs to philosopher kings and queens than the Dutch or even the American state.

But the paradox deepens. I am complaining about government, yet here at Erasmus and at home at the (state) University of Iowa I am a state bureaucrat educating more state bureaucrats.

Of course, I have answers, none of them very convincing. For one thing, I would in fact advocate making Erasmus and the University of Iowa private. As they are financed now they amount to a big income transfer from the average taxpayer to the above-average university graduates and their parents. For another, I am no more inconsistent than the socialist employed in a capitalist market or the advocate for compulsory charity through the state who does not give money at church to the poor.

But face up to it, Deirdre. There is some inconsistency. It is a deep one, the inconsistency between ancient and modern freedom. Like you, I want to be a respectable member of a community. As Aristotle said, people are political animals. To put it another way, like you, I need love. The loveliness of my experience at Erasmus is feeling part of a family. Yet I also want modern freedom, as a teacher, writer, woman.

You are familiar with the conflict. You want to be respected among your friends and family. And yet you want autonomy. It is the female principle of connection and the male principle of separation. We are all androgynous in wanting both. The two freedoms interfere with each other. If you make a *res publica,* it has to be paid for by compulsion. If you overstress autonomy, you erode fellow feeling. Likewise in a family or a group of friends.

We humans need both. As the American poet Walt Whitman said: "Do I contradict myself? Very well, I contradict myself." That's the price of living, to be always toggling between the two.

Love or Money

Just after the beginning of my transition, in the Eastern Economic Journal *(winter 1996).*

One more thing about gender, with apologies. Apologies because I don't plan to make this column into an account of the Perils of Deirdre (for that you'll have to read the forthcoming book *Crossings: A Memoir*—a very, very exciting book, I promise, from the University of Chicago Press, soon to be a motion picture [dream on, Deirdre] or at least a TV miniseries). Anyway, the Perils have turned a little boring lately. Tolerant Holland is just the place to "transition," in contrast to the busybody state violence and macho inconsiderateness of the US of A. I'm able to focus for the year on my topic, the history and philosophy of "bourgeois virtue" (another forthcoming book, that—but not I'm afraid a motion picture). The Dutch ease and tolerance reduces the gender task to finding walking shoes in European size 43 and learning the local customs of interaction among women. Believe me, size 43 is rare, so you have to search; and Dutch women are not as effusive as are American women, so you have to turn down the heat. Wonderfully boring, this business of being Mevrouw professor McCloskey.

The one more thing about gender I'd ask you to think about a little is perhaps the most embarrassing word to economists, and especially to men economists: *love.* The word is "about gender" only because women think about it more than men do, so there's a large gender difference in its valuation for the science. I mean think about it, not need: we all need it, but for a thoughtful analysis you'll probably do better talking to your sister than to your brother. Not always, but usually.

By *love* I mean Aristotle's third and highest form of friendship, the part that cannot be explained in turn by interest alone. The other two are friendship for pleasure and friendship for utility (we would now combine them). The third kind is friendship for the friend's own sake. I do not claim that such love is always a good thing. Having been the subject recently of some very bad love by an economist I caused to be hired at the University of Chicago and whom in other ways I loved well, I should know. After all, Hitler loved Germany, but look what his love did to it. People don't always know what's best for their friends. Jack High at George Mason University points out to me that love may have a comparative advantage in small scale rather than in large, a mother's love rather than German nationalism or Russian socialism, two recent excesses of large-scale experiments in love.

The word is embarrassing to a profession dominated by men. A male economist once called economics the "science of conserving on love," by which he meant that society must depend mainly on prudence, not altruism, in the style of Paul Samuelson's prudent maximizer or Gary Becker's loveless "family." It was not always so in the science of scarcity. Economics drops love early, but not as early as you may think. It's customary to think of Adam Smith as a sort of neoconservative in knee britches, but he in fact wrote two books in his lifetime, and only *The Wealth of Nations* celebrated Prudence. The other book, which I think most economists must not have heard of, much less read, was *The Theory of Moral Sentiments*. It celebrated Love. (Well, at least it mentioned it, along with the other four virtues of a complete human personality: in truth the book *celebrated* Temperance.)

Here's what Smith would say about the numero uno, country club Republicanism that elevates Prudence Alone to a philosophical axiom: "though, perhaps, it never gave occasion to more vice than what would have been without it, [it] at least taught that vice, which arose from other causes, to appear with more effrontery, and to avow the corruption of its motives with a profligate audaciousness which had never been heard of before" (*Theory*, Part VII, section ii, chap. 4, para. 13) .

Now, of course, certain low-status groups, such as women and Christians, have long talked about love, urging economists to bring love into their ken and to stop encouraging vice. But economists after Bentham have kept love out of it. Like other men after 1800 (before it was quite different), they think of love as sentimentality, an inability to face facts. They regard talk of love as preaching, in the sense that a teenager regards her Aunt Deirdre's wise suggestions about how to handle boys and homework as preaching. And the economists, of course, preserve their simple view of the word by never ever listening to experts on love, such as anthropologists or theologians (two exceptions are the Dutch economist Arjo Klamer, who does listen to anthropologists on social solidarity, and the American economist Robert Nelson, who does listen to theologians on spiritual love, as in his amazing book *Reaching for Heaven and Earth*).

Keeping love out of it has been fun in a little-boy way. It has been fun to try to find a Prudent reason for everything, from the provision of one's dinner by the butcher or the baker all the way to a genetic predisposition to altruism itself. Running economics without love continues to pose puzzles that economists delight in shocking the bourgeoisie by solving. Hah. You thought it was the love of social solidarity that explained why one businessperson is polite to another, but look at the incentives and notice that in long-term relations people are more polite. Hah. You thought that crime was a matter of passion, but look at how it, too, follows the law of supply. And on and on through *The Theory of Price* and *The Applied Theory of Price* and Steve Landsburg's charming latest. It's like a little boy showing off his magic tricks to a family audience. Cute. Boyish.

But after all, some aunt remarks, when you come right down to it people also do love each other. In the men's way of thinking the aunt's remark is supposed not to matter (and after all a woman said it). The men rely unconsciously on an unproven separation theorem, which says that in a world in which, admittedly and unfortunately, love is a complication, nonetheless you can strictly ignore the love for economic purposes. Prudence doesn't explain everything—this even the average male economist will admit after 5:00 P.M.—but in doing an analysis based on Prudence, he claims, there is no need to bring in the fact of love. "What does it matter?" he'll ask, a little belligerently.

I don't think the separation theorem is correct. So I don't think you can leave out the love. Often you can't do the prudential analysis correctly without love. To use another mathematical analogy, there is sometimes a large cross-partial derivative between the two. Or another, statistical analogy: they are not orthogonal.

For example, what is the effect of aid to dependent children? It depends on the context of love in which the unwed mother finds herself. The state's intervention can make the mother behave like an asocial monad and undermine the love. I repeat that love is not always wonderful, and so here. It may be good social policy to free the mother from her own mothering love, or it may not. But in any case the point is that you can't get the economics of charity even approximately right without including the nonstate, nonorganized charity of loving relations and how it is affected by and affects the aid.

Or take the age gap between men and women (the love I have in mind includes any passion, good or bad—thus the bad passion for a workplace segregated by gender). Yes, yes: I agree, *some* of the gap is explained by human capital. But Claudia Goldin, among other students of the matter, notes that not all of it is explained. Looking back on her work, she remarked: "The [strictly economic] framework had to be bent to fit the historical reality. We economists still don't know how to incorporate changing norms, and I was researching a subject in which norms played a major role" (1998, 107).

The attempt to run social science without love goes way back. One might call the central-puzzle-to-be-amusingly-solved The Hobbes Problem, in honor of the person who was first obsessed by it. The English political philosopher, who with Machiavelli and Mandeville brought the economistic sin into the world, and all our woe, asked essentially this: Will a group of solitary, nasty brutes (short, too) form spontaneously a civil society? We now call his answer the prisoner's dilemma: No, not without the compulsion of a Leviathan state. The economists (with a single-mindedness in the public choice literature that strikes outsiders and especially women outsiders as a trifle cracked) have been pursuing the Problem ever since, trying to show *on a blackboard* that civil society can arise without any love at all. Jim Buchanan, whom I admire extravagantly as an economist (more people like him and Gordon Tullock and Ronald Coase and Armen Alchian, and we'll get back to doing economics instead of fourth-rate nonapplied math), has this one fault, that he simply *loves* the Hobbes Problem.

The Hobbes Problem, a woman economist would say, is off the subject. Like a lot of what economists do these days (Jim has a wonderful collection of essays called *What Should Economists Do?* that makes the point), it's like the drunk searching under the lamppost because the light is better there, even though he lost his keys in the dark. It's off the subject because the subject is actual societies, of *already socialized* men and women, not a collection of unsocialized brutes. The already socialized people have bonds of affection that radically alter how they react to the prisoner's dilemma—thus recent experimental findings or the way (as Klamer has noted) that Washingtonians at a crucial, unposted junction on Connecticut Avenue during rush hour have fallen into a convention of alternating from the left and from the right, even though the right-hand always has the official, Leviathan right-of-way. The change that love makes in the prisoner's dilemma is not simple. It requires analysis. It requires, in fact, economic analysis but an economic analysis of people, not of blackboard phantoms.

If love is such a good thing to have in the analysis, why did it drop out of economics? I have a couple of simpleminded theories. One is that the Devil made us do it. The Devil is Jeremy Bentham, who for reasons I do not understand was able to seize the intellectual agenda in economics and drive love out of it, even though his disciples were sometimes evangelical Christians in love with God's love. Another theory is, to return to my current obsession (I promise . . .), is that, for reasons I now understand a little better, the men have always run economics and since 1800 have fled from a "feminine" love (before 1800, I repeat, no man had trouble with the word or emotion of love: the modern embarrassment is unique in the history I know). Thus socialism, a secularized Christianity at its birth filled with love, becomes in Marx's hands toughened and "masculine" and loveless.

The historical puzzle is why Adam Smith and other men of the eighteenth century had less trouble than their nineteenth-century and twentieth-century followers in keeping love in the analysis. We women can only hope that the men of the twenty-first century will get a little more relaxed about it, in that urbane eighteenth-century way. It will make for better men, and better economics.

Rule 2
Make Your Economics Courageously Part of Your Identity, and Vice Versa

Aunt Deirdre's Letter to a Graduate Student

I received an e-mail from a student in distress, as most graduate students in economics are distressed nowadays, and responded in my Eastern *column in the spring of 1997.*

Dear Mr. Smith,

I got your eloquent e-mail. In the past few years, it may comfort you to know, I've heard from a lot of graduate students with the same question. They ask me because they hear I criticize the establishment in economics. I do. I refer the students to Arjo Klamer and David Colander's book of interviews with graduate students, *The Making of an Economist.* Every intending graduate student should read the book. It's comforting to learn that *everyone* feels that the first year of graduate study in economics is a waste of time, demoralizing and unscholarly. You have to go through it, like marine boot camp or all-nighters in medical internships. Makes a man out of you (the men say—men say a lot of strange things when they get into this man-making mood).

You ask, in a nutshell, Is it worth it? Is this what I signed up for?

You say: I entered economics because I wanted to save the world or make a scientific contribution, or both. I see no signs of either. Help!

First off, you really need to give yourself a pat on the back for asking the question, Is it worth it? If anyone could go through the fourth-rate pure mathematics and the misapplied theoretical statistics that make up the Theory and Econometrics Sequence in modern departments of economics *without* asking The Question he would be a poor candidate for the profession. No person who does not have such doubts is going to be much of an economist.

And, yes, it's that bad. The "theory" is focused on existence proofs, an unscientific obsession taken from the Math Department (not from the Physics or Engineering Departments). It's puerile. Worse, the latest proof becomes obsolete quickly—not because of scientific advances but because of scientific fashion. The half-life of the so-called theory you just suffered through in the first year is five years in macro and a maximum of ten in micro. I, for example, in 1964 suffered through instruction in something called "activity analysis," which they told us (I mean Bob Solow and Paul Samuelson and Robert Dorfman told us, people you wanted to believe) was going to be the way that economics was expressed in the future. A lot like game theory now. So I know how to solve a linear programming problem better than anyone 10 years younger than I am. Why don't younger people know how to solve such problems? Because 5 years after I learned it the fashion of activity analysis was dead as a doornail. The residue is that I still talk in metaphors of "slack variables" and the like, translating marginal productivity into linear algebra for no scientific gain. The only result is that we old folks can communicate with each other over coffee (decaffeinated).

But don't laugh too hard. You yourself know how to translate market analysis into game theory for no scientific gain. Congratulations. Enjoy it while you can; in 10 years it will be as dead as activity analysis, recommended once by all the best authorities.

The econometrics is just as bad. I think you know my views on statistical significance. If you don't, I advise you find out, since they will save you having to remember a lot of pseudoscience beyond the final exam. Econometric estimation is a good thing, using the world's facts—though it does tend to cause lack of interest in collecting the facts, at least in some people who study it. But absent a loss function, econometric testing, as against estimation, is not worth anything at all. Its marginal product is zero. It's a result of a prisoner's dilemma game. It's a slack variable. Really.

So you show good taste by being depressed after the first year. And you show even better taste by going on to worry about the topic of your dissertation, worrying that it, too, might not survive the best question that can be asked of any intellectual production: So What? Is it worth the effort to produce yet another Three Minor Points of Theory in Search of a Scientific Justification? No, it's not. Aunt Deirdre is here to tell you that if you want to be an economic scientist you have to do economic science. And economic science is *not* searching through the hyperspace of assumptions or through the *t*-statistics of 50 different specifications. Economic science is like other sciences: it consists of finding things about the world and explaining them so that they stay explained. There's a new book on German guilt in the Holocaust that meets scientific standards, as do many books in history—before you sneer at the soft little people over in the Department of History you might reflect that when they learn something it stays learned, and history therefore makes the kind of scientific progress that economists should envy. Or go attend some seminars in geology, and notice what sorts of arguments impress the geological scientists. Existence theorems? Statistical significance? Policy conclusions from same? Not.

It's pretty simple to know when you have a dissertation worth doing. It will come from The World, not from The Literature. You will care about it, because (if you are wise) you will have chosen an area that just plain interests you—some part of the economy your family has long been involved in, say, or some fact (for example, corruption in building contractors) that excites your indignation or your love. You will look into explaining it from every conceivable angle, interviewing the people involved, reading history books, talking to sociologists, dreaming up six entirely different mathematical models for it, getting the statistics from dusty archives or from actually going out and watching what happens in the economic world. You will read an essay by C. Wright Mills, the great American sociologist of the 1950s, called "On Intellectual Craftsmanship" in his collection *The Sociological Imagination* (you will find it in the library because you will realize for the first time today that only the most *recent* books are in the electronic catalogue). From this you will learn that being a serious scientist is a way of life, not the following of a formula of Fashionable if Transient Theory + Fashionable if Illogical Econometrics = Publication.

For example, in my dissertation at Harvard in 1970 I studied the question "Was the British steel industry in 1870–1914 more stupid than the industry in the United States?" It turned out that some bits of theory and econometrics just invented could be applied (total factor productivity, for example: that same Robert Solow led the way, although, as I explained in the dissertation, his method had actually been invented in 1933 by a student of Alfred Marshall writing economic history). Why Britain? I had been there as a child; I liked English literature and history; I was lousy at languages (when as a graduate student I went to see David Landes over in the Department of History he threw me out of his office as soon as he realized I did not know German). Why steel? I had second cousins who worked in Gary, Indiana; we would drive past the furnaces in the 1940s; big pieces of capital equipment are exciting, especially to young men. Why stupidity? It's always interesting to ask if capitalism is wise or stupid, and was especially so in the 1960s, because I and a lot of other people were just then shifting politically from the stupid camp to the wise. Why ask such a question? Historians such as Landes had asked it and said, "Yes, the British businessmen were stupid, especially in iron and steel," on what seemed to me unimpressive evidence.

You can do it. You can be an economic scientist. Ask what matters to you. Do it. Find out something about the world. Really find it out. Really explain it, with reference to the great conversation of economics since 1776. Really. (You will find that the rubbish you learned in the first year of graduate school is not much use for real economic science; but you've already figured that out.) I know, I know: fear. "Will I get a job? Will I be a success? Oh, gosh. Maybe I should just take a piece of The Literature and run a new assumption or a new regression."

Please don't. It's not dignified. It's not ethical. It's not true to yourself. It does not advance economic science. (There's even some evidence that it's not prudent. People with the Three-Essays sort of dissertation are finding it harder to get jobs than people with the Look-What-I've-Discovered sort.)

There's an odd little economic argument for doing the right thing and breaking the cycle of nonscientific economics that your supervisors are locked into. It is that by choosing graduate school in the first place you incurred an opportunity cost that it would be irrational now to second-guess. You knew that you would make more money, get more settled employment, if you went to business school or law school. Or just got a job and worked—you are an intelligent and hard-working person. (How do I know? People who go to grad school in economics are, and the one good thing about the first year is that it is an IQ-and-brute-energy test—though teaching and testing you in ancient Greek would have tested the same qualities and would have had more lasting value). So it's not rational to suddenly get silly about job security now. If you had wanted job security, you could have had it. You've revealed that you value glory or goodness more. All right, go get it. The only way to get it is to face up, now, to the unscientific silliness of modern economics and to do the right thing.

But I don't want to rest the argument on prudence alone. I think economists have gotten carried away with prudential arguments, fouling them up because they do not trouble to include the other springs of action. But if you wanted to make another strictly Benthamite argument, it would go like this. You have shown that you have a low rate of time discount by going to grad school in the first place. How did the famous people in economics get famous? By following the literature? No. By doing their own thing. I speak of Ronald Coase and Robert Fogel and John Hicks and nearly every Nobel since the beginning.

But forget about prudence. Be true to yourself, for God's sake. Be brave. I can see you thinking, "She's in a poor position to say that—after all, she has a good job with tenure." All right. But I didn't get it by being a coward. (True, if I *had* been a coward, I would have a *better* job, the tenure I did have at the University of Chicago, actually; but I have to look at myself in the makeup mirror each morning, kids.)

When I was a graduate student I went in to see Richard Caves, a serious and scientific economist among a dwindling number. I asked, Is it worth it? He said, in the words of Scripture, This too will pass. He was right. I went back to work and tried to forget my doubts. Unconsciously, I sidestepped the sillier of the economic fashions some of my classmates became entangled in. But mainly I just went stupidly on, and only later came to realize that finding out things and explaining them is our central scientific duty as economists. I'm not recommending sleepwalking of the sort I engaged in. I'm recommending open-eyed courage.

Please, please, my dear, be brave and remake our splendid subject, the intelligent study of prudence among the other virtues, by bringing it back to science. I'll hire you, if I can. And you'll have a worthwhile life in science.

"Better than Plowing," Says Jim Buchanan

A review of his book of that name in the journal Constitutional Political Economy *in 1993. Buchanan had just won the Nobel Prize.*

Buchanan has here collected autobiographical pieces, with a selection of quotations from other writers which shed light on his thinking. The whole is organized as a rough chronology, with backtracks, from Middle Tennessee State Teachers College (B.A. 1940), through the war in the Pacific, the University of Chicago (1946–1948), a crucial year in the 1950s learning Italian and reading the clear-minded classics of Italian public finance (no Italian imagines the government to be a neat bunch of fellows from Yale), Virginia (1956–68), VPI, and George Mason. The character of the pieces is apparent from their titles: "Early Times," "An Easy War," "Born-again Economist," "Italian Retrospective," "Virginia Political Economy: Some Personal Reflections," "Nobelity," "Threescore Years and Ten."

Naturally, Buchanan tells his story in an economic way. Even his country lyric, to be expected from a Tennessee boy, stresses opportunity cost:

> There are too many forks in the road,
> There are too many forks in the road:
> And I never could learn
> Not to take the wrong turn.
> There are too many forks in the road. (37)

We ought to get together. I have a tune, an agent in Nashville, and another verse:

> There are too many forks in the road,
> There are too many books in a load,

If I heed all their lies
There'll be no Nobel Prize.
There are too many forks in the road.

The first thing an economist wants to know about another one is "Is he smart?" (We ought to rethink the question, which overvalues intellectual abilities that peak at age 19; economists put too little value on being wise or civilized or factual).

Is Buchanan smart? He says he's not, and in one sense I believe him. As he has noted elsewhere, few people are Nature's economists, like Jim's former friend Gordon Tullock or, from my own experience, Steven Cheung or Joseph Reid. Most of us sweat it out, learning to be "worldly philosophers," in Bob Heilbroner's phrase, only after experiencing the world.

Buchanan experienced it early, before graduate school at Chicago. He was for one thing a nonshooting aide to Admirals Nimitz and Spruance through Midway and the island-hopping. Spruance described Buchanan's work in the navy as "mighty fast and fairly accurate" (54), a description Buchanan relishes.

For another thing, Buchanan had farmed, at which he was also mighty fast and fairly accurate. The phrase "Better than plowing" is what his mentor Frank Knight said about his own career at Iowa and Chicago, but it expresses literally Buchanan's opportunity forgone by going to college. A lively sense of scarcity implanted by work as a boy on a hard-scrabble dairy farm makes it easier to grasp economics. Other farm people in economics (there have been lots of them; Theodore Schultz, Margaret Reid, and D. Gale Johnson are three I've known pretty well) would have had a notion of economics from childhood. Buchanan remarks, "I do not envy the youngsters in modern suburbia, who lack a sense of scarcity along any dimension" (23). Yes: and that's one reason why economics is so hard to teach to them. Most suburban kids come from a socialist paradise in which there is More to be had by just asking Dad. At age twenty-six, Buchanan notes, as a veteran of war and the milk shed, "I was, somehow, ready for the understanding of the economic process" (5).

So Buchanan isn't smart; he's educated. Like most of us, he's had to work at it, and, unlike most of us, he has kept at it (his only deviation from the keep-at-it theory is his notion that if you didn't study Latin and Greek as a child you can't do anything about it as an adult: get to it, Jim; sign up for a Latin course next term). He's always read books, which puts

him in a small minority of economists. Most economists reckon they
have completed their philosophical or literary or scientific educations by
their mid-twenties, which was when Buchanan really got going. Think of
the bookshelves in the average economist's home. A handful of economists keep reading. Every sentence from Leland Yeager, for example,
expresses a lifetime of reading books. Bob Solow reads a lot, too. Jim
Heckman is startlingly well read. I hear that Armen Alchian read the
entire two volumes of Maitland's *A History of English Law before the
Time of Edward the First* (2d ed., 1898). I know for a fact that he, like
Buchanan (142), has read Boswell's *The Journal of a Tour to the
Hebrides with Samuel Johnson*. Frank Knight, another book reader in
economics, shared with his student Buchanan a passion for Thomas
Hardy's poetry. Not smart; educated. Maybe we ought to educate our
young economists better, in the world and in the library.

And, second, we always ask about another economist, "Is he a nice
guy?" (The question doesn't arise for women, who *have* to be "nice" by
the conventions of American womanhood.) It's another question that
warrants rethinking, because as usually phrased it overvalues *social* abilities that peak at age 19, that is, the uncritical amiability that most adolescents show toward one another. On the contrary, what we should be
asking about, and sometimes are, is the ethical standing of the person as
an adult in scholarship. That on my testimony George Stigler and on
Buchanan's testimony Jacob Viner were emphatically *not* "nice guys"
and, equally emphatically, Milton Friedman and Theodore Schultz (as
Buchanan and I agree) *were* nice guys reflects on their work. We want
ethical goodness and scholarly excellence to correlate. They may not in
fact correlate, but anyway we want them to and feel uneasy about the
scholarly excellence if they don't.

Is Buchanan a nice guy? He doesn't claim much in the way of 19-
year-old amiability, though a person who has organized as many
research groups as he has must have some gifts of social dealing. He
claims no interest in academic politics and admits exercising instead the
exit option with a certain brio. In a courteous Southern way he says that
he doesn't think people campaign for the Nobel Prize. (His hypothesis
makes it a little hard to account for the number of late-middle-aged
American economists who summer in Sweden, but maybe they just like
saunas and birch forests; you should all read Herbert Simon's amazing
autobiography [1996], in which he tells, on the level, how he *did* campaign.) Buchanan noticed in his first teaching experience that he carries
"a natural aura or sense of authority" (44), a trait I have observed also in

Robert Lucas, Gary Becker, Alexander Gerschenkron, and Robert Mundell. What comes through in original scholars and successful teachers like these is not niceness, quite, in the usual amiable sense, although sometimes they have that, too, but the ethical quality of courage.

The San Francisco dock worker and sage Eric Hoffer made a distinction between hope and courage (German *Hoffnung* and *Mut* was what Hoffer, whose first language was German, was talking about). It applies to Buchanan. Hoffer wrote: "There is no hope without self-delusion, while courage is sober and sees things as they are. Hope is perishable, while courage is long-lived. It is easy in an outburst of hope to start a difficult undertaking, but it takes courage to bring it to conclusion" (1983, 28). A tough, poor, intelligent boy from Middle Tennessee would have courage rather than hope.

Buchanan's main personal trait seems to be this stubborn courage. The word *courage* figures heavily in his tributes to scholars he admires (for example, 75–76). In a good life in economics it means being something other than a first-derivative economist. A first-derivative economist follows the scholarly trend line to a close approximation, like a Taylor's series. If evolutionary game theory is in, he's onto it a split second after the original thinkers. The question always on the lips of the first-derivative economist is, What news on the Rialto?

To heck with the news, says Buchanan. Read, think, and gird thyself. "What is critically important for all those who may enter the game at some apparent disadvantage . . . is the attainment of the ability to resist discouragement and despair. This ability . . . depends on the achievement, early on, of a constrained and realistic, but finally unshakable, self-confidence" (47). He quotes Nietzsche—Buchanan is the only economist I know who quotes Nietzsche—as regarding the phrase "having the courage of one's convictions" as "a very popular error"; "rather it is a matter of having the courage of an attack on one's convictions" (140).

Buchanan has fended off his share of attacks on his convictions. Academic attacks usually depend on sneering, which has the advantage of requiring no laborious attention to the position attacked. The establishment economists, as long as they could get away with it, merely sneered at Friedman, Buchanan, Hayek. Buchanan sees a connection between intellectual and regional sneering. In the navy he ran into "blatant discrimination . . . against southerners, midwesterners, and westerners," which "served to reinforce in concrete [his] populist preconceptions" (49). Buchanan's pleasure in his Nobel Prize is in part and sincerely on behalf of we other hicks outside the BoWash corridor. (At one of the main barns in Massachusetts for the Eastern herd of independent minds I once overheard two people in two separate conversations use within a few seconds of each other that talismanic phrase among the coasties, the standard by which something is Really Important, "a front-page story in the *New York Times*.") Buchanan never was a member, say, of the National Bureau of Economic Research, never had a grant from the Sloan Foundation, and he would not fit in at Harvard.

So Buchanan isn't nice; he's courageous. Maybe we ought to be giving our young economists lessons in courage, the courage to live away from the Charles River and the first derivative.

Buchanan's scholarly character is plain in his story. He says truthfully that he has done practically no empirical work and claims also, less plausibly, that he does not engage in "ordered scholarship" (87; if learning Italian to study economics is not ordered I do not know what is). He is an Economist Thinking, though a persistent reader and a courageous arguer.

Buchanan views the subject of economics as exchange, not maximization (a view he has expressed most thoroughly in *What Should Economists Do?*). When he and Warren Nutter were students at Chicago in 1948 they decided in the foyer of the Social Science Building "that technique was replacing substance" in the field (94). As early as that. The agent of the replacement was Paul Samuelson, who the year before had published *The Foundations of Economic Analysis,* the program for turning economics into the study of maximization under constraints, the study of that strange monster in modern economics, Max U. In 1944 von Neumann and Morgenstern had invented the theory of games. In 1951 Kenneth Arrow published the book that set the tone for highbrow theory, *Social Choice and Individual Values*. Buchanan would have none of it: as a young professor he published an attack on Arrow's notion that a society is best viewed as a problem in maximization. Not a good way to get a job at Harvard.

The special character of Buchanan's kind of economics, I want to emphasize, is *not* its lack of math. That's not what Nutter and he meant by *technique*. Buchanan's theorems could just as well be put in mathematical terms, and some have. He leans as much as the next economist does toward abstraction. Economists have always been in love with abstraction (Schumpeter called it the Ricardian Vice), and Buchanan is no exception. His recent interest in the Hobbes Problem (101)—will a random assortment of unsocialized SOBs produce in time a civil society?—is typical of blackboard economics down the ages. (Strictly speaking, the answer to the Hobbes Problem will answer no concrete question about an economy made up of already socialized people, French people, say.)

What is special about Buchanan's approach is that it is Coordinationist rather than Maximizationist. Markets coordinate a complex society, sometimes better than the state could. Who cares if they maximize exactly correctly by a standard of perfection? Here Buchanan declares himself a disciple of Knight and the Austrians, especially Hayek. The Coordinationist coloring also shows through in the Good Old Chicago School, with which Buchanan has had, like Knight, an uneasy relation. The questions Knight or Friedman or Stigler asked were not about a particular maximizing monad. The Good Old Chicago School detested Max U (until finally in the 1980s Chicago gave in and become one of Max's main homes). George Stigler in the 1960s and 1970s made merry of the various mechanical first-derivative models of oligopoly coming out of MIT, proposing instead to ask the question why the oligopolists did not set up as a monopoly. It took a long, long time to extract an explicit model of monetarism from Friedman, long after Tobin had expressed himself in fixed metaphors of maximization. Friedman was on the lookout for principles of Coordination—rules versus authority, say, or the revival of the gold standard or letting speculators in foreign exchange put their money where their mouths were—not a model for Maximization. In a manner of speaking, Buchanan and his ilk, may their tribe increase, are looking for stories rather than metaphors, tales rather than models.

Tales after all carry multiple meanings easier than do models. An educated mind delights in multiplicity, without confusion. The computer age provides a metaphor of the mature mind: one "toggles" on a computer between this or that view of a word-processed document, moving from one perspective to another without confusion. The literary critic Richard Lanham (1993) describes toggling as the master skill, namely, the mature ability to hold two perspectives.

So does Buchanan, and it summarizes his method well. He speaks of the "relatively absolute absolute" (78; and in his earlier writing), by which he means toggling: while you are looking at the text in, say, Gothic letters, then that's how you look at it; but you bear in mind that another perspective is a toggle away. He quotes Scott Fitzgerald (from a review in the *Times Literary Supplement:* Buchanan is the only American economist I know aside from Jim Heckman who reads the *Times Literary Supplement*): "The test of a first-rate intelligence is the ability to hold two opposed ideas at the same time, and still retain the ability to function."

Toggling courageously between two opposing ideas, coordinationist and maximizationist, books and the blackboard, Tennessee and Italy, Buchanan has handled pretty well those too many forks in the road.

The Economic Tourism of Armen Alchian

One of my Eastern Economic Journal *columns (summer 1996).*

I've been doing a lot of moving from one economy to another. I am for a year in Holland, at Erasmus University of Rotterdam. I've made a few lightning visits back to the United States (I have to stay out of the country for 35 days in my tax year to get a $70,000 off-the-top reduction in my taxable income: we professors on visiting appointments in other counties join in saying, God bless the oil companies). I just spent a month in Australia and New Zealand. And I've done some short trips to England and France. It's hard duty, but someone has to do it. I'm proud to take up the onerous responsibility of buying fashionable hats in Paris (as I came out of the hat store with Nancy Folbre an elegant Frenchman passing by said, "Un beau chapeau, Madame!" I could have kissed him.)

The point: When you travel from one economy to another your attention is drawn to economic peculiarities. If we could use that sense of wonder in economics, trying to see ourselves as tourists even in our own neighborhood, the field would make rapid progress.

The best example I know of the point is the life of Armen Alchian. On my way out to Australia I stopped at UCLA to see some friends, among them Armen, the heart of the (former) distinctiveness of the Department of Economics there. ("Former" because UCLA, like every other department in the country, has remade itself with some difficulty into a pale imitation of MIT circa 1980.) Armen was as always the soul of courtesy. He was not the slightest bit put off by my recent change, and we had a nice two hours in his office and over coffee at the Business School, talking about economics.

Talking about economics with Armen Alchian is like talking about painting with Pablo Picasso. What you notice after reading Armen or listening to Armen is that none of his art comes from abstraction alone.

This is unusual in our strange field these days, which in Ronald Coase's phrase consists mainly of "Blackboard Economics." Armen's economics (and Ronald's and Barbara's and that of a handful of our colleagues) comes from experience of life. When he talks about the housing market you discover soon that he is holding vividly in mind the first house that he and Pauline bought in Los Angeles. When he talks about the subsidization of the middle class implicit in the distinction between California State at Fullerton and the University of California at Los Angeles you can hear his experiences with his own children or echoes of an argument decades ago with a university administrator, not an economist. Armen has gone through life as a tourist in his own economy, noting with wonder the existence of transactions costs, the expensiveness of establishing property rights, the strange rhetoric of vested interests.

I've urged him to do an autobiography consisting just of his successive Encounters with an Economy, from his boyhood paper route to the pricing of golf clubs (physical and institutional). It would be better than most textbooks in economics. Not better than his own, of course, which is full of this living sense of the economy. The textbook is coming out in a new edition from Oxford University Press soon, for which praise the Lord. Buy it, people. I learned more economics from his and Bill Allen's old *Exchange and Production Theory in Use*, earnestly pressed on me by his prize student Steven N. S. Cheung when we were both beginning teachers at Chicago, than from any 100 pounds of tomes I could name in Blackboard Economics.

The job is to get away from Blackboard Economics and get closer to Alchian Economics. Be a tourist.

For example, I immediately noticed as a long-term tourist in Holland how hard it is to shop. The stores are mainly closed—a proverb has it that Holland is a good place to save money because the shops are never open. If you work during the day you are in serious trouble getting the grocery shopping accomplished. When the stores are open they are thronged with goods-starved people, especially women, with a crazed look in their eyes. Holland had until recently the lowest labor force participation rate among OECD countries of women with children, and one can see why. You have to choose between having a job or having milk.

And the stores are widely spread. I don't have a car—for the good, Alchian, relative price reason that gasoline costs nearly three times what it costs in the United States—so I do a lot of walking when I shop. I mean a lot. I've been eating cheese nonstop since I arrived in January (and a wonderful pudding concoction called *vla*) but have not gained an ounce.

That's because I have to walk miles to shop. You'll find one, and only one, pharmacist or grocery store or clothing shop per square mile.

All this is the result of an amazing set of laws, enforced by the local governments (which, as Adam Smith noted, are run by shop owners). The law says that to open a new grocery store you have to have the permission of the local government, and the local government *asks the existing grocery store owners* whether there is really a "need" for another store. Actually, such laws, you begin to learn from economic tourism, are not that amazing—at any rate they are not rare. We have more mercantilism alive and well and living in modern economies, especially European economies, than you might think from the textbooks, especially American textbooks. The historian Macaulay, who was very wise about economics, noted in 1824 that "free trade, one of the greatest blessings which a government can confer on a people, is in almost every country unpopular." It's very unpopular among existing store owners in Holland, for example. People complained so much that at length the store owners allowed *avondwinkels,* evening stores, where you could buy a loaf of bread after 6:00 P.M., or sometimes 5:00. The *avondwinkels* are by law closed until the other shops have themselves closed.

I can't think of a better project for a class of Dutch undergraduates than to examine the reason that retailing is so much more expensive in Holland than in the United States (German and Japanese undergraduates would have a similarly good time). Or for a class of Australian undergraduates than to examine the reasons Australia imposes visas like the United States does (that was why I spent an extra day in Los Angeles) and has explicit and insulting airport taxes imposed openly on passengers and does not support competition among airlines on Pacific routes. Or for a class of American undergraduates to dig into the economics of homelessness and why it was not a perceived problem before the middle class introduced zoning and building codes into poor neighborhoods then took the neighborhoods away.

Economic tourism doesn't always come to Chicago School conclusions, I have to admit. The bread in Paris is just unbelievably good. Combined with the coffee and the wine, what would be the point of eating anything else? Yet the production and price of bread in Paris has been strictly regulated for many centuries. I mean seven. Again, European cities from Bergen to Catania are pretty—much prettier than American or Australian cities. Why? Because of zoning laws and building codes that Americans and Australians would regard as fascistic. In most European cities large and small the old downtown is still where people shop, and not because they are quaintly attached to The Old Ways. The town councils simply do not allow strip malls to develop on the outskirts. So the outskirts are charming country scenes, and the downtowns are charming urban relics. And I say—I bite my lip when I say it, but I say it still—there's something to be said for it. If you could see Gouda and Delft you'd wonder whether we libertarians should fight to the death for the Coralville strip in Iowa City.

Economic tourism makes plain—oh, so plain—the importance of transaction costs. Just knowing where to go to get this or that and which this or that is worth getting is a set-up cost of consuming that takes years to bring up to local standards. (Of course, it helps to be a woman: unlike the men, we ask for directions.) I spent hours looking for a fabric store to get a clasp to repair a skirt. Or, more exactly, I spent a lot of alertness, that crucial input, as Israel Kirzner has emphasized, to anything but an economy of utter routine: instead of looking for another kind of store while I rode the trams, I looked for fabric stores. My former colleague at Chicago Larry Sjaastad was fond of joking that the reason the prices are higher for tourists is to give the natives an incentive to learn their own language. Actually, in an extended sense of "language" he's right.

And economic tourism shows you the cultural differences in attitudes toward work. It's easy to overstate their importance. Sheer hard work is not what makes America rich, although together with Japan the United States has the lowest rates of vacation-taking of any country in the world. (By contrast, in Holland, as I write in early August, out of a population of 15 million fully 8 million are at present on vacation, and an astounding 6 million of them are outside of Holland. No wonder the game experimental theorist and student of art economics Judith Mehta wondered at the emptiness of Rotterdam streets when she came to visit me last week: they've all defected.) What makes America rich is the absence of obstacles to innovation, for one thing, and, mainly, the high achievement of modern technology if adopted. Still, one notes different attitudes, good and bad, in the workplace. Dutch academics are not quite so businesslike as Americans. Australian workers really do believe they are just as good as management.

Travel is good for your economics, then, if you allow it. But it's more than allowing it, and its more than travel. It's an attitude of wonder. In the Blessed Adam Smith's *History of Astronomy* (yes, and he wrote things like *Lectures on Rhetoric and Belles Lettres,* too, though none of these as published books) he emphasizes the scientific importance of a sense of wonder. We would all do well to follow Smith, and Alchian, in this, and to wonder about economic phenomena instead of the next pointless turn in the Literature.

The Persuasive Life of
Friedrich Hayek

A review of Stephen Kresge and Leif Wener, eds., Hayek on Hayek *(Chicago: University of Chicago Press, 1994). It appeared in the magazine* Reason.

The simplest mark of a comedy is a happy ending. In the late 1940s, as the notorious author of *The Road to Serfdom,* estranged in marriage, Friedrich Hayek did not view his life as a comedy. Yet his life ended in 1992 on the whole happily. An antisocialist born in Vienna in 1899, who saw socialism triumph, he flourished into his 90s and to communism's collapse. An economic theorist regarded until 1945 as the equal of Keynes, yet who five years later was spurned for an appointment in Economics at the University of Chicago, he lived to get a Nobel Prize in the subject and to see his ideas again taken seriously. It's a sweet story and a painless way to begin reading Hayek.

Stephen Kresge is the general editor of *The Collected Works of F. A. Hayek* being published by the University of Chicago Press in 19 volumes, of which this book is a supplement. The two sources are autobiographical notes by Hayek himself and numerous interviews, some published (one by Tom Hazlett in *Reason* a couple of years ago). Though Kresge and Lief Wener have worked diligently at the weaving, the result has naturally some disproportions. The index of persons, a good idea, is uneven and inaccurate. The long and chatty introduction by Kresge is worshipful. Hayek said thus and such, and "Einstein has said much the same thing." The portraits include one of our hero's great-great-grandfathers. Altogether it's an unsteady book.

Yet it's the best route to Hayek I know, much better than Hayek himself. Reading the great man's works can be a trial. Hayek said that the introduction and the first couple of chapters of *The Road to Serfdom* was the best writing in any language he ever did, as writing. Here is the opening sentence of the introduction: "Contemporary events differ from history in that we do not know the results they will produce." And the concluding sentence: "It was the prevalence of socialist views and not Prussianism that Germany had in common with Italy and Russia—and it was from the masses and not from the classes steeped in the Prussian tradition, and favored by it, that National Socialism arose." *Oy.* The prose of his academic books is not up to this standard.

Hayek himself explained why he was such a poor writer. Some people, unlike him, "are able to restate chains of reasoning that they have once learnt," and they are the good writers—the Keynes and Schumpeters of this world. He, on the other hand, "had painfully to work them out anew almost every time." I know just what he means.

Further, Hayek's kind of working out did not lend itself to storytelling. He was a seeker after patterns, metaphors, timeless structures. Not a page of Keynes or Schumpeter lacks a story. By contrast it's hard to find even one in Hayek's books. Aside from the story of socialism's rise, expressed abstractly, Hayek had no tales to tell. He made even evolution sound boring.

Approaching his thought through the story of his life, then, is a better idea. For example, Hayek said that he would have become like his father a biologist but for the timing of World War I. As an Austrian officer on the Italian front he "served in a battle in which eleven different languages were spoken. It's bound to draw your attention to the problems of political organization." He was not a superb student at school or university, being too undisciplined and slow. Contrast again Keynes and Schumpeter, who remind one of Thomas Mann's description of the brightest high school boys in Germany around 1880, "small, ambitious lads, far ahead of their age, who were brilliant in subjects that could be got by heart."

Hayek's thinking by his own account often came from his slow-witted attention to the very words, what I would call the rhetoric: "in that process I often discovered the flaws or inadequacies of the generally held views." He attributed one of his main ideas to reflection on the redundancy in an economist's phrase, a subject of merriment around the London School of Economics when he was there, "given data" (the merrymakers were noting a point about Latin: *data* means literally "things given," so it was "given things given," which only a non-Latinist could utter). "That led me, in part, to ask to whom were the data really given. To us [the staff at the LSE], it was of course to nobody. . . . That's what led me, in the thirties, to the idea that the whole problem was the utilization of information dispersed among thousands of people and not possessed by anyone."

The fulcrum of the Hayek bildungsroman is the triumph and disaster of *The Road to Serfdom*, published in Britain in 1944. Suddenly famous in the United States on the strength of a skillful condensation in the *Reader's Digest*, Hayek was surprised to be rushed off on a book tour, speaking to thousands. He notes, "I discredited myself with most of my fellow economists by writing *The Road to Serfdom*, which is disliked so much." That the book alienated so many economists, especially in the United States, shows how optimistic the average egghead was about socialism at the time and how cross he became when his optimism was challenged. Much looser books by socialists such as R. H. Tawney's egregious one in 1932 about China, for example, or Karl Polanyi's fairy tales about modern economic growth also published in 1944 were taken seriously and praised.

Hayek wrote the book when there were 12 democracies left in the world and prophets like Anne Morrow Lindbergh were saying that totalitarianism, after all, had some good points and was anyway the wave of the future. From the other, left-leaning side in 1945 Charles Merriam and Maynard Krueger at the University of Chicago argued optimistically that "the political process" would overcome socialism's flaws. It's how we thought in that bright dawn before Vietnam, urban renewal, and the war on drugs. Greater fools we.

A fellow Austrian (in the merely geographical sense of the word) shows up Hayek's isolation. Joseph Schumpeter's book of 1942, *Capitalism, Socialism, and Democracy*, did not admire socialism but did not argue against its rise. The book became fashionable with statists like Merriam and Krueger (I knew Krueger as an old man and taught with him in Chicago's freshman course on the social sciences; Krueger has the distinction of being the only economist mentioned in an important English poem, by Auden). Schumpeter was a rhetorical fatalist. Hayek notes that, like many modernists, "Schumpeter had, in the last resort, really no belief in the power of argument. He took it for granted that the state of affairs forces people to think in a particular manner. . . . Schumpeter's attitude was one of complete despair and disillusionment over the power of reason" (155). (I note that George Stigler had a similar pessimism about argument and therefore similar arrogance about his conclusions. The English professor Wayne Booth has made a similar point at length about Bertrand Russell [1974, chap. 2].) Schumpeter had written in 1942 that "the case for capitalism . . . could never be made simple. People at large would have to be possessed of an insight and a power of analysis which are altogether beyond them. Why, practically every nonsense that has ever been said about capitalism has been championed by a professional economist." So he surrendered to fate—unlike Hayek, who argued and argued and argued with the socialists about economic histories and economic futures. And won.

As an early-nineteenth-century liberal, Hayek believed throughout in the power of argument—as does, say, Milton Friedman. The pessimists about argument like Schumpeter and Stigler look clever at the time, men of the world not fooled by mere words, rhetoricians who sneer at rhetoric. But in the long run they join the greater fools. In *A History of Economic Analysis,* on which he was working when he died, Schumpeter put the clever, unargued case this way: "We may, indeed, prefer the world of modern dictatorial socialism to the world of Adam Smith, or vice versa, but any such preference comes within the same category of subjective evaluation as does, to plagiarize Sombart, a man's preference for blondes over brunettes." Finely put; so much more clever than Hayek's leaden prose (Stigler was a better writer than Friedman, too). But in the long run it is fool's talk. Words matter and are worth earnestly disputing.

Hayek's optimism did not extend to scientific method. Unlike Friedman, he did not swallow the modernism of "prediction" as the master virtue in science, perhaps because of his training in biology, which is a pattern-finding discipline, not predictive (neither for the most part is economics predictive, of course). Hayek's ideas were impossibility theorems. He said it's impossible to predict more than the larger patterns of social life. It's possible to predict that government control of prices will do damage. It's impossible to plan production for an entire country. And, he claimed, this time mistakenly, it is in the long run impossible to be a socialist and remain a democrat.

But people want predictions—of the coming Great Depression of 1990 (I bought Ravi Batra's book of this title in 1994, cheap) or the coming greenhouse catastrophe of 2010—not denials that prediction and control is possible. "This is, incidentally," Hayek remarked, "a reason why my views have become unpopular." Friedman and many other economists have fallen under the modernist spell, articulated, for example, by Wesley Clair Mitchell in 1924: "In economics as in other sciences we desire knowledge mainly as an instrument of control. Control means the alluring possibility of shaping the evolution of economic life to fit the developing purposes of the race." More than any other economist, our Hayek was out of step with such erotic fascism of prediction and control.

In another way that left him out of step Hayek disagreed with his predecessor as doyen of the Austrian School, Ludwig von Mises. Hayek gradually realized that he himself had more in common with the Scottish Enlightenment than with the French and that Jeremy Bentham symbolized the French element in British thought.

> I believe I can now . . . explain why . . . [the] masterly critique by Mises of socialism has not really been effective. Because Mises remained in the end himself a rationalist-utilitarian, and with a rationalist-utilitarianism, the rejection of socialism is irreconcilable. . . . If we remain strictly rationalists, utilitarians, that implies we can arrange everything according to our pleasure. . . . In one place he says we can't do it, in another place he argues, being rational people, we must try to do it.

It's what's wrong with much of modern economic thought, this utilitarian rationalism—in Stigler's political economy as against Friedman's or in Richard Posner's law and economics as against Ronald Coase's. The philosophers and literary people call it the "aporia [contradiction, indecision] of the Enlightenment project," which is to say the contradiction between freedom and rationality. Hayek was two centuries behind the times, a virtual resident of Edinburgh rather than Paris, an exponent of bourgeois virtue rather than of a new aristocracy of experts. By the end of the twentieth century, though, he is old-fashioned enough to be postmodern.

You read it here: Hayek in his courageous and slow-witted and badly written originality had more in common with Jacques Derrida and Gayatri Spivak than with Bentham and Comte and Russell.

Some Buried Female Lives in Economics

A review for the Times Higher Education Supplement *(May 31, 1996) of Mary Ann Dimand, Robert W. Dimand, and Evelyn Forget, eds.,* Women of Value: Feminist Essays on the History of Women in Economics *(Brighton: Elgar).*

Aristotle wrote that a society wastes half its human resources if it neglects its women. You would think that such an argument for efficiency would have had some appeal to economists, but economists have mostly been men, sharing the frailties of that office. *Women of Value,* a collection of 10 essays on the history down to 1940 of women economists in Britain and the United States, tells how the little society of an increasingly professional economics neglected its women yet how the women nonetheless achieved.

Economists don't give a fig for olden times, and 1940 is inconceivably olden in their minds. Why bother? Well, for one thing, if economics is going to get beyond its present limitation to boys' rules of play, it needs to reflect on women of value and on women's values and on the value of women. For another, as one of the editors, Robert Dimand, points out, the claim of many economists that all worthwhile economics is already embodied in the latest journal article by one of the boys is patently false. The essay by the late Michele Pujol on Harriet Taylor (1807–58), colleague and wife to John Stuart Mill, and the essay by Mary Ann Dimand on Charlotte Perkins Gilman (1860–1935) show thinking about women and marriage and the household better as economics than most productions on similar topics in last year's *Economic Journal* and the *American Economic Review.* Thus Gilman in *Women and Economics* (1898): "The labor of women in the house . . . enables men to produce more wealth . . . and in this way women are economic factors in society. But so are horses. . . . The horse is not economically independent, nor is the woman."

The volume is filled with stories of women's lives in the science of value, from Jane Marcet, author of the best-selling economics book of the early nineteenth century, down to still active women economists, such as Anna Schwartz. As Harriet Martineau wrote in 1834, even economics is best told by stories rather than by the male method of abstract proposition, "not only because [narrative in economics] is new, not only because it is entertaining, but because we think it is the most faithful and most complete [method]."

The fact told faithfully by the stories—known to every woman but still puzzling to some men—is this: a life of teaching and scholarships in economics, as in all fields dominated by husbands and brothers, was once almost impossible for a woman and remains hard. Mary Paley Marshall (1850–1944) had done her feminist duty by achieving distinction in the moral sciences tripos in 1874 and becoming "the lady lecturer from Newnham." To expect her to have pieced together a research career as well, against the conventions and the money fellowships of the day, and against the loudly expressed conviction of her economist husband, Alfred, that research would debilitate the mothers of the race (Mary never agreed), would be anachronistic.

Alison Cornish Thorne, in a memoir nearly worth the book's price, tells of announcing in 1937 to Elizabeth Hoyt, her thesis supervisor at Iowa State, that she was now betrothed to the agronomist Wynne Thorne. Said Hoyt, ladylike in her expletives, "Oh, shoot!" Everyone knew that marriage ended a research career, because rules about nepotism then in force would make it impossible for Alison to get the job she deserved at her husband's (isolated) institution.

What chiefly intervened was the womanly duty of care, a topic just now coming back into economics, in the work of Nancy Folbre and Edith Kuiper and Irene van Staveren, two centuries after Adam Smith proposed it and Jeremy Bentham disposed of it. Thorne says of a contemporary, also mentored by the extraordinary group of home economists at Iowa State University and the University of Chicago, that she "returned home to Massachusetts because her mother was unwell. As for me, I had babies." That was, and is, The Fact.

In 1996 the book is not startling, after so many studies in other fields documenting The Fact, and documenting all the baby facts The Fact has spawned. We know already from Evelyn Fox Keller and Sandra Harding and others that early in the twentieth century women, mostly unmarried, increasingly participated in science, breaking the gender bar of the nineteenth century—though in economics the women were often segregated in women's colleges and in home economics. Women did not segregate themselves. They did not deal exclusively with "women's" issues. "By 1935," writes Forget in her essay, "men and women were virtually indistinguishable insofar as area of specialization was concerned."

Yet a "woman's way of knowing" often characterized their scholarly contributions, such as the persistence among women of methodical observation, a willingness to listen with care apparent in Marie Curie's work in physics or Barbara McClintock's or Rosalind Franklin's work in biology. In economics one can see it in the work of Margaret Reid of Iowa State and the University of Chicago, Dorothy Brady of the University of Pennsylvania and the Women's Bureau, or Anna Schwartz of the National Bureau of Economic Research and New York University.

After 1930 the Great American Gender Reaction set in (it started a decade earlier, it seems, in economics). Women started disappearing from universities in the United States, on the way to the 1950s and the height of the feminine mystique. The decline begins before the raising of the mathematical stakes in economics, so it's not that the women couldn't handle the math (anyway, the eminence of such women as Cecilia Payne-Gaposchkin in math-intensive fields like astronomy makes this sound silly). In sociology, as Barbara Laslett has shown, the expulsion of women was associated in the 1920s with quantification. But women in economics were and still are great quantifiers. Brady and Schwartz, for instance, can be counted as founders of a quantitative economic history, carried on by Claudia Goldin and Elyce Rotella and Susan Carter.

American academic women had research careers disproportionately in the big state universities of the Midwest and West. When in the 1930s the places like Iowa and Berkeley began to sell their birthright and imitate the Eastern private universities, they imitated the old-boy misogyny of Yale and Harvard, too. The book's terminus of 1940 leaves the worst of the Great American Gender Reaction offstage, and unexplained, appropriate for the purposes of the book—which is not to solve one of the bigger puzzles in modern European history (namely, the rise, fall, and rise of women).

Certainly by the 1950s academic life in Britain and the United States had become aggressively masculine (my father was a professor then, and I can remember the appalling sexism). Since the 1960s the academic positions lost in economics after 1920 have been regained and increased, now with no marriage test. And yet in macho fields like economics women are still rare. The second woman president of the American Economic Association just served her year in office. A social science that underacknowl-

edges half of humankind is going to look strange, and modern economics looks very strange—and very masculine.

Viewed from the history of science, then, the book is one of many
contributions to the acknowledgment of women. Though it is not going
to attract a wide audience—it is too miscellaneous and specialized for
that—it is nonetheless a sample of what can be done to repair the neglect
of women economists. It points to growing literature on the subject by
Peter Groenewegen, Maxine Berg, Margaret O'Donnell, Jannett Highfill,
William Weber, and the editors and contributors themselves. When it
moves beyond the present task of collective biography and bibliography
the literature will arrive at issues raised by the new rhetoric of science and
British sociology of knowledge.

But viewed from the mainstream of economics, what Pujol calls in
the feminist jibe the "MALEstream," the book is shocking stuff. Marcet
wrote early in classical economics a popular book superior in vision to
the men's books but forgotten. Harriet Martineau, the J. K. Galbraith of
the 1830s, was blamed by men for making books rather than babies. Harriet Taylor was effusively lauded by her husband, Mill, as the muse for
his *Principles* of 1848 and all his later work but was not acknowledged on
any of his title pages. Charlotte Perkins Gilman, a leading unorthodox
economist circa 1900, is ignored in books that dote on Thorstein Veblen.
Joan Robinson of Cambridge, acknowledged even by her numerous male
enemies as one of the handful of greatest twentieth-century economists,
was not deemed worthy of a bare lectureship until she had published to
acclaim not one but two pathbreaking books in economic theory. Nor
was she later deemed worthy of a Nobel Prize. The "new" household
economics of Gary Becker and his mainly male followers, for which
Becker won the vaunted prize, was pioneered 50 years earlier by Elizabeth Hoyt, Hazel Kyrk, and Margaret Reid, who figure hardly at all in
Becker's footnotes.

And so forth. It reminds one of conventional male attitudes toward
women as servants and ornamental furniture. To most men, wrote Taylor, who, as Pujol shows, was much more radical and economically clear-
minded about the emancipation of women than was Mill, "it is agreeable
. . . that men should live for their own sake, women for the sake of men."
While you're up, honey, could you run me another regression?

But of all moral sentiments, Adam Smith pointed out, indignation is
the hardest to share. It unintentionally arouses sympathy for the target of
the indignation, in this case the men in economics, who still dully insist
that the field is gender neutral, that women could make it if they would

only join more enthusiastically in the boys' games in the sandbox—such futilities as game theory and existence theorems.

The contributors occasionally make use of an appeal to moral sentiment that might possibly work with male economists: imagine, if you can, how a male economist of the stature of Joan Robinson could possibly have failed to get the Nobel year after year. Then imagine historical silence about a male economist winner of the Nobel *Peace* Prize. Emily Greene Balch was just such an economist, removed from a tenured professorship at Wellesley College in 1918 precisely because of the pacifist activism that won her the prize. (Compare the parallel case of Bertrand Russell.)

It's hard, though, for male economists to maintain much indignation on the subject. As Mill put it in *The Subjection of Women,* "persons even of considerable moral worth . . . are very ready to believe the practices, the evils of which they have not experienced, do not produce any evils." (Or is that Harriet Taylor's thought and prose?) The women must do it for themselves and have shown that they can. This book honors the women pioneers. The field is open now to women to overcome the failings of a science devoted to sandbox games, an economics altogether too complacently masculine. Go, team, go!

Rule 3
Get Ethics beyond "Have a Nice Career"

"He's Smart. And He's a Nice Guy, Too."

Another column for the Eastern Economic Journal *(winter 1995, an eventful time for me).*

Share $100 if you say the magic word, a word American economists use every day to describe an economist they approve of. "Well informed about the economy"? Get serious. "Wise about the place of economics in the conversation of humanity"? Give me a break. "Imaginative, energetic, empirically sound, or scientifically reliable"? Ho, ho, ha, ha, hee, hee. / My name is Pinky Lee.

The word is: *smart,* as in "He's very smart" or "Boy, is he smart." The economist being evaluated has never met a farmer or worker or businessperson. He doesn't have a clue what American national income was last year. He makes up "stylized facts" about history as he goes along. He has no idea how economic advice works out in practice. He couldn't convince a freshman about the virtue of markets on a bet. He's never read *The Wealth of Nations,* not to speak of *The Theory of Monopolistic Competition* or *The General Theory of Employment Interest and Money.* But, I'm telling you, he's smart. He's not scholarly, scientific, learned, curious, thorough, patient, serious, imaginative, broad-minded, humane, involved. He doesn't read books. He doesn't talk to sociologists or historians or philosophers. He's never thought in depth about the society he's in. But he's smart.

Then the American economists will add, oddly, a two-word judgment on the guy's character. (In these capsule evaluations it's a guy, not a gal. The vocabulary for describing women economists is underdeveloped and doesn't allow two dimensions.) Share another $100 if you say the magic words. "Possessing integrity"? Don't be absurd. "Exhibiting courage, prudence, temperance, and justice"? Don't make me laugh. "Faith, hope, and charity"? What planet do you live on?

The magic words are: *nice guy.* If the judgment is favorable by the relaxed standards of America in the late twentieth century, they'll say, "And he's a nice guy, too." (You can see it's a male business, the phrase, since female economists are assumed to be nice without it needing to be mentioned.) The evaluative vocabulary of economic science in America consists of two adjectives, *smart* and *nice,* plus the adverb *not very.* About "guys."

The words are genuinely American and genuinely economic. In Paris the nice-guy talk would not get you very far. In Japan being nice means conforming rigidly to a social role in a strict hierarchy, which is not what makes Bob Solow the classic nice guy in American economics. Bob has been "smart," too, since the 1950s. In Britain *smart* means "well dressed," which is not obviously relevant to economic science. The corresponding British word is *clever* and is usually deprecating, as in "too clever by half." In Dutch economics the smart young people are called "whiz kids" (using the English phrase; you know about the Dutch and languages), with just that degree of doubt in the voice. Among historians even in America to call someone "smart" would simply be puzzling. Smart, schmart. What books has he written? Among biologists being smart doesn't sound like it would win NSF money, if not combined with care and imagination in running experiments. Among political scientists being "bright" entails reading more hard books at a younger age than a smart economist would believe humanly possible—at any rate it entails such reading among the political scientists who have not abandoned their craft to become second-rate economists. Even mathematicians don't usually talk about how smart a person is in the economist's sense. I suspect that the only other field in which being smart has the same valence as in economics is theoretical physics, which from popular accounts (chiefly

Richard Feynman, I admit) appears to consist of smarty-pants guy under-graduates who prefer drinking and practical jokes to studying. But, boy, are they smart.

The word matters because it sets the intellectual agenda of modern economics. Back when economists were not consumed with a desire to be reckoned smart, they were better empiricists and philosophers (not usu-ally simultaneously, which was a problem). Smart says: Don't read much. Figure it out yourself. Think fast, not deep or thorough. Force the assumptions to do the work. Fake it.

But the other part, the "nice guy" part, matters, too. Anyway, peo-ple talk about it a lot. And in truth, contrary to the received view on the Method of science, character does matter in science. The received view is that The Facts or The Truth Will Out, regardless of character. Thus the journalist Steven Levy on the obnoxious biologist Gerald Edelman: "Ulti-mately, of course, none of Edelman's personal traits will matter when it comes to determining whether or not his notion of a neuronal-group selection is valid. Science, Edelman's god, will administer the test. The facts will out" (1994, 73). One wonders why science journalists write so much about character if they actually *believe* in fact- and truth-outing. The hypothesis is contradicted by every modern historical and sociologi-cal study about how science works and is contradicted even by the stories by the science writers themselves. A page earlier Levy quotes the philoso-pher Daniel Dennett explaining why Edelman's work is often ignored: Edelman "makes it impossible for people to listen. He's gone around and offended people, criticized people, and misrepresented and insulted them. He's brought a lot of this on himself" (72). Dennett's indignation does not sound like The Facts or The Truth Coming Out. It sounds, as it often does when economists are explaining why they ignore some non-power-ful person who is "not a very nice guy," more like a childish excuse for not bothering to face the facts or the truth. Heh, shoot the messenger. It sounds like a complaint—irrelevant under the hypothesis that The Facts Will Out—that Edelman is not a nice guy, so it serves him right, and we have permission therefore to remain ignorant and misled about what he is arguing.

We could improve our evaluations of economists if we dropped the words *smart* and *nice* and started using the more grownup and compli-cated word *good*. *Good* is complicated because it has a 3,000-year history of written thinking behind it. *Smart* and *nice,* by contrast, have no think-ing at all behind them.

The trouble with *smart* is that it celebrates intellectual qualities that reach a maximum around age 19. That may be OK in mathematics, but it's bad in economics, which makes important use also of qualities that peak at 29 or 39 or 79. Of course, if you define economics to be a depraved form of mathematics, as we tried doing for a while, then *smart* in the IQ sense is going to be all that matters. But an economics back on a factual track, an economics in the 1990s, cannot really believe it, can it? So *smart* won't do for grownups in science, will it, now?

Likewise with *nice*. It celebrates ethical qualities that reach a maximum around age 19. Everyone is "nice" at 19, because all 19-year olds want to be popular, and none has a position of authority to abuse. You learn whether someone is a mensch despite surface brusqueness, the way Harry Johnson was, or on the other hand a momzer despite surface wit, the way George Stigler was, only when a Johnson or a Stigler has had mature opportunities to screw people.

Ethical goodness—"ethos," as the Greeks called it, which is to say "character"—would be irrelevant to scientific goodness only if science actually worked the way the high-school version of scientific method says it does. But we all know it doesn't, though we won't let the students hear us saying it. Science in fact depends on ethics (I argue hopefully), which is one connection between the Good Economist and the Good Person, the smart and the nice and a lot more. A man like Tom Sargent who listens when people argue with him about, say, politics and tries to see how they could hold such strange views is more believable as an economic scientist than an ideologue who evaluates everyone against a party line in the first 30 seconds of conversation. A woman like Barbara Bergmann with evident integrity and straightforwardness, who in other ways would not think of dissembling, is more believable as an economic scientist than is some game player and power lady.

It's deeper than the correlation. Science actually does operate on norms and trust, right down at the level of language. The philosopher Hilary Putnam observed that "To say that a belief is justified is to say that it is what we ought to believe; justification is a normative notion on the face of it" (1990, 115). Or, as the social psychologist Rom Harré puts it, "To publish abroad a discovery couched in the rhetoric of science is to let it be known that the presumed fact can safely be used in debate, in practical projects, and so on. Knowledge claims are tacitly prefixed with a performative of trust" (1986, 90). If you watch yourself when conversing with another economist unknown to you or when examining her paper in a job interview, you will find yourself asking, "Is she honest and intelligent enough to be believed?" You hardly hear the details of what she says. Once you believe Tom Sargent as a person, you believe almost any nonsense that comes from his mouth (his students do). And if you don't believe, on this ethical basis, then no amount of cleverness is going to change your mind.

So I propose a new matrix of possibilities: Good Economist, Bad Economist, Good Person, Bad Person. At least it brings the discussion of scientific and personal merit up to age 39 and suggests as a hypothesis that there may be a quality, "goodness," that figures in both. I've known people who fit into all four cells of the matrix. (I'm not of course going to fill any of the Bad cells with living economists—I've got enough enemies.) To speak of olden times, it is evident that Keynes was a Bad Person in lots of ways, though in most people's reckoning an exceptionally Good Economist. Marshall appears to have been a surprisingly Bad Person. Marx was of course more so, an all-around louse, and we are therefore unsurprised to learn that as a scientist he never visited a factory or a farm. Adam Smith was the kind of friend one would want to have, at least according to David Hume, himself a Good Person by most accounts. And so forth. You can fill in the matrix with your own personal lists and then think about what correlation, if any, the 2 x 2 classification reveals. My notion of the Good Economist/Good Person cell would include: Theodore Schultz, Otto Eckstein, Milton Friedman, Robert Solow, Clopper Almon, Margaret Reid, Gordon Tullock, Armen Alchian, Barbara Bergmann. By "good," you see, I don't mean just overwhelmingly smart or conventionally nice. Good has more to it.

You often can't discern goodness in a person without thorough acquaintance. Dr. Johnson said, "Judge ability at its best, character at its worst." The best of our abilities get published in the *American Economic Review* for all to see; the worst of our private deeds are often hidden from view, unless the observer gets a lot of views. If you've never been someone's employee, for example, you are missing important evidence about her inclination to do good or evil. Some people, contrary to the maximizing model of man, are ethical with students, unethical with colleagues. I know two professors like that, both Good Economists, one a former colleague at Chicago, the other a former colleague at Iowa. And I know one very Good Economist who is a Bad Person only to his boss and behaves worse the higher up the boss. You can imagine how well he has done in worldly terms.

The business is tricky yet determines our judgment of the scientist. Startlingly, for instance, some people say that the economic historian at Chicago, Nobel laureate and pioneer of cliometrics Bob Fogel, is not a Good Person. Their ideology or their chagrin has blinded them to his obvious goodness as a human being. (I said "good," not "perfect," as I've found recently, in his reaction to my gender change, but pretty good by the standards of our amoral science.) Equally startlingly, some people— Paul Samuelson, for example—say that Ronald Coase is not a Good Economist. They must not be reading his work, a disability in judging it that is surprisingly widespread among people with opinions on the matter. In the other cells some of George Stigler's followers are always telling me that he was in fact a Good Guy, contrary to my daily experience in 12 years as his colleague. For sure he was funny, very, very funny, and very, very smart. But he was cruel, arrogant, dogmatic, and willfully ignorant beyond even the challenging local standard in such matters in Economics at the University of Chicago. At a seminar over in the Law School he once made a grown man weep. Yet Stigler was just about the Best Economist I've ever known. It makes me want to join the man in weeping.

Ask yourself, then, what the connection is between goodness in scholarship and goodness in character. The English poet Philip Larkin said that "a writer's reputation is twofold: what we think of his work, and what we think of him. What's more, we expect the two halves to relate: if they don't, then one or the other of our opinions alter until they do." The smart/nice talk suggests that we would like the off-diagonal cells of the matrix to be empty. Unhappily, the data don't seem to line up that way. And yet who doesn't believe that ethical goodness has a positive marginal product in science?

Whatever the answer to that empirical question, as a policy matter let's go for the grownup Good and stop using those adolescent categories, smart and nice. Please. That's a good boy.

What You Read Is
What You Are

*Wayne Booth introduced me to the ancient study of rhetoric in
1980, my last year at the University of Chicago. I wish it had been
my first year. Here I review for the* Chicago Tribune *his book*
The Company We Keep *(1988).*

When the Chicago City Council went over to the Art Institute last year
and seized a portrait of Mayor Washington in a garter belt, the alderman
showed that they don't know much about art. But they know what they
don't like. They don't like the dirty parts. The experiment in criticism
gave everyone a laugh, from Mike Royko on down.

Behind the laughing was a modern sentiment, beloved by some professors: don't get on your high horse about the writer of *Lady Chatterly's
Lover* and the painter of *Mayor Washington in Drag,* you mope. Or, as
Oscar Wilde first put it: "There is no such thing as a moral or an immoral
book. Books are well written or badly written. That is all."

But wait a minute, says Wayne Booth, Distinguished Professor of
English at the University of Chicago. Do professors and novelists and
painters get off the ethical hook so easily? Booth's long, sweetly written
volume of literary and ethical criticism says, No, they don't. Wilde is
wrong, and the aldermen in their screwy way are right. The aldermen
may not know much about art or much of anything else, but at least they
know this: that if a book or painting is powerful it has the power to do
evil as well as good and that good and evil are worth worrying about.

The evil is not a matter of "ethics" in the Watch-and-Ward sense,
the sense that turns out to have a lot to do with sex. In Booth's thinking
the ethics is one's whole "ethos," in the old Greek word—that is (in the
old American word), *character*. Books have their way with us. To read
any story, from the "Goose Who Laid the Golden Egg" right up to *Oth-
ello* the reader must at least for the moment "embrace its patterns of

desire." When reading *Ulysses,* say, we embrace for the moment "Joyce's implied notions of what women in general and Jews in general and Irish people in general are like; to say nothing of the insistent . . . elevation of artistic sensibility over all other human values."

Booth writes charmingly about hundreds of novels and stories and poems and advertising jingles from the ethical point of view. Understand, he doesn't slot them into categories of G, PG, R, and X. The effect on character is more complicated than a rating system. It depends for one thing on who reads. A Disney movie can have a worse effect on the character of a six-year-old than can free access to Réage's *Story of O* to the same innocent child. Booth is trying to think seriously about the ethical effects, beyond the too-simple categories of the aldermen or the embarrassed silences of the professors. What makes his book a stunner is that no one else had thought of doing it.

Booth has noticed that books are potential friends. After all, as you read this sentence you are magically thinking my thoughts. Writing says, Let's be friends. Booth's motto comes from Wallace Stevens: "The house was quiet and the world was calm. / The reader became the book; and summer night / Was like the conscious being of the book."

But is the book a good friend by Aristotle's definition, a friend who "has the same relations with me that he has with himself"? Answering the question is what Booth's ethical criticism is about and, incidentally, explains his title. The company we keep, as our mothers told us, makes us who we are. If we keep company with rotten friends, we'll become rotten, too. Most people can't read the Marquis de Sade without damaging themselves ethically, just as they would be damaged by him if they got together for a little fun and games through the personals in the Chicago *Reader.* Resisting such temptations is the "lifetime project of building the character of an ethical reader."

The professors have long admired a frivolous, chocolate ice cream theory of ethics; ethics, according to them and their sophomores, is a mere matter of taste, like the taste for chocolate ice cream. Hey, you either like the Holocaust or you don't. It's like a man's preference for blondes over brunettes, as two great thinkers about the economy put it, idiots on matters of ethics. It's a matter of taste. Booth is saying to his fellow professors, and anyone else who cares to listen: Get serious.

Booth's writing is serious, and his ethical purpose is serious, but he believes that being serious does not require being obscure, boring, or somber. You have to pay attention, but the attention pays. For example, chapter 13 is, as they say, worth the price of the book, a long conversation between the author and himself "that might get somewhere—not just a sharing of subjective opinions but a way of learning from one another about the ethical value of narratives." In the chapter Booth ran an experiment in ethical criticism on himself about authors he liked (Jane Austen and Mark Twain) and an author he disliked (D. H. Lawrence, whom he admits to calling once a "confused and pretentious little author"). Can their books be his good friends? He comes out with surprising results. Maybe, he reckons, Austen can be faulted for presenting too persuasively a society in which all is well; maybe Twain does deserve some harsh words for using Jim as a mere stage prop; maybe Lawrence is more than a sex-mad woman-hater. The outcome of the criticism matters for "real" life, "that part of life that we perhaps ought to call less real, since its friendships are often less concentrated, less intense, and less enduring than those offered by story-tellers." Nowadays when Booth wants to remind himself "how it feels to grapple seriously with religious issues divorced from established answers" he rereads "pretentious little Lawrence."

I don't want to fall, as Booth puts it, into "a sentimental tone of over-praise for the works I like—as the weekly reviewers do at their worst." His book is a wonderful friend, but nobody's perfect. The explicitly economic and political parts of the book, such as the early parts of chapter 11 about Mailer's *The Armies of the Night* and chapter 10 about an unfunny joke that a lawyer once told to a jury, are skippable. Maybe Booth doesn't have enough economist or sociologist friends, in books or in person.

Yet Booth's is a great book, profound and learned, the mature fruit of a lifetime spent thinking about why we tell stories. Give yourself a learning break, and keep the company for a while of Wayne C. Booth. You'll be better for it.

Cheating as a Scientist

A review of Marcel C. LaFollette's Stealing into Print *(1993) for the* Journal of Economic Literature.

"Now the klieg lights are on," writes Marcel LaFollette. "What began as private discussions among professionals stands unshielded in the spotlight of national politics" (1993, 2). Her book, which has made a considerable and justified splash, surveys the scandals in science that have brought camera crews and members of Congress pushing into the lab— or, rather, into the editorial office, her focus being on scholarly publishing, especially journals. LaFollette does not believe, as claimed by the New York Police Department and by the pitchmen for big science, that fraud is a matter of a few bad apples. She offers what amounts to an economic explanation: the gains from big science are so big, and the number of people involved so large, that comity has broken down. Can economics itself be far behind?

"Fraud occurs when an author, editor, or referee makes a false representation to obtain some unfair advantage or to injure deliberately the rights or interests of another person or group" (LaFollette 1993, 41). The NSF estimated recently that 2,000,000 scientific articles are published annually in 200,000 journals. The detection of fraud is therefore difficult, and difficult for the scientists to believe: "the community often engages in wholesale denial of the problem's significance" (2f). One is reminded of the denial in economics of the problem with statistical significance. The denial stage is chronicled by LaFollette in embarrassing detail. Time and again the establishment figures in science, and often the very journals *Science* and *Nature* (denying most vehemently), have had to eat their words. As the journalists William Broad and Nicholas Wade put it, science has a "rotten barrel."

LaFollette makes a useful distinction between the whistle-blower— an insider who cries foul—and a new breed, the nemesis, an outsider to a research team who exposes its fraud, "attempting singlehandedly to punish unethical behavior through dogged publicity." A pair at one of the National Institutes of Health, Walter Stewart and Ned Feder, is a double-headed version of Nemesis. We could use a few of them in economics.

The book is compulsively readable, a gripping story filled with news from the science wars. LaFollette's source and to some degree her subject is the science press, which she covers in a rhetorically sophisticated way. The implied audience for the book is someone outside scholarship, or someone just beginning, who will be surprised that referees do not double check everything in a submitted paper or that journals do not certify as true and original everything in a published paper. (And yet, as LaFollette notes with astonishment, when the *Journal of American History* in 1986 stopped checking in the Indiana University Library "the accuracy of every footnote citation," it *apologized*. Economists take note of what real scholarship means.)

LaFollette does not offer much in the way of closure for the problem of fraud—although she can hardly be blamed for not solving a problem that lies at the heart of science as a community. No economist would object to her mild suggestion that "mistakes or errors within the system may simply represent a price paid for a free market in scientific information" (1993, 4). LaFollette observes that a routine of blind refereeing is recent in all the sciences (the routine started in sociology, introduced only in the 1960s to increase the objectivity of reports). She quotes a chemist suggesting we initiate nonanonymous refereeing: "If science is really supposed to be the most honest game in town then why not referee our publications above board?" (128). She rejects the suggestion for a "journal centered data audit" on grounds that do not seem persuasive. In economics we have become alerted to the problem precisely from such audits, as for example the *Journal of Money, Credit, and Banking* audit or Cooley and Leroy's classic article of 1981. Here she reveals a lack of statistical savvy (she appears to think that sample percentage rather than sample size is what matters), claiming that "to produce statistically useful results, an audit would have to examine several thousand papers" (198).

Who doubts that such cheating is a serious problem in economics? LaFollette's book is a good place to start in thinking about fraud in science, even in the science of prudence. She clears away the folly that peer review is enough, noting that in the 1980s "fraud had not been discovered by traditional peer review checks and yet those mechanisms were continually proposed in congressional testimony or in statements to the media as the means of insuring that fraud was rare" (1993, 24; I *do* wish we could get rid of peer review; it has made journals idiotically conformist and has driven deans and other academic central planners completely whacko; the science it produces is mostly useless). She uses a variety of evidence to explore the problem—novels, for example, such as C. P. Snow's *The Affair* and Kingsley Amis's *Lucky Jim* (the hero of which is one of the two portrayals in literature of an economic historian, the other being the unspeakably boring husband of Hedda Gabler). And through-out she makes good use of the literature on forgery in painting: "An unscrupulous author might craft a manuscript to fool experts likely to review it. This phenomenon has not been systematically studied for sci-ence, but it is well-known in art" (123).

But—here is my main complaint—she does not know enough about the sociology and history of science. Largely British, the "Strong Pro-gramme" has since the 1970s transformed our understanding of science by getting down into laboratory life. The 300-item bibliography contains three mentions of Strong Programmers (Barry Barnes, David Edge, and Trevor Pinch) but mentions none in the index or the footnotes or the text.

LaFollette therefore understates the normality of fraud in science. The historians John Farley and Gerald Geison, for example, have discov-ered that even the mighty Pasteur kept double laboratory books. Saying that science has a good deal of fraud and always has, since Galileo fibbed about his experiments and Newton engaged in a little alchemy in calcu-lating the speed of sound, is not to say that science is a Bad Thing. It is to say merely that scientists are humans, not romantic supermen, which is the main discovery of the Strong Programme. Humans trying to under-stand a complicated world are going to have to stretch. As the late Lewis Thomas put it, "there is in fact . . . a shared common earth beneath the feet of all the humanists and all the scientists. . . . It is called bewilder-ment. . . . What we have been learning in our time is that we do not understand this place or how it works, and we comprehend our own selves least of all" (1983, 157). LaFollette does not recognize the deep truth in what John Maddox, the editor of *Nature* and an establishment bad guy, admits: "Journal editors, if they are honest with themselves, will acknowledge that much, perhaps most, of what they publish will turn out to be incorrect" (quoted in LaFollette 1993, 40).

Furthermore, as the anthropologist Jonathan Marks points out in a review of LaFollette's book in the *American Scientist,* the naughty behav-ior is not properly confined to fraud. Leaving it at literal fraud will leave unasked the wider ethical questions of a scientific life. It's like the discus-sions of political ethics that focus on whether or not the congressman has committed an actually indictable offense. LaFollette's own definition extends further than she notices. "Making a false representation to obtain some unfair advantage" is unhappily routine in science and scholarship, though it's not always called fraud. In our own field it's called "playing hardball on the recruitment committee" or "using statistical significance mechanically" or "dismissing economics originating from other schools without serious reading." Marks observes that the young people who get caught doctoring their slides may well be imitating their elders:

> Junior people . . . are not necessarily the ones who establish sexual liaisons with graduate students [I know numerous famous economists who did], bend rules to get jobs for their lovers [I know a famous economist who did], write review articles promoting discoveries made by biotechnology [or investment advice] firms in which they hold stock, shoot down their enemies' grant proposals under the cloak of anonymity [it's been done to me: I caught him], or any of the dozens of other ethical breaches that aren't subsumed by "fraud" but are of a piece with it. (1992, 381)

In other words, in science as in human life generally there is a good deal of naughty behavior. There is no reason to expect economics to be any better than biology—probably worse, since a large minority of economists have adopted Prudence unadorned as a guide to ethics. Much of the naughty behavior is going to be in aid of arguments that in the end prove mistaken, such as Kelvin throwing his weight around in an attempt to squash Darwin; or, worse, such as Karl Pearson inventing neopositivism and eugenics in the same program, or Freud, in order to spread his theory to a big Swiss madhouse, dropping his principled insistence that mental patients volunteer for treatment. Fraud, with other scientific misbehavior, is not eliminated merely by Being Scientific. Some of the best scientists do it.

In charging or defending fraud the scientific establishment has misbehaved often enough to suggest a generalization. "Power tends to corrupt" would be a catchy way to put it. The Nobel laureate (and now president of Cal Tech) David Baltimore attempted in 1988 to ruin the reputation of a whistle-blower who had worked in his laboratory (he later apologized). The rhetoric Baltimore deployed is that she was a "publicity seeker," a charge the establishment always uses against inconvenient people. Yet, as LaFollette points out, "Baltimore himself turned out to be a skillful manipulator of press coverage" (1993, 153). Another case, with which I am personally acquainted, is the tarring and feathering in 1983 of a young historian by the eminent historians Henry Turner of Yale and G. D. Feldman of Berkeley. Again, the establishment proved the better publicist, sending poison pen letters to recruitment committees nation-wide. Similarly, the furor over cold fusion brought out the worst in the establishment physicists, who were granted free access to the columns of the *New York Times* for making lengthy complaints about the awful uses of publicity by Pons and Fleischman. (The episode is not discussed by LaFollette, since fraud was not the issue; but if you think it was an open-and-shut case of bad science, read Eugene Mallove's book *Fire from Ice*.)

Note well: even the first-rate, or maybe especially the first-rate, sci-entists engage in rhetorical thuggery. They get accustomed to being believed every time they open their mouths. The temptation to cash in the rhetorical capital is hard to resist. (Do you know any Nobel laureates in economics who behave like this, class?) A distinguished mathematician from Yale (a good example of a nemesis figure) engaged, for instance, in an utterly loony witch-hunt against a political scientist nominated for the National Academy. The mathematician was cashing in his scientific chips for a Left political purpose. Being Scientific, or at Yale, no more than Getting Referee Reports, is no guarantee of virtue in science.

And yet, says the editor of the *New England Journal of Medicine* (Arnold Relman, who comes across as an establishment mensch), "the whole system is based on trust. You can't run science the way you run a criminal investigation" (qtd. in LaFollette 1993, 127). That's right. LaFol-lette points out that, "in retrospect, it may seem remarkable that no one questioned [John] Darsee's phenomenal rate of production [as a researcher in cardiology in 1981 at Harvard Medical School] or asked to see his data, but such a level of trust among co-workers is normal and, indeed, encouraged among scientists" (9). Stephen Toulmin, Rom Harré, Hilary Putnam, and others have concluded that scientific truth is a mat-ter of persuasion within a speech community: "Knowledge claims," writes Harré, "are tacitly prefixed with a performative of trust" (1986, 90).

The trust means that science is a matter of human persuasion. But the persuasion in science, like the persuasion in the economy, is not self-correcting, if the notion is that we can rely entirely on greed without attention to love. Many economists miss the point, and have missed it since Hobbes. As Adam Smith understood, an economy that gets 90 per-cent of its fuel from Prudence nonetheless requires the other 10 percent to warm the market, the 10 percent that Smith called in his other book "moral sentiments." So too in science.

The implications for graduate training are not that we need courses in ethics (a while ago the Harvard Business School was given $20 million for such purposes: all the ethics that money can buy). We need to expose students to standards of scholarly integrity harder to meet than "Have a career." That's going to be hard for the science of Prudence, where doing well is identified with doing good. An essential part of the good in science is a public provision, on which the baddies find it easy to free ride. Perhaps it's time to start thinking about the free-riding on integrity in economic science. Start with LaFollette and keep going.

Rule 4
Follow the Brave

The Career Courage
of Amartya Sen

For the Eastern Economic Journal, *early 1999.*

Amartya Sen, as you know, won the Nobel Prize. About time. It put me in mind of something I've noticed about the Prize: that many of the people (need I mention the scandal that they have all been men?) have shown courage in their careers—Maurice Allais (1988), Herbert Simon (1978), Friedrich von Hayek (1974), to name three. They took intellectual chances, and so they spent time in the wilderness. Unlike the sleek imitators and *A*-primers who fill the Best Journals, they were not always rewarded with the Best Jobs: Allais was not at the center of French academic life, Hayek could not get hired by the Department of Economics at Chicago, Simon worked in Pittsburgh.

Imagine a swiggly curve, not necessarily differentiable, plotting some index, any index, of economic ideas against time. I dunno. Prevalence of nonequilibrium arguments. Mathematization. Belief in state action. Attention to historical context. Whatever. If you like, think of it as a vector function. The *A*-primers follow the curve. If they have the Best Jobs, the undignified offers from Columbia or the crazy advances on a textbook they haven't started, they are often epsilon behind it. Some Nobel Prize winners have been such *A*-primers. When you look down the list, though, not many. The original minds in economics—the Coases

(1991) or Alchians, the Buchanans (1986) or Tullocks, the Nashes (1994) or Schellings, the Beckers (1992) or Hirschmans, the Robert Fogels (1993) or Vernon Smiths, the Bob Mundells (1999) or Steve Resnicks—don't follow the curve. They leave it. They anticipate it by decades or return boldly to themes long forgotten. They use their tenure for something more noble, and Nobel, than a good raise at salary time and the accolades of the ignorant. Sometimes they lose. Among the most original minds I know in economics has spent his career at a major department without having had the slightest impact on the discipline, chiefly because he kept inventing it before the letter and writes poorly. He did game theory, for example, fifteen years before its recent rise and fall. But the courageous scholars, whether they receive the laurel wreath or not, have the satisfaction of virtue, which as you know is its own reward.

Take Milton Friedman (1976). We now think of Milton as a globe-straddling colossus (well, a 5'1" colossus), the Moses of modern macro (with Bob Lucas as Aaron), above all the prophet of pro-market politics, guru to Thatcher and Reagan. He is our age's leading "liberal" in the nineteenth century and European sense. Think of the past twenty-five years without Milton. He mattered, in economics and outside.

Yet the best way for a professor to raise a laugh in a Harvard classroom in the early 1960s was to mention the name of Milton Friedman. Just mention. He didn't have to marshal any actual *arguments* against the Little Giant. Sneering sufficed and protected the Harvard faculty of economics during its historic low point as an intellectual center (which is why I made sure to study there) from having to think through flexible exchange rates or no minimum wage or school vouchers or MV = PT. (Admittedly, when I decamped to Chicago in 1968 I found that the mere mention of the name of Ken Galbraith or Bob Solow [1987] or (to mention the scandal of the woman who first should have got the Prize) Joan Robinson had the same effect there. George Stigler [1982] didn't have to marshal *arguments* against Robinson's Marxist work or, for that matter, her work on imperfect competition. He needed merely to sneer, and the students and assistant professors would join in the fun.)

Milton Friedman was for many years a laughing stock in economics, the anti-Keynesian fanatic from Rutgers and Chicago. That the other economists were laughing at an original statistician, a devoted empiricist, and the author of *A Theory of the Consumption Function* (1957), which no economist of taste can read without thinking, "Wow: this guy is good," just shows how stupid the conventional wisdom can be and how important it is to read before sneering. When Milton finally got his Prize, his wife and fellow economist, Rose Director Friedman (whose brother Aaron at the Law School really was an Aaron to Milton's Moses), said to me that, nice as it was to get the Big One, a smaller prize and a modicum of respect in the 1940s, 1950s, and 1960s would have meant more.

Or take the entire Chicago School (please?). I won't remind Princeton (one, in 1979, shared) or Stanford (one half, in 1972, shared, if Arrow is assigned half to Stanford and half to Harvard) that cranky little Chicago has been a more courageously innovative place for economics than they (people whose creative work was done there won the prize in 1976, 1979, 1982, 1990, 1992, 1993, 1995, and 1999). When I was at Chicago in the late 1960s and 1970s it was pound-for-pound the best collection of economists ever assembled (assembled in Economics itself with Friedman's help by Theodore Schultz, laureate 1979, who had done the same trick in his youth at Iowa State; since I left in 1980 Bob and Gary and Sherwin have done a thorough job of disassembly, staffing the place with *A*-primers and curve-huggers; Chicago will have no more Nobel Prizes). In the 1970s it was: Harry Johnson. Buz Brock. Sherwin Rosen. And that was the second string.

But in 1968 the place was under siege. Hard as it is for any economist under 40 to believe, in the 1960s everyone hated the Chicago School. I admit I have been amazed how well a little group of Scandinavians has chosen the Prize (though I would rather see it lapse, because its scarcity blights the declining years of so many male economists). That people at first hate you, laugh at you, sneer at you, write you out of the game is almost a test of real intellectual merit—thus Bob Lucas (1995) in the wilderness at Carnegie-Mellon. The time of scorn is not *sufficient* for merit, which is what confuses monetary cranks and others who think that because they are scorned they must be geniuses. But it's something like necessary. Normal science is often so idiotically wrong (need I mention statistical significance, class?) that the *A*-primers and curve-huggers almost never generate real intellectual merit.

All right. What about Sen? He got the prize, according to the muddled citation, for his early work in social choice, such as *Collective Choice and Social Welfare* (1970b), and for his later work on poverty and ethics, such as *On Ethics and Economics* (1987). Courage or curve-hugging?

Both. Sen's early work is strikingly unoriginal. It dots the *I*s and crosses the *T*s on Arrow's Impossibility Theorem. It looked unlikely in 1970 that Sen would ever be worthy of the glittering prize. A good, workmanlike job, yes, and a smooth path in a career, because second-raters can get most enthusiastic about second-rate work done beautifully, and the second-rate provide most of the faculty votes and almost all the deans. That's what makes Schultz's double performance as chair at Iowa State in the 1930s and 1940s and at Chicago in the 1950s and early 1960s so astounding. He could pick 'em, and the kind of people he picked were first-raters like George Stigler (whom he hired at Iowa State in 1936 and rehired at Chicago) and Margaret Reid (who was at Iowa State from 1930 but whom Schultz encouraged when, in 1934, he became chair and then brought to Chicago; she invented permanent income and coinvented household economics; note well, ye misogynistic Scandinavians, and weep).

Sen, however, proceeded to do something with his tenure and his A-prime eminence. Beginning with his little essay in the *Journal of Political Economy* in 1970, "The Impossibility of a Paretian Liberal," he embarked courageously on a program of reminding economists that we live in an ethical universe. We live not in that best of all possible worlds that Stigler liked to suppose but a universe of good and evil, a universe in which the Coase Theorem rules (not Stigler's So-Called Coase Theorem but the real one), under which human arrangements can have inefficient outcomes. People can starve in the midst of plenty, and, Sen argued, in 1943 in his native Bengal, they did.

To get economics off the Benthamite line that any evaluation outside of money is mistaken is a great accomplishment, though only a beginning. Up to 1970 Sen's work is A-prime, and after 1970 it is prime. It is for books like *On Ethics and Economics* that he deserves the money and the wild adulation he has gotten now in India.

If your reaction is, "What's she talking about? That's normative economics. I do positive economics," I suggest you grow up and start reading ethical philosophy more serious than "De Gustibus Non Disputandum Est." You would do well to pick up a nice little undergraduate text by James Rachels, *The Elements of Moral Philosophy* (1993). What Sen has shown is that you are already doing ethical thinking. You might as well get serious.

In the fall of 1997 I started to read C. S. Lewis again. As a bookish adolescent I had read *The Screwtape Letters* (1942) and much later, as a youngish adult, his autobiography, *Surprised by Joy* (1956). Lewis, you know, was a professor of literature at Oxbridge, a writer of children's books, and a Christian apologist, specifically Anglican, active in the 1940s and 1950s. In *Mere Christianity* (1952, based on lectures published in

1943–45) Lewis was arguing for the existence of a Moral Law, beyond convention or evolutionary prudence, and points out that:

> there is one thing, and one only, in the whole universe which we know more about than we could learn from external observation. That one thing is Man [Humanity, if you please!]. . . . In this case we have, so to speak, inside information; we are in the know. And because of that, we know that men find themselves under a moral law, which they did not make, and cannot quite forget even when they try, and which they know they ought to obey. . . . Anyone studying Man from the outside as we study electricity or cabbages, not knowing our language , . . . would never get the slightest evidence that we had this moral law. . . . His observations would only show what we did, and the moral law is about what we ought to do. (Lewis 1952 [1996], 35)

What we really, truly know, Lewis is arguing, is this extra-behaviorist fact about our ethical selves. I think, therefore I judge.

As you would expect, on the same page Lewis drew theistic conclusions from the fact of the moral law:

> We want to know whether the universe simply happens to be what it is for no reason or whether there is a power behind it that makes it what it is. . . . There is only one case in which we can know whether there is anything more, namely our own case. And in that one case we find there is.

Eerie. But the way I am using Lewis's argument does not depend on a belief in God (he elaborates it on pp. 17–39; Lewis was not the originator of the argument; it is found in Kant, I think). A prejudice against belief in God need not stand in the way of admitting Lewis's original observation: what we Know is *ethical.*

What we together know, small *k*, as reality, small *r*, is what we should agree on for practical purposes (but you see the intrusion of ethics even into small-*k* knowledge in that *should*). What we Know as Reality, capital *K* and capital *R*, if we know anything at that exalted level, is *only* ethical. Ought, not Is. So it's silly to think of ethical thought as something nonscientific. This we know.

Prudence (self-interest, Max *U*) is a virtue. We do want to have people around us who can take care of themselves. But there are other virtues that economics should acknowledge operating in the economy and which in any case work in the lives of our ethical heroes. Nobels do not come only from Prudence (Debreu) but from Love (Solow), Temperance (Coase), Faith (Buchanan), Hope (Hayek), and Justice (Sen). And there's Courage in it all, to leave the curve of dull-normal science.

The Coolness of
Alexander Gerschenkron

I wrote the piece in spring 1992 for the American Scholar. *That's a magazine economists who are serious about becoming scholars might want to subscribe to. The magazine's title comes from Emerson's essay of 1837, another item every aspiring economistic scholar ought to read.*

We must have had teachers who made us teachers. In my own case from the sixth grade to my first teaching job they were (I write them out in a verse) Stanton, Melcher, Brisbois, /Gustafson the Moghul,/ Meyer, Gerschenkron, Temin,/ and Bob Fogel. Alexander Gerschenkron was not the best teacher or the best economist or the best historian among them, not even, I think, the best human being. But he was the best scholar I have known.

Gerschenkron was an economic historian and a comparativist, writing on the European past and the Soviet present. He taught from 1948 to 1975 in the Department of Economics at Harvard, producing, if that is quite the word, scores of graduate students and writing a moderate number of books. He made an impression. Students and colleagues lived in awe of him, and not only because they were merely economists while he was everything, a polymath ranging over statistics and Greek poetry. Other people who also know everything—the Bernard Lewises and the Albert Hirschmans of the scholarly world—tell stories about Gerschenkron's erudition and wit as though they too were impressed.

He was born in Odessa in 1904. We think: like his friend the medievalist M. M. Postan, a fellow Russian residing among the gullible Westerners, he liked to tell his students vivid stories about his life. We students were never quite sure when he was ornamenting the stories for effect. He came from a bourgeois, Orthodox family, long converted from Judaism, and was raised by a French-speaking governess. His family fled the civil war in 1920 to the comparative calm of Austria (he told a story of his father and him fording a river into Romania on their way to Vienna), where he received a gymnasium education, adding Latin, Greek, and German to his Russian and French.

Later he acquired languages with astonishing ease, Swedish one week, Bulgarian the next. The story circulated that he needed Portuguese for some minor purpose and, knowing all the other Romance tongues, found the grammar the job of an afternoon. Starting to read a stack of easy Portuguese that evening, he at first found the going a little tough but gradually easier. Suddenly it clicked, and he was reading fluently. Ah, success. Several minutes into his triumph, however, he noticed that the text he had picked up was not in fact Portuguese but . . . English: *he had not noticed the change in language.* Italian he knew very well, Dutch, Swedish, Lord knows what else. He wrote a somewhat Latinate English well. I seem to recall that in retirement he worked at Chinese, too, but perhaps that is an extrapolation by a dazzled monolingual.

Gerschenkron studied economics and politics at the University of Vienna, managed a motorcycle firm for a few years, and worked during the 1930s as an economist in Viennese research institutes. The Anchluss drove him to the United States in 1938, a double refugee in the intellectual migration. He told a story to students about coming across to Switzerland on the passport of a St. Bernard dog, but this version was one of his spoofs. (The correct story, which he told to colleagues, was that he was to join his wife, Erika, already in Switzerland, by crossing with a companion on a day-pass for mountain walkers. The border guard was annoyed by the vagueness of the pass—"This says, 'Admit two,' Admit two what? That could be a man and a dog. If it is two men, say two men. If it is two dogs, say so"—but then let them through.) During the 1940s he taught at Berkeley and worked as a flanger on Liberty ships in the Oakland shipyard, his contribution to the war effort and his melding with ordinary Americans. His grandson, a journalist who is writing a book about him, tells of Gerschenkron having said once: "I seriously considered staying in the shipyard. I liked the contact with the anonymous mass of Americans. And the work doesn't follow you at night and into your dreams." After the war he worked for the Federal Reserve Board in Washington. His Austrian dissertation, translated into English as *Bread and Democracy in Germany,* combines a historian's and an economist's intellectual values, no easy matter but characteristic of his intellectual life.

American academia, stuffy and second-rate though it was then, absorbed many of these astonishing people from *Mitteleuropa*. I later lived in Iowa City next to the philosopher and junior member of the Vienna Circle, Gustav Bergmann; and wrote about Karl and Michael Polanyi; and fell under the influence of Hannah Arendt, among the hundreds and thousands of first-raters who made America the center of intellectual life after the war. I was impressed. Academics of my generation think of real intellectuals and scientists as speaking with a heavy German or Hungarian or Russian accent. I do not know what possessed the stuffy and second-rate Harvard faculty of economics in 1948 to hire Gerschenkron as the replacement for the great historian of technology Abbott Payson Usher. Perhaps Gerschenkron impressed them too.

Beyond Gerschenkron's early work in measuring Soviet industrial output his main scholarly contribution was a "theory of relative backwardness," which gave an account of the differing ways that European countries industrialized. He first formulated it in 1952, at age 48, and tested and elaborated it for the rest of his life. He argued that a country like Russia, backward relative to Britain when it started industrializing, did not go through the same stages. It leapt over them, using the state as a substitute for the missing prerequisites of economic growth. Growth was force-fed in Russia, and to a lesser extent in Germany, with consequences for the character of the places. Russia grew with giant enterprises instead of small firms, centralized control instead of competitive markets, an overbearing military-industrial complex instead of peace-loving capitalists.

I first met Gerschenkron in the fall of 1964, when he was 60 and eminent for these thoughts, in the first week of my graduate education. He was teaching his yearlong course on European economic history required of all the would-be economists. Harvard had, to my relief, just gotten rid of the language requirement for the Ph.D. degree in economics (you were allowed to substitute mathematics and statistics). It had shortly before gotten rid of the requirement that economists learn the history of their discipline. Later, in Harvard's final contribution to breadth in economic education, it got rid of this very requirement in economic history, the study of which Henry Rosovsky (an early Gerschenkron student himself) has described as "virtually the only course in the graduate economics curriculum that directly assaulted the provincialism of most students." But until Gerschenkron retired you had to take a full year of him, writing two long papers applying economics to some event in economic history and suffering an assault from a most unprovincial man.

In 1964, as it happened, Gerschenkron puzzled us for a few weeks with the theory of index numbers, his great formal love in economics (there is still a proposition in index numbers known as the Gerschenkron Effect), and then fell ill before getting to any economic history. A bad heart plagued him throughout the 1960s and 1970s, and this was another long episode. One of them, not this one I think, was brought on by a heroic sprint along the platform of the subway at Harvard Square to stop a despondent Soviet visitor from throwing himself under the wheels of the train. When I first encountered him he was slight of build, thinned down, I was told, from a pre–heart attack plumpness. His office was littered with bottles of brandy, a glass of which he offered to all comers. The brandy was supposed to be for his heart, you see, although Rosovosky remembers it from before the heart trouble. Again, one never knew.

One never knew much with Gerschenkron. William Parker of Yale, another distinguished economic historian, fleetingly Gerschenkron's student, has complained bitterly about the master's skill at keeping everyone around him off balance. Paul David of Stanford, also distinguished and also his student, describes Gerschenkron discovering one day that this particular student was not a morning person; henceforth all their meetings were scheduled for 7:00 A.M. at the Faculty Club.

He was on sick leave the entire academic year 1964–65, and I therefore was not taught economic history by the man in a classroom. Albert Imlah of Tufts University and Barry Supple, a young Englishman then at the Business School across the river, filled in for Gerschenkron that year. But we did the Gerschenkron reading list and papers, the papers being the only opportunity for creativity in a mind-stunning program of mainly useless formalisms (economic education has not changed, though the mathematical ante has risen), and the subject intrigued me.

So did the man, from a distance. My father was his colleague (over in the Department of Government) and like all the faculty was filled with admiration for Gerschenkron. They were friends, in the nonintimate way that two such men could be friends, exchanging sporting news and learned witticisms over the Long Table at the Faculty Club. I have my father's copy of Gerschenkron's most well-known work, *Economic Backwardness in Historical Perspective: A Book of Essays* (1962), inscribed, when my father was in the hospital after a botched appendicitis operation: "To Bob, this small offering to Aesculapius with warmest personal regards and all good wishes, Alex, January 1963." The classical reference was characteristic and the Socratic echo appropriate, too.

It was from my father about then that I first heard the Ted Williams story. Gerschenkron, who was a serious student of baseball and basketball—it was part of his commitment to his new nation—claimed to know Ted Williams, the retired star of his beloved Boston Red Sox. "Williams, you know," he would say, "is no boob. In fact, he's quite well read, and has a special interest in economics and history. But he expresses himself, naturally enough, in baseball terms." Oh, is that so? What does he think about Ken Galbraith? "He says: 'Galbraith hits very high flies to very short left field.'" What about Arnold Toynbee, the theoretician of history? "Ted says, 'Toynbee hits a homerun every time he steps up to the plate. But he forgets to touch the bases as he runs it out.'" Here was a scholar. The next academic year I signed up for his seminar.

There began two years in which I learned my trade in the seminar, with students like Richard Sutch, Barbara Solow, Peter McClelland, Bob Zevin, Knick Harley, Dick Sylla, Tom Sargent, David Loschky, Stefano Fenoaltea (the last briefly: it was a fault in Gerschenkron that he could not stand the aristocratic arrogance of a young man who went on to become the leading student of Italian economic history and of more; they quarreled over a criticism Fenoaltea had made of Gerschenkron's pioneering work on Italy, and Fenoaltea was banished). To say that Gerschenkron "taught" us would be too Anglo-Saxon and direct. The Latin is better: we were educated, drawn out. Gerschenkron never intervened during the main business of the seminar. He sat puffing his pipe (a substitute for cigarettes), watching the graduate students teach one another.

I recognize now that he had a brilliant sense of ceremony and honor. He always scheduled his seminar in the evenings, once a week, and arranged for proper seminar rooms, never classrooms, which gave the seminar a dignity hard to achieve between 10:30 and 11:50 A.M., TuTh in PHBA 213, with chairs bolted to the floor. He played the judge listening to the attorneys quarreling in the well. No other faculty were allowed to attend, except his own student McClelland, an assistant professor until moving to Cornell. A paper would be presented, distributed in advance, and criticized by the other students. (I learned from the experience, and from Fogel's workshop in Chicago, that this is the way to run a seminar: *never* allow the speaker to read or even present the paper; *always* have the paper distributed beforehand. It's the only way to create the right incentives to read beforehand and to discuss with seriousness during.)

Gerschenkron's only direct contribution would be a delphic comment at the end, before closing the proceedings. Often it would be evaluative, and the students would ache for a hint of approval. Approval was never more than a hint, to preserve its scarcity value. A particularly unimaginative paper on subject X, which had been utterly demolished by the junior attorneys, evoked only the summarizing remark, formed of delicate irony, "Well . . . we certainly know more about subject X than we did two hours ago."

Honor, he understood, is crucial for intellectual work. People do not go to graduate school, even in economics in the boom time of the late 1960s, to make money. They go and stay for honor. I later tried to persuade university administrators that honor is a good substitute for cash in bad times, but they are obsessed with budget cuts and the *numerus clausus* for registered races and could not hear. Gerschenkron gave out honors as though they mattered. An A in his course was something special, based wholly on one's performance on the big paper. He often did not get around to reading the final exams, which irritated the students but made pedagogic sense. The point of graduate school is scholarship, not quiz mastering, something that departments of economics might take to heart. The interviews in his office were made into little ceremonies. Conversations in the hallway were made to tell. He gave fellowships from a foundation grant that he got when he realized that a new economic history, more analytic than the old, was coming into being, and he gave out the fellowships with a gravity suitable to the honor.

He scrounged for us honored economic historians some office space in the attic of an old building on Linden Street, which housed mainly the Harvard Bureau of Study Counsel and, across the hall from us, the magazine of the American (really, it should be said: the "Northeastern and especially Bostonian") Academy of Arts and Sciences, *Daedalus,* before the AAAS moved to Norton's Wood. In the attic we were to have a Workshop. The word *workshop,* with *laboratory,* was a Gerschenkron favorite. Scholarship was work as in a motorcycle repair shop; it was as the chemists and biologists would say a "bench science" in the laboratory (the word is Latin for *workshop:* Gerschenkron's Latinism). In a preface to the book by his student Albert Fishlow he praised "the statistical appendixes in which the author offers a full insight into his laboratory and without which no real appreciation of the importance of the study and of the validity of its interpretative results is possible." It was an honor to labor in the Workshop, though Gerschenkron would have been appalled by our ignorant motto, characteristic of young economists, which we hung over the door (he never came up: more laissez faire): "Give us the data and we will finish the job." "Give us the data, the facts given." Good Lord, my children: *find* and *take* and *make* them, dears.

What Gerschenkron understood about teaching graduate students, which most professors do not, is that their tribes are important for their educations. He did not wish to be our friend; he was willing to be our totem, our untouchable king, a remote and sardonically amused father from whom honor derives. The Baker Report from the University of Chicago around 1980 made this point about the later years of graduate school, stressing that graduate students need an honorable social life connected to their intellectual life. Again no administrator has listened.

One can justify in such terms a practice that will seem unjustifiable otherwise. Gerschenkron "supervised" dissertations with a notably light hand. In my case, which was not unusual, we had in four years from start to finish many chats, much sparring about the defenestration of Prague (May 23, 1618, a favorite topic for exhibiting erudition) or the merits of an Anglo-Saxon as against a Latinate vocabulary in writing English or the chances this season for the Celtics but exactly one discussion about my dissertation and that desultory.

In this he was practicing a theory of graduate teaching, not merely avoiding students. On the contrary, he interviewed at length every one of the 50 students in his graduate class each term as preparation for their papers. Unlike many economists, he was not always rushing about advising governments or giving seminars (I never got him to come out to Chicago to give a paper, for example) and was available for student talk. But when you were embarking on the first piece of independent work as a scholar he would not let you whine about it or let you receive detailed instructions from the master. I later learned that some professors have the opposite theory, that a graduate student should be led in detail: Gregg Lewis at Chicago (and then at Duke) was the master of this technique. It results in the giving of many degrees and the production of much normal science. Whether it results in creative scholars is not so clear.

Gerschenkron taught by example, but in his office, not on the lecture circuit. Waiting in his astonishingly chaotic office for an interview one day I received from the nearest of numerous stacks of books and magazines a lesson in the scholarly life, the sort of lesson that professors sometimes forget they give. The stack contained a book of plays in Latin, a book on non-Euclidean geometry, a book of chess problems, numerous statistical tomes, journals of literature and science, several historical works in various languages, and, at the bottom of it all, two feet down, a well-worn copy of *Mad* magazine.

Ceremony was the key to such a mythologized theory of teaching, as when his graduate students were invited up to his dacha in New Hampshire for an annual meal, filled with ironic ceremonies. There was for one thing the ceremony of the ride up, if you went in his car. He drove like a madman, at Italian speed but without Italian skill. One time the car broke down, and I went out and fiddled with the carburetor, accidentally fixing it. Gerschenkron ever after touted my mechanical ability (of which I had little), by contrast with his European and upper-class ignorance of the internal combustion engine. Come to think of it, the pose was odd in view of his stint selling motorcycles and his bourgeois, if privileged, origins. Probably it was one of his little jokes.

The compulsory croquet game at the dacha was certainly one of them. The students and spouses would participate, but Gerschenkron always won. By cheating. He would make up house rules of great ingenuity to his own advantage. If nonetheless it appeared he might lose, he would abruptly adjourn the game: it was suddenly time for drinks indoors before dinner. We learned at one of these dinners that he was tone deaf, unable to distinguish one tune from another. It seemed to us the only flaw in an otherwise complete cultivation.

The visits to New Hampshire were occasions to meet Erika, who did not have the cheerful disposition of her husband but had some of the same cultivation. She was I think Austrian and had in any case been taught like her husband to keep on teaching herself after school. They wrote an article together about translations of Shakespeare, published in a literary journal. Gerschenkron delighted in publishing in literary journals—it was claimed, not inconceivably but, I take it, falsely, that when Roman Jakobson retired in 1960 from his chair in Slavic literature at Harvard the economist Alexander Gerschenkron was offered it.

If honor was important for maintaining scholarly standards among students and colleagues, then dishonor had to have a place, too. Gerschenkron could be harshly evaluative in a way that makes the American-born, with their cult of niceness, wince. He wrote, for example, a devastating review of a translation from Russian of a book in economics, attacking in detail the author's apparently feeble command of the language. Later at a conference the translator had the temerity to approach Gerschenkron and say amiably, "I want you to know, Professor Gerschenkron, that I am not angry about your review." Gerschenkron turned on him and replied: "Angry? Angry? Why should you be angry? Ashamed, yes. Angry, no."

The scholarly ethos of care was prominently commended in Gerschenkron's reviews and in his footnote polemics. Carefulness in the European scholarly tradition consists of avoiding error in detail and putting forward conclusions with suitable modesty. Gerschenkron here did not inhabit the world of modern economics, in which theory is said to provide a check on facts and in which a blackboard exercise is said to have "policy implications." Most particularly, he detested theories of history that can in their rigidity supply bridges across evidential voids— Marxism most notably—and favored theories such as Toynbee's that provide merely a way to shape the facts into a story.

Sir John Hicks, later a Nobel laureate, wrote a lamentable book in 1969 called *A Theory of Economic History,* based on his ruminations without enough trips to the library concerning what medieval life must have been like, theoretically speaking. (I learned later that Sir John read only Oxford University Press books, because as a syndic for the press he could get them free; but Oxford's list could have provided him sounder factual material than he used.) In the book Hicks advanced the notion, which some other equally close students of the period have adopted on Hicks's authority (or on their own lack of reading: thus Douglass North), that manorialism and serfdom were voluntary exchanges of labor for "protection" between lord and peasant. In his review of the book Gerschenkron noted with a characteristic turn of phrase that "the possibility that the main, if not the only, danger against which the peasant very frequently was in need of protection was the very lord is not mentioned."

He wrote judgmentally about scholarly discourse, raising up or breaking down this or that other scholar's ethos, "character." Such judgments are usually suppressed in scholarly prose. In *Europe in the Russian Mirror* he admired Tugan-Baranovskii (6ff: "valuable contribution"; "probably the most original Russian economist, . . . amazingly broad in his interests"; and, his greatest compliment, "a serious scholar"). Such compliments served more to honor the author than the subject—which of course was their rhetorical purpose. The author exhibited the good taste to admire the best work. The old Russian economist's "amazingly broad interests" turned out to be merely subjects within economics, whereas the writer himself, also a Russian economist, ranged over mathematics, Western literature, and the history of baseball.

A long time ago David Riesman wrote, in his *Constraint and Variety*

in American Education, of academic life that "looked at from the perspective of our national problems, it . . . seems remote and crazy like a
sport, and it so strikes perhaps the majority of students. But . . . we
always hope that if we run well enough, some students will run the race
too, and become as crazy as we." Gerschenkron's theory of teaching was
successful at making his students as crazy as he.

Gerschenkron was able to get the newly crazed students to run the
race approximately as he wanted them to do. Yet the students deserve
some of the credit. It was not merely that the Harvard students were
smart. Smartness does not go very far in scholarship. Lots of people are
smart. I've known beer-soaked day laborers who were as "smart" as
many of the best scholars I've known. What made the Harvard students
better, as I've noted from teaching at a lot of other places, is that when
they admired a teacher they did what he or she advised them to do. When
Gerschenkron advised me one year to support myself in part by teaching
in the then left-leaning Social Studies Program, I saluted and went off and
taught Marx-Durkheim-Weber for a year with an anthropology grad student named Renato Rosaldo. As a result, I have never sneered at sociologists and anthropologists or at Marxists or at left-leaners, which most
mainstream economists do without knowing what they are sneering at. It
was good advice. When Gerschenkron advised me to go to England to
complete work on my dissertation on the British iron and steel industry
(a wonderful book: read it and join the fun) I bought a ticket. No whin-
ing about needing to get a job earlier. As a result, I came in contact with
economic historians of a less technocratic type and again lost my sneering rights. The Harvard students took advice well. I have noticed at
Chicago and Iowa and elsewhere that less able graduate students do not
follow advice well—this, not their lower IQs, is their main disability.
They substitute instead their own and necessarily defective scholarly
tastes.

To speak in rhetorical terms, Gerschenkron taught by ethos. The
beginning, or exordium, of a speech is meant in the classical system to
establish an ethos, the good character warranting attention. Gerschenkron's presentation of self was largely "ethical" in this sense. He
did not teach by *explicatio* or *amplificatio* but by ethos.

A person's life is an argument. We think less of Marx for his neglect
of Jenny and his ignorance of physical work; and we think less of the
modernist heroes of economics now for their frank appeals to selfishness,
exhibited in their lives. Gerschenkron shaped his life to better values.
Although I do not think he was a paragon (his treatment of Fenoaltea

was disgraceful), he stood the bigger tests. In the year of tested values, 1968, for example, this private man spoke publicly against nihilism at Harvard. He gave a famous speech to one of the tumultuous faculty meetings (at which my father played whip to the economist John Dunlop's parliamentary leadership of the "conservatives"), "The Most Amazing Thing." It was based on the Hans Christian Andersen story in which the lout wins the hand of the princess by wrecking an amazing clock, an act more "amazing" than the clock itself. (The year of the louts proved a strain on my father, who had a heart condition himself, unknown; he died the next summer.)

The year after the violence Gerschenkron retreated for a while to the Institute for Advanced Study. Another Gerschenkron tale was generated, a tribute more to his erudition than his originality. An administrator from Princeton came out to the Institute with the strange purpose of discussing a proposal for a Black Studies Program. Academic life was abuzz with the Black Power intimidations at Cornell (I later got a conservative's-eye view of what had happened there from Allan Bloom when he interviewed for a job in Social Thought at Chicago). The Princeton administrator had an understandably difficult time getting the fellows at the Institute, Gerschenkron among them, to see merit in the proposal. Sweating under the strain, the administrator finally gave up rational argument and blurted out, "Well, we have to do something: after all, they have the guns." A stunned silence descended on the group, into which after a pause Gerschenkron dropped the reply, delivered in his bass Russian voice: "Ven I hear the vord *guns* . . . I reach for my culture."

About the same time the Soviet tanks rolled into Prague, Gerschenkron spoke eloquently to the meetings of the American Economic History Association, at Brandeis that year, against participation in a forthcoming conference at Leningrad. His eloquence, like that at Harvard, was unsuccessful, and the Association decamped to Leningrad, honoring the tyrants. But Gerschenkron had established his ethos clearly enough.

You can see why his students worshiped him. He was, as the kids say (and so did we), cool, that is, witty, self-possessed, courageous, outspoken—an ethos attractive to the young, and most particularly to young men. In his case it was combined with a mature scholarly purpose.

What did I learn from such a walking exordium? It was not his particular theories of economic history (assessed later in a book edited by two other students, Richard Sylla and Gianni Toniolo). It was his way of life, and especially his mixing of genres, mixing democratic with highbrow amusements, literature with science, economics with history, mathematics with words. Sylla tells a story of attending to his thesis up in our attic workshop one spring afternoon and getting a phone call from Gerschenkron. Sylla was also a basketball fan and could hear in the background the radio in Gerschenkron's study blaring out the NBA finals, in which the Celtics were playing. The student thought to please the master. (Henry Rosovsky had found a quotation from *The Sayings of the Masters* for the festschrift for Gerschenkron, *Industrialization in Two Systems* [1966], which expressed all our anxieties on this score: "The day is short, and the work is great, and the reward is much, and the Master is urgent.") So Sylla bragged a little to Gerschenkron that, instead of listening to basketball, he was working on his thesis. Gerschenkron saw his chance. "Oh, Dick," he exclaimed in mock disappointment (he always called his students by their first and informal name; more Americanism, this), "You're not listening to the Celtics?! And I thought you were an *intellectual*."

I formed an image of a complete scholar, the American scholar, though from Russia and Austria. The American scholar, as Emerson said, is not thinking man but man thinking, not a specialized thumb or brain strutting about but a whole person exercising all human powers.

The image was of course unattainable. None of the students could come close to the master in foreign languages or worldly experience, to name two accomplishments of the complete scholar. But holding the image up does keep at least one from sneering at other knowledge. Specialists comfortable at being partial humans get angry when someone says what is true of us all, that we are shamefully ignorant. Gerschenkron would reply: Angry? Angry? Why should you be angry? Ashamed, yes. Angry, no.

I think all his students learned this. Something I learned which does not appear to be shared by many of his other students is a belief in the importance of words. That is, I learned from his example that wordcraft, rhetoric, runs even a mathematical and quantitative field like economics. It became one of the main themes of my scholarly life. Gerschenkron himself recognized the rhetoric in science, and especially he recognized social theories as metaphors. He was aware that words are not mere tags for things behind them but are tools in the scholar's workshop. His main contribution to scholarship was to revise radically the metaphor of social "stages," which had dominated nineteenth-century and much twentieth-century social thought. Henry Maine, Auguste Comte, Friedrich List, Karl Marx, Werner Sombart [he of blondes and brunettes], Bruno Hildebrand, Max Weber, and, latterly, Walt Rostow and then the "new" growth theories of the 1980s thought of a nation as a person, with predictable stages of development from birth to maturity. The stage theorists took the child to be the father of the man. Gerschenkron was the new Freud, noting the pathologies arising from stages missed or badly taken, casting doubt on the iron law of succession, noting substitutes for prerequisites in development.

Gerschenkron justified his substitute and economistic metaphor in a mainly Kantian rather than a Baconian way. He appears to have become over time more Kantian, becoming more convinced as Kant said that "concepts without perceptions are empty; perceptions without concepts are blind." The Kantian point of view, when you think of the matter in economic terms, is similar to weights in a statistical index of industrial output. That is, it's at choice, for some human purpose on which we must agree, not given by God's universe. Facts lie around, but interpretations, which anyway are involved in all facts, are a human business *about* the circumambient facts. Failure to grasp this obvious point has ruined much hard work, as in the absurdities of statistical significance and positive economics. William Parker has argued that Gerschenkron's experience of repeated transplantation from Russia to Austria to America led him to the problem of point of view. Parker's story fits Gerschenkron's fascination with manner of viewpoint problems: index numbers, relative backwardness, and literary translation (most notably a devastating assault on Nabokov's translation of Pushkin's *Eugene Onegin,* in *Modern Philology* [May 1966]; Nabokov got back at him by introducing into *Ada* [1969] a fictional pedant named "Dr. Gerschizkevsky." Gerschenkron remarked, "A small man's revenge").

He was the best scholar, I would say, because he was the best rhetorician. I mean *rhetoric* not in some cheap definition favored in the newspapers but in its oldest and most honorable definition, what Werner Jaeger called "the first humanism." Words, Gerschenkron recognized, are what we have in common, not things.

A rhetorical reading of Gerschenkron does not reveal him as a nonscientist, a mere word spinner. He shaped in his work a story of his own life, one of attention to the words themselves. Master scientists from Galileo to Gould are master rhetoricians, word spinners in no dishonorable sense, or else they do not remake the sciences. Gerschenkron's science was model building but also storytelling. It used the capacities of language, self-consciously. He showed that science is rhetoric, all the way down.

The Passion of
Robert Fogel

*For a conference honoring Fogel's work (mainly by doing some),
published as Claudia Goldin and Hugh Rockoff, eds.*, Strategic
Factors in Nineteenth-Century American Economic History
*(Chicago: University of Chicago Press, 1992). I had just written a
piece nominating Fogel, and Douglass North, for the Nobel Prize,
so I was primed with praise.*

Officially, I was not Fogel's student but his colleague, from 1968, when I
arrived at Chicago as an assistant professor, until 1975, when Fogel left
for a sojourn at Harvard (he came back to Chicago in 1981, but by that
time I had left for Iowa). Being Fogel's colleague, though, felt like being
his student. The feeling was reinforced by the students he had gathered in
1968, such as Jacob Metzer and Claudia Goldin and Joe Reid and Hugh
Rockoff, who were about my age and knew a lot more economics than I
did. One could not be around the best historical economist since Schumpeter for any length of time without learning a lot, even if such a one
were not a great teacher. But Fogel was. Gladly would he learn and
gladly teach.

Fogel's personal qualities smoothed the way and taught their own
lessons. He is for one thing the soul of wit and warmth. Wit is common
enough in academic life, and especially so among economists, irrationally
proud of their quickness. William James called it the "Harvard indifference": "the smoking of cigarettes and living on small sarcasms."
Warmth, however, is rare. The average academic applies his small sarcasms indiscriminately to his students and junior colleagues and certainly
to his rivals. Fogel refrained from "applying" his wit to people. Anyone
in Fogel's presence, from the cab driver waiting in front of the Quadrangle Club to the president of the university, gets treated with the same
warmth, spiced—not poisoned—by his wit.

Fogel, in other words, is more of a democrat than most of us. He therefore does not commit the characteristic sin of academic life, sneering. In the three decades I have known him I have not seen him sneer, not once, despite his numerous opportunities. Fogel's personal and intellectual tolerance shames us. I once complained to him about the rank favoritism that William Parker exhibited in his hiring at Yale, disregarding merit (mine, for example) in favor of his former students. Fogel laughed tolerantly: it is not the worst of sins, he said, to favor one's own. I once tried to persuade him at lunch that certain activities in mathematical economics, hostile to his empirical values, were not good for economics. No, said he, we cannot tell; the investment in today's existence theorem may pay off in 50 years. Fogel can teach because he is willing to learn from the least of us, ready to see merit in the misled, ready to attribute admirable motives to his enemies.

So the first thing he taught students and colleagues was a simple, democratic, even American openness. The openness is hard to learn. The political theorist Judith Skhlar described snobbery as "the habit of making inequality hurt." Snobbery and sneering are antidemocratic vices. American democracy has always been uncomfortable with scholarship, as an elitist activity devoted to making an inequality of knowledge hurt. But in Robert Fogel's case being a superior scholar does not entail making others hurt.

His easy relations with his students and junior colleagues were something new for me. Fogel and his wife Enid took the social responsibilities of academic leadership seriously. My supervisor, Gerschenkron, had been amusing and courteous in a European way but no drinking buddy with junior faculty and graduate students. At Chicago circa 1968, however, drinking with intellectual buddies was the style, the most serious teachers in this line being Al Harberger, Larry Sjaastad, Bob Mundell, Harry Johnson, and Bob Fogel. Fogel would meet the students and faculty after the weekly economic history workshop for beer and too many bowls of potato chips at the Quadrangle Club. He would pick up the bill when the last student tottered home then walk up 57th Street with Harry Johnson to the apartment.

The talk at the drinking table was about economics. The students learned economics personally, by discussing real economic institutions with a first-rate economist. We never talked about sports, seldom about public or academic politics. The questions were, what do you make of this or that economic argument? Does it fit the historical evidence? What kind of evidence? How would you get it? How do you know?

The evidence Fogel favored was quantitative. He approved of the remark by Lord Kelvin, slightly misquoted in the stones of the Social Science Building at Chicago: "When you cannot measure it, when you cannot express it in numbers, your knowledge is of a meagre and unsatisfactory kind. . . . It may be the beginning of knowledge, but you have scarcely in your thoughts advanced to the stage of science."

Even in conversations outside of class Fogel pursued quantitative science. He pursued it with algebra, not geometry. Fogel believed that when one could not express an economic argument in algebra your knowledge was of a meager and unsatisfactory kind. Many lunchtime hours in the solarium of the Quad Club were spent in communal attempts to convert someone's geometrical or verbal argument into algebra, and this for two reasons.

First, Fogel thinks algebraically. He will not believe a proposition until it has been put through his algebraic tortures, complete with cunning asterisks and subtle subscripts and mind-stunning tables of variables. The mathematician Ian Stewart notes what others have, that there are two kinds of mathematicians: "Most work in terms of visual images and mental pictures; a minority thinks in formulas." And so in other fields: "Johannes Müller, a famous biologist, said that his mental picture of a dog was like this: DOG" (Stewart 1990, 95). Fogel's mental picture of American slavery seems to be something like this: $P^* = H^* - i^* + X^*$.

Second, if one is going to do more than speculate in a pointless *A*-prime, *C*-prime, way on the direction of effects, you need the algebra, because only then can you use actual measurements. Here was the great principle: measure then measure again then measure yet again. Fogel is like a carpenter of history, spending as much time in measuring and remeasuring as in sawing or hammering: measure twice, cut once. He agrees with John Clapham, the first holder of a chair of economic history at Cambridge: "every economic historian should . . . have acquired what might be called the statistical sense, the habit of asking in relation to any institution, group or movement the questions: how large? how long? how often? how representative?" (Clapham 1930, 416). Substitute *social scientist* for *economic historian,* and add to "institution, group or movement" the phrase *alleged explanation,* and you have Fogel's procedure exactly.

The procedure meant that as little as possible was left to blackboard speculation. Other economists might be content to note the *likelihood* that social savings of railroads were small, the *possibility* that economies of scale in sectors served by railroads were large, the *existence* of miscegenation among slaves and masters, the *presence* of nutritional effects in death rates. Fogel insisted on measuring them. He sought oomph. As he wrote about declining mortality since 1700, "the debate . . . revealed that the critical differences were quantitative rather than qualitative" (Fogel 1986, 105). The "debate" (a favorite Fogel word) was always "revealing" to him that the issue was quantitative. One suspects that he didn't really need the debate to know that it was. How large? How representative? Oomph.

Fogel takes fewer shortcuts in measuring things than any student of society I know this side of the medievalists. He even eschews the short-cuts "implied by theory," as the optimistic phrase among economists has it, much used, for example, by Douglass North. I have tried repeatedly to persuade Fogel that Harberger's Theorem suffices to show that the static effect of railroads on growth was small: if you multiply together the share of transport in national income, the share of railroads in all transport, and any rough estimate of the cost savings of railroads over canals (not-ing that all three numbers are well below unity), you are going to get a small number. Fogel was and is unimpressed. He says that to really know you have to scour the records of the industry and write a 296-page book.

Paul David (1969) speculated once that railroads induced economies of scale. In Fogel's astonishing Presidential Address to the Economic His-tory Association (in 1978, published in the *Journal of Economic History* in 1979; see esp. 39–44), the longest ever, delivered one September night in a mock-Tudor college hall in Toronto, he actually measured the alleged economies of scale and showed them to be small. The measurement showed the frailties of the *qualitative* reasoning that David and most other economists usually rely on. Fogel stands with Newton in saying, *hypotheses non fingo*, I do not express mere hypotheses, "For what I tell . . . is not Hypothesis but the most rigid consequence, not conjectured . . . but evinced by the meditation of experiments concluded directly and without any suspicion of doubt." Maybe this is why Fogel is so tolerant of the sterile rigor of mathematical economics, seeing in it a shadow of the rigid consequence of fact. The empiricist and rationalist traditions of the West, British and French, meet on the grounds of certitude.

When I first met Fogel's rigid consequence, reading *Railroads and American Economic Growth* in a graduate seminar with Gerschenkron in 1965, I detected a fellow positivist. Since then I have grown critical of the philosophical position that Fogel believes goes along with being quantitative. As most plainly revealed in his little book of 1983 with Geoffrey Elton, Fogel believes that a quantitative science follows the pre-cepts of philosophy of science circa 1950 (Fogel and Elton 1983). He has since 1983 shifted ground some, especially in consequence of his work on religious conviction as a force in British and American abolitionism. Yet he is still in his philosophy of science loyal to the older received view. He would reply: there is no sin in such loyalty. Surely he is right. Fogel keeps the faith. The positivistic faith that inspired Robert Fogel, Milton Friedman, Paul Samuelson, and the rest may now strike us as crude philosophy, but judging from results it served once to motivate a lot of good science.

Other features of his personality taught us, too. His convivial but intellectual socializing was presided over by Enid, between her or his airplane voyages to and from their second jobs in Rochester (I was charmed to hear that Enid and Bob were accustomed to having dates in O'Hare Airport, as their travels crossed, and this before such jet-setting was common). The Fogels together taught that intellectual life was worthy of ceremony. I think Bob was for this reason exceptionally pleased with his year as Pitt Professor of American Institutions at Cambridge: boy from the Bronx sips 100-year old port and smokes Havana cigars after dinner with the fellows of Kings.

Fogel's socialist background made a big impression on me and taught me to outgrow the remnants of my own socialism. Here was a man who had been a paid organizer for the Communist Party. (Enid was scornful of the "paid" part. She told me once that being herself from working-class parents, unlike Bob, she expected the boss to actually *pay* the employees on payday, even if the boss was the Revolution—or the paymaster the FBI.) And yet he was reasonable. I had heard the Yogi-and-the-Commissar line, that once a radical always a radical, of the Right if not of the Left. The line is a sort of McCarthyism of the middle (I pause to note the analogy with the anti-Chicago McCarthyism in the 1960s among coastie economists, from which Fogel suffered, gracefully). Fogel in the flesh, however, was nothing like either the yogi or the commissar. He described himself quite accurately as a Scoop Jackson Democrat and argued genially with us about the good sides of Nixon, Vietnam, and Mayor Daley the Elder. One learned that people could change their minds on reasonable grounds and then go on to argue with civility about things that mattered.

One learned also from Fogel the nitty-gritty of being a professor. Only my time as a research assistant for John Meyer on his projects in history and transportation economics made as much of an impression. Fogel, for example, sends draft papers out for comment on a massive scale. His students have adopted the practice. Invite criticism and take advantage of it. Mail is cheap. "I'd rather be criticized in private by a friend," says Fogel, "than be savaged in public by an enemy," and unlike most of us he actually believes it. He believes deeply in the conversation of scholarship, often starting a new project by writing long, sweetly reasonable letters to other scholars, whether or not he has been introduced.

Fogel does not spurn the nitty-gritty of scholarly administration. He has assembled numerous research teams, larger and larger and larger. With his longtime assistant, and big sister to us all, Marilyn Coopersmith, he has repeatedly created new institutions and taught his students the desirability of doing the same. His workshop in economic history was one of many in the Chicago Department of Economics—the institution of workshops is Chicago's main contribution to the administrative culture of the field—but his was suffused with warmth as well as rigor (that Ted Schultz and Margaret Reid were always in attendance helped). Some of the other workshops at Chicago seemed to spring more from the dark side of the Force. Chicago had a stream of foreign visitors coming to study with Fogel, because Fogel does not view demographers and historians as engaged in some other enterprise that we economists can safely ignore. Like most economists, he believes in intellectual specialization. But, unlike most economists, he is consistent in his economics: after the specialization he also believes in trade, rather than the piling up of exports unsold in the backyard.

Fogel embraced with enthusiasm the nitty-gritty task of financing all this work. He taught us that a scholarly life was worth paying for. He got fellowships for his visitors, he argued for appointments (my own, for example), and he paid for much of the resulting intellectual activity out of his own pocket. He spent what seemed like enormous sums on cameras and tape recorders and other equipment, using them to record first drafts of papers in seminars and to photograph participants quarreling with each other at conferences. A tape of the last seminar ran as background music for the famous annual Indoor Picnic at Bob and Enid's.

All these unifications of Fogel's life with his work were corollaries of the Great Nitty-Gritty: *put scholarship first*. Always, always, scholarship came first. Moses Abramowitz, a student of Simon Kuznets, as Fogel was, tells how difficult it was for he himself to encounter Kuznets, because the older scholar would invariably ask, as though to a graduate student who was not making very good progress on his dissertation, "Well, Moses, what are you working on?" Fogel likewise behaved as though Kuznets were about to show up in a few minutes and pop the overwhelming question, "Well, Robert, what are you working on?" He worked, and works, incessantly, to a plan that Kuznets would recognize as the most serious of scholarly work. When the Nobel Committee called in the wee hours to tell Fogel that he had got the prize, it found him awake . . . and at work.

The work is guided by Fogel's 50-Year Rule, which he taught us all: will it matter in 50 years? Because he really does believe the rule, Fogel has been calmer in controversy than you or I would have been under similar provocation. He does not worry about short-run defeats, such as the politically poisoned reaction to his book with Stanley Engerman, *Time on the Cross: The Economics of American Negro Slavery*. What matters is the reaction in 50 years. As the driving instructor advises, Fogel aims high in steering. (A Latin motto: *Intendete alte in gubernando*.)

The 50-Year Rule, aiming high, entails thinking big, which Fogel does himself and encourages in his students and colleagues. He still has the detailed thesis proposal presented to Kuznets on January 14, 1959. The seminar participants at Johns Hopkins heard a 19-page paper entitled "Notes on the Influence of the Railroads on American Economic Growth, 1830–1890." It begins, "The railroads exercised a decisive influence on the course of American economic growth in the nineteenth century." There follows a Schumpeterian/Rostovian paean to the iron horse and a two-page outline of the proposed dissertation. Think big. The outline covers most of the railroad subjects written about since then, such as the economies of scale and the population growth attributable to railroads, capital formation in railroads, and comparisons of social savings in other countries. The long book that finally resulted from this exercise in scholarly chutzpah, it turns out, covered only 2 of the 17 proposed subjects. Here was someone building a monument for the ages, more durable than bronze.

But he was always willing to change the plans for the monument as the building proceeded. As a graduate student, he changed his mind on American railroads, moving from a pro- to an anti-Rostow position after looking at the evidence. As a professor, he was enthusiastic when students and junior colleagues (such as Jacob Metzer of Hebrew University and John Coatsworth of Chicago and Harvard) came to contrary conclusions about the role of railroads in other countries. People who have not been close to Fogel cannot believe that he has a flexible mind. They see only the vigorous advocacy in the short run. Dogmatists interpret advocacy by others as a dogmatism like their own. Fogel could say more truthfully than could most of his critics, *dogma non fingo*, I do not express mere dogma. Fogel has changed his mind on railroads, on slavery (he started as a doubter of the Meyer and Conrad view), on abolition (he started as a doubter of the force of religion), and on death rates (he started as a doubter of the importance of nutrition). He has changed his mind more than any scholar I know—although one must admit that the competition in this line is not especially fierce.

It was of course his astounding scholarly productions that most kept our attention as students and colleagues. The man could have been a cold, colorless, inflexible curmudgeon and still have taught us a lot. Fogel is the master of historical economics, taking it to the frontiers of economic and historical study. His works on railways, slavery, abolitionism, and mortality have carried out the program of using modern economics to understand history. No economist or historian combines the scholarly values of economics and of history more thoroughly.

Fogel believes that the example of historical economics will make other parts of history and of economics broader. A profession that aims at *histoire totale* can be improved by analytic and computational techniques applied to historical facts. And, as the historical evidence improves (indeed, as the present becomes the past), economic history will take an increasing share of the argument in economics itself. The antihistorical frame of mind in economics cannot last, no more than can the antiquantitative frame of mind in history. It would be a strange aberration in the history of astronomy if astronomers resolved to concentrate exclusively on the solar system or to concentrate exclusively on the red side of the spectrum. The stars in all their radiation nonetheless remain and will at last be studied. The interesting but narrow questions of what caused last year's economic downturn or why women participated more in the economy over the past decade will yield to the broader and longer-term questions of what causes the business cycle in capitalist economies or what causes the sexual segregation of the workforce.

Fogel believes we should study all the evidence with all the techniques. We cannot achieve all things in historical science by scrutinizing the conventional sources, he says, nor all things in economic science by staring for a long time at a blackboard. We have to look at the evidence hard, as genuine scientists, and then argue the case, hard.

Fogel is above all a hard economic arguer about the evidence, an attorney for the factual prosecution. He takes an empirical idea—such as that one might measure the social savings of railroads—and asks, What conceivable doubts might someone have that the answer is so-and-so? Before the trial gets under way he imagines every move of the opposing attorney. While others build their cases on a rough-and-ready plausibility, such as might persuade their mothers, using observations "consistent with" the hypothesis (and therefore, statistically speaking, ignoring power), confusing existence with magnitude, Fogel builds his case on excoriating, quantitative doubt. It is the scholarly standard that Karl Popper and others have held up as the ideal for science. Recent studies of science have shown that even in the physical and biological sciences the standard is seldom achieved.

Fogel meets or exceeds the standard for factual inquiry—to pick a few comparable scholars in various fields, of Simon Kuznets in economics, Louis Namier in British history, V. O. Key in political science, and Ronald Syme in Roman history. That puts him with the great scholars of the twentieth century. No stone is left unturned. Repeatedly, the ingenuity of critics swarming around him is made to look foolish when their main point turns out to have been anticipated in an obscure footnote by the master himself. After Fogel's address to the British Economic History Society in 1976 an English economic historian, well disposed toward him but unable to resist taking advantage of a rumor that Fogel was worried about a certain calculation concerning the slave trade, rose in criticism. "About that calculation concerning the slave trade, Professor Fogel." Fogel waited until the fellow had finished his apparently devastating remark; then, smiling broadly, Fogel allowed as he was glad the question had been asked, because in the month since the news had gone out that he was having difficulty on the point he and his coworkers had collected observations bearing on it to the number of 40,000. Fogel then proceeded to reestablish the calculation beyond cavil.

Fogel's opinion, voiced repeatedly since his earliest work, is that "the major obstacle to the resolution of [most of the issues in history and economics] . . . is the absence of data rather than the absence of analytical ingenuity or credible theories." His opinion is worthy of respect for two reasons. First, economics has had a long run with blackboard reasoning. Perhaps the time has come to take economic magnitudes seriously. Second, Fogel backs his opinion with analytic ingenuity and credible theories in quantity but most of all by supplying enormous, Tycho-Brahean masses of data. Not data, really, which means "things given," but *capta,* "things seized," or *facta,* facts, things made.

Fogel makes and seizes from every source. He measured the social saving of railroads by mastering the engineering literature. He measured the efficiency of slavery by making use of dozens of Southern archives, tens of thousands of prices of slaves, and detailed knowledge of the manuscript censuses. He measured the sources of mortality by using an array of epidemiological and nutritional studies, the records of military recruits, the Mormon family archives, the experiments of biologists, the records of hospitals. He set a standard of empirical seriousness that no economist in the history of the discipline has matched. He makes most other economists look like boys playing in the sandbox.

To put it another way, Fogel combines a superb analytic mind in economics with the highest standards of self-doubt in social inquiry and with what historians call "historical imagination." He is a "scientific historian," not in his own sense recalled from an acquaintance with the positivist philosophies but in R. G. Collingwood's sense: "scientific historians study problems: they ask questions, and if they are good historians they ask questions which they see their way to answering." Fogel sees the right historical questions to ask and sees his way to answering them. He brings the highest historical standards of factual veracity to economics. He is both the best of economists and the best of historians.

The difficulty of achieving such dual excellence late in the twentieth century is great. Scholarly standards in both economics and history have risen since 1950. What would pass for analytic brilliance in an economics article in the 1940s looks childish circa 1990 (consider Samuelson on the multiplier and accelerator). What would be considered impressive breadth of sources from a historian in the 1930s looks now crude and inexplicit (consider Marc Bloch on French agricultural history). Fogel has done it in both fields.

The dual excellence sets a standard that both economics and history might achieve, if they aim high enough in steering. It is peculiar, to pick one standard, that economics has allowed itself to ignore certain classes of evidence and argument. Ignoring evidence from opinion surveys or arguments from narrative is not a good idea. Yet the official methodology of economics urges this and other pointless narrowings of the evidence. Fogel does not. You can't read a piece by Fogel without bumping against the startling if obvious standard, borrowed from history for the good of economics: examine all the evidence.

The standard has resulted in large scientific advances. His friend and former colleague, the economist and business school dean Richard Rosett, is fond of pointing out that few scientists or scholars have the energy or ability to achieve one great scholarly success in the time allotted to them. In three decades Fogel achieved three.

First, he discovered that the iron horse, bestriding the economic historiography of the nineteenth century like a colossus, was important but not colossal. He was here testing the theory of Schumpeter and Rostow that modern economic growth has depended on certain great inventions, the analogue in economic history of great men. Transportation strikes the noneconomist as obviously fundamental in some vague fashion—after all, what would happen if we closed down the highways and railroads tomorrow? Fogel noted that the right question was one of long-run dispensability and brought to bear the latest insights of cost/benefit analysis.

The book (really, two books: his Master's thesis under Carter Goodrich at Columbia on the Union Pacific railway was part of the tale) created controversy. Fogel's argumentative style rubbed some economists the wrong way, and the less self-confident among the historians, frightened by the quantitative history that Fogel was advocating, were pleased to see the historical economists quarreling among themselves. The same story was to be repeated more bitterly ten years later in the controversy over slavery.

In any event, Fogel was right. He was complimented by imitation, in a dozen replications of his study for other countries and other branches of transportation. His argument was scrutinized in a way that only the most important scientific findings are, by the best critical minds in the discipline, inside and outside economic history. It lasts.

He turned then to American slavery, with his colleague at Rochester, Stanley Engerman. (Each successive project of Fogel's has involved more and more work by teams, as his ambitions for capta have grown; the scientific importance of the work has fallen, though, as Fogel has moved away from his comparative advantage as a lone researcher.) Unlike the railroad book, the essential plan of the work on slavery was not original with Fogel. The notion that one might view slavery, however vile its ethical basis, as an efficient market arrangement had been adumbrated by Kenneth Stampp, Alfred H. Conrad, and John R. Meyer. But adumbration is not the same as painting in oils. Fogel and Engerman in the two volumes of *Time on the Cross* and in their massive subsequent work with others have painted a picture of capitalism gone wrong, of slavery as an economic success that demanded political intervention to kill, and of a black workforce that achieved much in bourgeois terms despite the lash.

The uproar occasioned by *Time on the Cross* is hard to understand now. Some of the internal criticism, unhappily, arose from personal jealousies, as anyone attending the various conferences about the book could see. The book was favorably reviewed by the doyen of Southern historians in the *New York Review of Books* and reviewed at astonishing length and with great respect in numerous technical journals. Then came a reaction to the publicity. Some of the scholars seem to have been annoyed by the appearances of Fogel and Engerman in *Time* magazine and of Fogel alone on the "Today" show on television—one is put in mind of the fury that descended on the chemists who had the temerity to announce fusion in a bottle before clearing it with coastie physicists; or Hayek's travail after the popular success of *The Road to Serfdom*. Certainly any book that touches the American dilemma of race incurs the risk of being misunderstood, especially in the overheated days of the early 1970s. Fogel was attacked as a racist in some circles and a running dog of capitalism in others. It is hard to imagine labels less apt.

The sober truth is that he and the group of scholars he led increased our understanding of American slavery. Only ideology stands in the way of acknowledging the achievement. Fogel was slow to answer his critics, which proved fatal to his reputation among historians, but when his replies appeared they were crushingly persuasive. Fogel and Engerman were the first to take seriously the measurement of efficiency, of slave diets and physical conditions, and of the abuse of slaves. On other issues—such as the demography of the slave population—they permanently and substantially raised the level of debate. Any student of the compulsory labor systems that typified the workplace before the twentieth century must use Fogel and Engerman's work, extended by their students and colleagues and embodied now in the massive volumes of *Without Consent or Contract.*

To put it more broadly, neither the optimistic correlation of capitalism with freedom nor the pessimistic correlation of capitalism with misery make much sense. Fogel has done additional work on the abolition movement, tracing its roots in political economy and especially in religious conviction. He has found that abolition was a close call, not inevitable, no automatic result of "modernization." Nor was it a self-interested move of the middle class. A quantitative economist has ended by emphasizing the complexities of politics and the saliency of ethical freedom.

As if two home runs in a single game were not enough, Fogel pointed to a spot in center field and produced with a mighty swing an explanation of the fall in mortality, 1700 to 1900. The project is less controversial than his other work and, as I've said, in my opinion less important. It is international in scope (though emphasizing the American experience), undertaken with a still larger team (running into the dozens), and has moved further away from economics strictly defined. It has pioneered entirely new sources of data, especially military recruit-

ment records. The work is typically Fogelian in the catholicity of literature brought to bear. Fogel has ransacked the literature of human biology, the history of medicine, demography, social history, economic history, nutritional history, pediatrics, clinical nutrition, embryology,
historical sociology, tropical medicine, public health, historical geography, epidemiology, agricultural history, physical anthropology, gynecol-
ogy, international economics, industrial history, toxology, genealogy,
and development economics to discover the link between nutrition and
life chances. He has concluded that better food accounted for about 40
percent of the decline in mortality, mainly among infants, leaving a considerable unexplained fall in mortality well before the coming of modern
medicine. The work is in progress—another of Fogel's favorite phrases
borrowed from careful science is *preliminary results,* and he means it:
measure twice, cut once. What is clear is that the project contributes to
our understanding of how we grew, and how we grew rich. It is not as
original as his first work on railroads; not as historically salient as his
work on slavery; but, like all his work, it is *echt* science in a field that
long ago abandoned such a standard.

Rather than conjecturing on the causes of growth, Fogel has asked
throughout his career "How large?" and has seen the way to answer. He
has set a new standard for empirical thoroughness in economics and a
new standard of logical cogency in history. The historical economics he
helped invent can bring economics back to real science. The trick is simple to state but hard to do: emulate Fogel.

Rule 5
Work and Pray

How to Organize a Conference

Eastern Economic Journal *(spring 1994)*.

Economists and other talkers live for conferences. Teaching is OK, colleagues are swell, reading is nice, consulting is fun. But flying across the country in midwinter to sit in a quarter-full hotel ballroom listening to someone exceeding their allotted time—that's what the intellectual life of an academic economist is all about. I've been to a passel of conferences, some half-dozen each year. Over three decades that comes to about 180. Hog heaven.

Being public spirited and impulsive, I've organized quite a few conferences, too, about two dozen. There's a career path in such things. The first I organized was at Harvard in 1970, when I was an assistant professor at Chicago. I did everything, getting the money, drawing up the invitations, hassling the paper givers, setting up the microphones in Eliot House, and driving down Mass. Ave. before each day of the conference to get the donuts. I then edited the conference volume, down to transcribing the recorded discussion into indirect discourse (look it up: "Professor Landes then said such and such" [McCloskey 1971]). Everyone should have this experience at least once, like preparing an elaborate French meal from start to finish. It's like finding out where the data come from. After doing it once, you can move on to less intense experiences.

For example, I helped Victor Fuchs organize part of the American Economic Association conference for January 1995. I did nothing but read some proposals with care and then call round to see who could be roped into doing the actual work. Still, I suppose it counts as "organizing" a conference, and I've done on two occasions the harder job that Victor had. No one who has not organized a large association's conference knows what administrative hell is like. I lost one of the best secretaries I've had shortly after she had gone through the experience twice.

So I have some claim as consumer and producer to knowing how to organize a conference, at any rate if the two dozen I've organized were not a succession of bombs. There were a couple like that, but most were all right, and some—such as the 1984 conference I helped organize at Iowa that launched what we call "the rhetoric of inquiry" and one of the annual "Cliometrics" conferences held at Iowa—have been what intellectual life should be: in the words of the English political philosopher Michael Oakeshott, "unrehearsed intellectual adventure." And I've attended enough Conferences from Hell to have observed a wide range in the dependent variable.

Here are a few suggestions arising from the data. I think of a new one every time I go to a conference, so I confine myself merely to the more important ones.

1. Distribute the papers to the audience in advance. You want to maximize the time for discussion, not the time for exposition best left to the printed page. In the humanities and even in economics in some countries the presenter is expected literally to *read* her paper word for word, and in such fields the best people get to be pretty good at it. But it doesn't suit the genius of American economics. In American economics—and in math, physics, and biology—the format is called, revealingly, "the talk." Talk, not read.

2. But then keep the talk to a minimum in order to give the maximum time for discussion. The author can present a few further thoughts, five minutes at most, and then open the floor. If the paper is distributed in advance then the author has no excuse to filibuster. (Bob Gordon of Northwestern is notorious for sending a paper, reproduced and distributed, but then showing up at the conference with his own stack of a heavily revised version that puts him back in the driver's seat; his friends are not sure whether this is conscious gaming or just a desire to excel gone a little wacko—probably the latter).

3. In order for all this to work you as the organizer have to, first,

make sure the papers are on time by canceling the author's participation if he does not send it. Second, you must resist all suggestions that because "some of the audience may not have read the paper" the author should be allowed to babble on for 90 minutes. It turns out that it's not essential to have read the paper to participate at some level in a discussion, because the issues raised, if the paper is interesting at all, will be of a general character. Of course, to participate at a serious professional level one must have read the paper. But the nonreaders are not being cut out entirely, and the quality of the discussion is much higher if some people have read the paper with care. Get the incentives right: if you establish that the audience cannot expect the paper to be presented in full, then the paper distributed in advance will actually get read. You must tell all participants about the rules in advance, but if you do, and can affect a suitably grim demeanor, you will provide them with the incentives to have an unrehearsed intellectual adventure.

4. In a conference session with more than one paper you should "workshop" each paper by itself. That is, let Ms. Jones talk a little about her paper then open the floor to discussion of her paper. Then let Mr. Smith talk about his paper, with discussion from the floor. Then do the same with paper number 3, and so forth. The intellectual drama in a conference always comes from the discussion (and rarely from a discussion prepared in advance, unless you have chosen the speaker's worst enemy as discussant, which is often cruel: so keep the discussants' time short, too). It's torture for the audience to make it sit through three 20-minute presentations by A, B, C (who of course run over their time), then to hear three tediously predictable "discussions" from D, E, and F, and finally, 10 minutes before lunch, to get to the adventure.

It's hard I've discovered to persuade people of the merits of workshopping until they try it. Often they will object without thinking through the price theory that such workshopping is "unfair to the last speaker," by which they mean that everyone will poach on the last speaker's time, since he's last. The argument is only welfare relevant if the audience is for some reason regarded as the least important part of the proceedings and should get last *last* dibs, the better to be "fair" to one of three or four people who have talked longer than they were supposed to. Even with such a strange welfare function it is anyway only relevant in a second-best world in which the chair has not enforced the clock— and if that's the case the last paper giver is going to get shortchanged anyhow.

So it's Pareto optimal to workshop papers at *every* conference. If the chair does her job the 90 minutes (say) are split into three strictly enforced subsessions of 30 minutes each, so that every paper gets its fair amount of presentation and discussion. Fairness is maintained, but audience boredom is relieved. The economics of "we'll just follow the printed schedule and do all the papers without a break" is defective. The speaker gains from having her paper discussed—if she doesn't think so, she can in any case filibuster and absorb all the 30 minutes in presentation. The price theory is that establishing private property in each subsession—by workshopping—eliminates the incentive under the usual procedure for speaker 1 to overfish the common pool.

5. For the same reason, and using the same economics (left as an exercise to the reader; hint: think incentives), start exactly on time, regardless of whether all the speakers are there. Tell people you will do this, in advance.

And a few rules of politeness, which turn out to have intellectual consequences:

6. You can tell people how to behave at the conference, and on the whole they will do what you say. Amazing among a group of Max U-ers, but true. I learned this from the Liberty Fund, which holds superb, small conferences about which the fund has strict rules: participants must turn in their papers on time, or they are canceled; they must arrive on time; they must attend all the sessions, or they do not get their pay; they must attend all meals. The public or private instructions you give will work. For instance, you can tell the senior people in confidence to be gentle on the graduate students, and they will obey, contrary to one of the bomb conferences I attended, during the ruckus over Bob Fogel and Stan Engerman's *Time on the Cross,* in which someone—apparently to get at Stan, who was supervising the only graduate student presenting at the conference—attacked the graduate student's paper as "a term paper, not a professional paper." Not so nice, and not usual for the man involved. (Incidentally, the remark was incorrect at the time, and the graduate student has gone on to a distinguished career; Stan survived, too.)

7. Never leave people alone for meals, most particularly people you have specially invited. It's boorish and makes the specially invited speaker feel like a sucker: "For this treatment I left the bosom of my family and flew 1,000 miles?" In any case the best talk usually happens at meals, and you don't want to miss it.

8. For that reason meals are a good investment. By spending not

much money per person, which in a pinch you can even extract from the people enjoying it, you can arrange for people to break bread and have more of the unrehearsed intellectual adventure. By the way, crowded places are not good places to do it: the ideal common meal is at a deserted college dining room out of term, the more spartan the better. A monkish atmosphere seems to encourage serious conversation.

There are other rules. Get an assistant who is more intelligent, polite, firm, organized, and sensible than you are. Be warmly polite to people whose papers you reject. Consider poster sessions of the sort they run in the biological sciences, and make a big deal of them, allotting a couple of hours in which the entire conference is expected to attend. Announce rigid deadlines for proposals, but then don't be stupid about rejecting a superb paper just because it was a couple of days late. Have as much socializing as possible, preferably socializing that throws together people unacquainted with each other. Do the socializing early in the conference, not late: you want people to get over the pomposity and aggression as early as possible, to start having their intellectual adventure. Allow plenty of time for out-of-session schmoozing: if you don't, no one will attend your sessions. Prefer "plenary" (that is, whole group) sessions to parallel sessions: you're trying to start a conversation. Don't let the hotel get away with its Standard Business Conference Procedures: bother them about overheads and water and the functioning of microphones (this oldest of electronic technology breaks down in about a third of the cases). Try the NBER format of having the commentator present (briefly) the paper. Try not having any commentators at all: it makes the audience act less like free-riders. Do not be surprised or even annoyed if VIPs back out: at least they've let you use their name to gather the group for the adventure. Ask VIPs at least a year in advance, more like two years: the world gets nuttier by the minute. On the other hand, watch out for VIPs: they often do not do their homework (the dog ate it), and they sometimes expect prima donna treatment in a world in which most of us are seconde donne. And so forth. It's a little piece of academic business that we should learn how to do better, this giving of conferences, and can, if we'll try.

How to Host a
Seminar Visitor

Eastern Economic Journal *(spring 1995).*

Your chair asks you, a promising assistant professor just out of grad school, to supervise the biweekly Departmental Seminar. You are flattered and accept the assignment. The problem: you do not have a clue.

Fortunately, just in time to save you from your vanity, my advice comes to your attention. If you will follow it in every detail, which I urge you to do, you'll get a reputation for administrative skill. The reputation will serve you well, leading in future to department chairdoms and associate deanships and other agreeable by-employment.

First the objective function. Ask yourself: What's the purpose of a seminar series? (I mean, aside from such administrative imperatives as "make sure you spend every nickel this year so that our budget is not cut next year" or "do the job of hosting people with the minimum damage to your reputation and your clothes shopping time.")

The purpose of having people visit to give talks is twofold: partly to keep you-all in touch with the conversation of economics and partly to advertise the intellectual merits of your department. In truth (deans: take notice) the keeping in touch is better done per dollar by going to conferences and getting on Xerox and e-mail lists or, horrible thought, reading a book. (Read Bob Frank's latest, for example, whatever it is.)

But there's no better way than outside visitors to advertise your department. I still have a soft spot for Southeast Missouri State University at Cape Girardeau because of the nice way they treated me in the 1970s. The Economics Department at the University of Tasmania strikes me as a swell place and gets a good word from me every time it comes up, largely because one of its faculty back in 1983 took seriously my yammering about "rhetoric" and arranged while I was in Australia for the department to show its best side. On the other hand, I travel a lot, and

I've been on enough visits organized by the Three Stooges to know that a badly organized visit can do a department damage. I won't tell you the name, but a major department on the West Coast has earned my low opinion of its intellectual life with three—count 'em, three—horribly fouled-up visits. And I once visited a college of no great distinction that couldn't live itself intellectually out of a wet paper bag.

For most departments, in other words, the advertising of your reputation is more important than the keeping in touch, and easier to foul up. To get a unified objective function, suppose the weighting between keeping in touch and investing in reputation is set at about 20–80. The weighting toward reputation is contrary to the surface rhetoric of the visit, as understood by departmental secretaries and the millionaire endowers of lecture series. They talk as though the main point of a visit were The Big Speech. Their talk makes it hard to remember that it's you-all, the department, who are performing, not the speaker.

All right. How to do it?

Collect suggestions about whom to invite from your colleagues. It's wise to do it by letter, so that no one feels left out. View the suggestions as ideas, not votes. If you just take the suggestion with the largest number of votes (by three assistant professors, actually), you'll merely reproduce the latest fashion in the field. Curve-hugging follows the latest wiggle in economics as closely as the first few terms of a Taylor's series will allow. Taylor's series visitors do not provide education, because what they say is callow and will be obsolete in five years. And remember: the advertising of your reputation is the main point anyway. It's better therefore to invite older people, such as Lester Telser at Chicago, who is always about 10 years ahead of the latest fashion, or Richard Sutch at UC Riverside, who believes in collecting his own data, or Nancy Folbre of Massachusetts, who insists that economics should concern itself with important things. These are economic scientists, not trainees.

If you've "never heard of Professor X" (where X = such intellectual heavyweights as Tom Schelling or Barbara Bergmann), consider that at your age it may be your problem, not theirs. Consider that you may not yet have read everything in every field of economics, and that What's Hot in your infinitesimally small Ph.D. thesis neighborhood (a set of measure zero, actually) might after all not survive into next week, much less 50 years. So think big and think old. It's better for your reputation.

The success of the visit depends on details. Get them right. For example, do not use a travel bureau of your own to make the travel arrangements. You'll think it saves money or is something that people want done for them, but in fact it irritates a seasoned traveler. Her own travel agent knows what she likes and can get the best ticket. I know a big-deal scholar in nursing who was invited to give a big-deal speech once but was given a ticket that ran her all over the country to save a few bucks. Not big-deal thinking. She canceled out the whole trip when a little fog descended on her home airport.

Unless you are reading this from Harvard and the like, pick her up at your airport. Do it yourself, since visitors assume that whoever picks them up is the organizer of the visit. You might as well get the credit. If you have to send someone else, do not send a student: few students have spent enough time in airports to know what to do when something goes wrong, as it does about a quarter of the time. Picking up the speaker at the airport is necessary regardless of the age or rank of the guest, but neglecting it is particularly irritating to senior people, even if able-bodied. They have a lot to think about (more, even, than the average assistant professor), and figuring out how to get from the airport to the seminar is not one of their top priorities.

Actually read something—anything—the person has written. At a minimum it will give you something to chat about as you drive the guest from the airport. The drive is your personal chance to show what a good little scholar you are, and it's elementary human nature that the speaker will think highly of someone who knows her work. Unless you are running the series at the top 10 or so universities, the arrogance of not having read anything is not an available strategy. Nor is other arrogance, come to think of it. (Before one Harvard seminar I gave, a former colleague and supposed friend read a book half-concealed under the table throughout the luncheon; doubtless he had more important matters in mind, such as another plan to idiotically misuse statistical significance in his work.) Flattery, or even common courtesy, will get you everywhere. For example, if the person writes books, it's a good idea to inform the college bookstore a month or more in advance, so they can have the books on display. College bookstores like to do it.

Don't underwork the visitor. That means you should give her a full schedule of classes, lectures, luncheons, parties, one-on-one talking. I visited the University of South Dakota once to give a lecture in a series that two years before had been graced by my friend Theodore Schultz (born South Dakota 1902; Iowa State University 1930–43; Chicago 1943–68; Nobel 1979). They kept asking me if I was tired, to which I asked each time, "Did Ted do it?" It always turned out Ted, then age 90, had. By the end of the two days of following Ted's schedule I was exhausted. At least I had defended the honor of us 50-year-olds.

On the whole the students don't get much out of a visitor and should not be the focus of your use of her. A "special treat" of a class lecture by the visitor is too much like the substitute teacher in grade school (remember how you massacred her). If you must do it, make sure the instructor impresses on the students for weeks and weeks in advance how Incredibly Eminent the visitor is and makes the point by having the students read something accessible (test them on it beforehand). And for all lectures, talks, luncheons, and so forth make sure to give the visitor an exact schedule and tell her personally what the person she is talking with does and to what stage the class has gotten and, right on the spot as she begins her talk, what sort of people are in the audience that actually showed up. I visited a university Down Under at which my host took me from the tea room directly to an auditorium with 250 people already assembled "for the lecture," he said as I walked into the room unaware, "on Victorian economic failure," which he had not told me about. It was like a scene from a nightmare. I discovered that the human mind can work on three levels, speaking at one level, planning 2 minutes ahead at another, and planning 20 minutes ahead at still another, all at once. I think the lecture was all right, and no one was the wiser. But I was sweating. The rule: no surprises.

It's the faculty, especially the junior faculty, who earn the *imports* from a visit. Remember, though, that it's *exports* that you're mainly interested in. You are displaying your faculty. Meals are the best place to capture the imports. Make sure five people come but no more. More than five is a waste, since it's too large a group to talk with the guest in one conversation. At six or seven you will find that the conversation keeps breaking in two, only three or four people engaging with the visitor.

As for The Big Speech, remember who's on display. Get your colleagues to come and urge them to think up intelligent questions: export or die. The visitor has not left her home to speak to a half-dozen ignorant faculty with nothing better to do at 4:00 P.M. A big, informed, enthusiastic audience is what you want to aim for. Worry about it— though put a bright face on things if the big audience doesn't materialize. This means speaking to your colleagues personally about the visit, not just making a sign-up list available or posting notices the day before.

Undergraduate students again make poor filler for The Big Speech, unless they come with preparation and enthusiasm. I stutter, and nothing is more irritating to me than watching a couple of undergraduates in the fifth row giggle to each other about my *A Fish Called Wanda* performances. It doesn't improve my speech or my opinion of the place. I never allow it from my 430-student Econ 1 or History 101 classes. If there's anything peculiar like this about the speaker (old age, disfigurement, boring delivery, odd speech pattern, excessively highbrow ideas about speech making), make sure you warn the adolescents to behave themselves; or, better, instruct them to stay away.

Remember that for the best visitors some of your colleagues elsewhere will be interested, too, which will spread the name of your department within your own college and in neighboring colleges, which will be encouraged to think of you-all as Where the Intellectual Action Is. And remember that your administrators will want to press the flesh with the Nobel laureate, actual or prospective, that you have finagled into coming. Exercise judgment. If your dean is a fool, keep the visitor away from him. Export.

Talk economics and only economics. The visitor expects it and if seasoned knows how to do it. You don't make a good impression by asking about low-level professional gossip or How about Them Hawks.

Young people (that's less than 40 years old, my dear) will be happy to stay in faculty houses. But in that case you are committed to entertaining the visitor all the time. Older people will prefer a hotel, unless they have a close friend on your faculty. Accommodations on campus in quiet surroundings are the standard. For Lord's sake make sure the room is quiet and that the guest can get a decent night's sleep. Bed and breakfast places are much nicer than the local El Cheapo Motel, usually quieter, and always more characteristic of the part of the country you're in. Chances are you've never stayed in El Cheapo, or when you did stay in it you were interviewing for the job and were at an age when having your own TV and shower gave you a big thrill.

Convince your local accountants not to report reimbursement for expenses on the same form as honoraria. The one is nontaxable, the other is not, but many universities merge the two. Sure, the speaker can deduct the "unreimbursed business expenses," if she can remember to. Save her the trouble.

And many other tips, left as an exercise to the assistant professor. Don't worry. All that will happen if you foul up is that you and your colleagues will never be able to participate in the economics profession in a serious way, because you will have offended the people who run it. Relax. And enjoy the visit.

"To Burn Always
with a Hard, Gemlike Flame,"
Eh, Professor?

Eastern Economic Journal *(fall 1994)*.

Academic life, like any other these days, has a full in-box. A professor can stay busy merely answering her junk mail. Professors and other economists are employed by bureaucracies, after all, and it is the way of bureaucracies to generate tasks to fill the time allotted. The committees of a modern college or university grow yearly. So too in industry or in the government. The committees are too many and too large by a factor of about three, but you can make a career on them, attending to what appears to be your duty. And they are socially pleasant. Serving on a committee is a chance to get to know your colleagues, a chance strangely rare in academic and most other life.

The requests that come from outside by mail or phone or e-mail grow steadily. In academic life they grow because colleges are part of the 20 percent or so of national income, above the 35 percent now supplying alleged goods and services at some level of government, in course of being absorbed by the federal government without actually becoming government offices. Will the professor kindly fill out this report of how she spent her time, suitably jiggered to keep the Feds happy? They grow also because the time of professors at other universities is a common pool, which academic institutions have become careless in exploiting because it is not priced. Will she kindly act as referee for a paper generated by fear of tenure review? Will she kindly be one of a dozen or so people solicited to write meaningless letters of recommendation, interpretable only by the people in the identical field who know that Ken Arrow always exaggerates or that Stan Engerman always understates but read by committees of people in other fields who know nothing of this?

I am not recommending irresponsibility. Some refereeing needs to be done, and who better to do it than you or me? Some committees need to meet, even though the provost will then do what she already planned to do. Most first-class mail, and even some third-class, warrants a reply, if only a scribbled note on the bottom. Books should be reviewed. The students must be graded. I seldom miss a class, even for really important matters like attending conferences in nice places with my little Yorkshire terrier, Janie.

I affirm that many bureaucratic jobs really do need to be done and that it is shameful not to do them when asked, if you can. Everyone with gifts that way should be chair of the department for a while, crummy though the job is (it's like being a foreman in a factory—neither labor nor management, chewed up by both). The work has to be done. The journals do have to be edited (though the task would be lighter if we didn't need 10 mediocre pieces for tenure instead of 3 good ones). I growled for a long time at a friend who twice turned down the editorship of the *Journal of Economic History* for what seemed selfish reasons. He was willing to take honors from the profession but not to do the dirty work. Finally he gave in.

And yet. Harry Johnson and Robert Mundell are paired in my mind, both at Chicago in the early 1970s. Both were Canadians, both heavy drinkers, both world-famous in trade theory. Harry was the most responsible academic I have ever known, the very soul of professional care. His capacity for routine work was amazing. I came into the department once on a Saturday morning to find him with a pile of 50 Ph.D. core examinations on one side of the desk and a full bottle of scotch on the other. When I left a few hours later the pile and the scotch, both finished, had traded positions. Johnson inspired hundreds of other economists, traveling incessantly to universities off the main track, commenting on everyone's work, synthesizing, editing, teaching (his classes were models of preparation and clarity), attending committees (while opening his mail, all of which he answered promptly), running the invisible college.

Bob Mundell, on the other hand, is among the least responsible academics I have known (the competition is stiff). His office at Chicago looked like the result of a terrorist bombing. He never prepared classes. He was editor of the *Journal of Political Economy* for a while but was so negligent that Harry had to take over and straighten things up. And yet: Bob Mundell (Nobel 1999) in a brief spurt of creativity in the 1960s in Waterloo and Chicago reoriented the theory of international finance permanently, which will be remembered into the twenty-first century. When

Harry died, prematurely, with bitter pain to his many friends, his influence on economics ceased.

If you are going to do creative work that lasts, whether in the library or the classroom, you have to cherish the flame. You have to protect it from the puffing of bureaucracy. The examples from art are impressive, the most extreme case being Gauguin, who one day (it is said: the true story must be more complicated) left his banking bureaucracy and his family for a life of painting in Tahiti. That's a terrible thing to do, ethically indefensible. And yet.

The literary critic Edmund Wilson had late in life a prestamped postcard printed up, which he would use to reply to requests not relevant to his current projects. It said "Edmund Wilson regrets that he does not (1.) Write testimonials for books (2.) Attend conferences (3.) Comment on unsolicited manuscripts," and so on through the dozen ways of snuffing the flame. He would check off the relevant item and drop it in the mail to the person requesting. The technique is harsh, but you see the point.

My mentor early in graduate school was John Meyer, whose graduate course in transportation economics I had taken as a senior in college. He supported me for a couple of summers, and in part during the year, in exchange for incompetent assistance on the economics of slavery and the Colombian Transport Project. I saw him as an academic entrepreneur, more businesslike than most professors. But *businesslike* does not mean "methodical, orderly, time-keeping." The word is *businesslike,* not *bureaucracy-like.* It is what foreign academics can learn from American academics, using the best values of a commercial civilization for the study of economics or Greek.

Meyer's force and business reminded me of my grandfather, an electrical contractor in Michigan. I noticed in particular that Meyer was ruthless about his research time, as an electrical contractor had better be ruthless about his wiring time. One day, for example, I was standing in Meyer's office waiting to be told what to do (research assistants are like that, unfortunately) when his secretary, Marina, brought in a new book from the mail. Meyer tore open the package, turned at once to the index, scanned the pages he had looked up, then tossed the book aside, probably forever. In retrospect it's possible he was looking up (1) *Meyer, John;* or (2) *sex.* But at the time it struck me as an emblem of how a businesslike scholar works. Get right to the point. Dig out what you need. Don't read books; use them.

Read for pleasure, use for work. Since then I've rarely read a nonfiction book cover to cover, though I've used many thousands. As it was put by Francis Bacon: "Some books are to be tasted, others to be swallowed, and some few [very few, and mainly if written by your scientific opponents] to be chewed and digested." Good advice (though it should be noted from a man in other ways a scoundrel; Bacon was, for instance, the last man to use torture in England for official purposes).

My other mentor in graduate school, Alexander Gerschenkron, made his first impression on many people through his office, another lesson in cherishing the flame. It was an appalling mess, books and papers piled high, a long tunnel of stacked tomes to the desk itself, bottles of brandy littered within reach for his heart condition. Gerschenkron claimed that he knew where everything was because once a year he spent a day going through the stacks. It was one of the great messes of academic life. The prize in this regard goes in fact to Leo Goodman, the sociologist and statistician at Chicago, whose office had when I saw it thousands of pieces of unopened mail covering the entire floor, tilting up to the walls at the angle of repose of mail. Al Harberger's office in Economics at Chicago, despite the work of a super secretary, Elyce Monroe, was only an order of magnitude or two below Goodman's on the entropy scale. Gerschenkron's lay somewhere between Harberger's and Goodman's.

The messy academic offices make the point. Gerschenkron, Goodman, and Harberger were brilliantly creative people, masters in their field and beyond. The moral is given by the joke: "If a messy desk is a sign of a messy mind, what's an empty desk a sign of?" I once saw at the University of Virginia the office of Ralph Cohen, a great student of literature, and it reminded me so strongly of Gerschenkron's that I told him so. Cohen, Gerschenkron, and the rest did not waste time being neat about inessentials. They were neat when it mattered, for this footnote or that equation—and then fanatically neat, willing to go to absurd lengths of precision, Fogel style—but not as a rule in matters far from the creative flame. Being neat about inessentials is like attending all committees and answering all mail or, in the modern mode, reading the manual from start to finish before starting up the computer. In the way of John Meyer, Gerschenkron was businesslike and neat when it mattered, for compiling a statistical table on Russian agriculture in the late nineteenth century or for writing English better than most native English speakers. But for the rest, well . . . clean up in a dull moment.

"To burn always with this hard, gemlike flame, to maintain this ecstasy, is success in life," said the English critic Walter Pater a century ago. Heady stuff, but also soberly correct. Routine science is satisfactory and pays the bills. The bureaucracies that pay us must be served. Yet we should each of us cherish our hard, gemlike flame, however small, because it is success in the scientific or teaching life. Neglect the committee that is not accomplishing anything; avoid the student who is merely buttering you up; do not respond to the Nth request for a recommendation of a colleague you don't know or care about. Or, to be exact and economic, watch for the opportunity cost in cherished flame forgone.

How to Work

How do I work? Messily, cleaning up in dull moments. And I imitate my betters. And I cherish my little flame.

I learned how to cherish my flame from experts. My mother's passions for painting, singing (she started a promising career in opera), studying Greek, writing poetry, fixing the house, have been for me models of how to work. In 1995 I attended a conference at Temple University on writing, at which a woman professor of composition gave a paper called "Writing on the Bias" (*on the bias* is a term in sewing, guys). She said she learned to write by watching her mother make beautiful clothing. The inspiration to work is the same, she was saying, whatever the medium. I agree. My mother's way of tearing down a wall and rebuilding it is a way of doing science.

My father was a professor, too (as is my kid sister, a psychologist; professing is the family business). He was well-known in political science in the 1950s and 1960s, a fine scholar. I watched him goof off a lot between deadlines. He would read two mystery novels a night, for example, and read many other books not on his professional list (his profession was to study the American Supreme Court). I say "goofing off," but that's not right, because he showed me that wide reading makes a flexible scholar. From him I learned to make time for reading outside British iron and steel, 1870–1914, my dissertation subject, or British economic history, my specialty, or even my wide passion of the 1980s, rhetoric. The result was, for example, that in early middle life I had a way of learning something about the humanities, in order to see the rhetoric of economics; and in late middle life I could see the relevance to economics of ethical reflection.

But the "pleasure" reading kept becoming work reading. I would read about astronomy for pleasure but then find 10 years later that I was using what I had absorbed about the scholarly attitude of astrophysicists to compare real sciences with Samuelsonian economics and its math department values (I was joined in the astrophysics hobby for a while at Chicago by an economist colleague, Gilbert Ghez; I was charmed to learn a while ago that his daughter has become at UCLA a distinguished young

. . . astrophysicist). I would read about linguistics for pleasure—if I had it to do over again, I think I would become a linguist, although probably unhappily, linguistics in my day being one of the most violently contentious fields around (be thankful that *our* Great MIT Leader is the amiable Paul Anthony Samuelson instead of the vicious and vindictive Noam Chomsky). But then 10 years later I found that the linguistics illuminated how an economy operates. In the early 1980s I read Thomas Mann's first big novel, *Buddenbrooks,* because I was ashamed I had not. I found it enthralling and recognized later that it was one of the few sympathetic portraits of a businessman in modern literature (another is David Lodge's recent *Nice Work*). It started me thinking, at Arjo Klamer's urging, about the role of persuasion in the economy and then of ethics and our times.

Flame-cherishers are rare, so you have to pay attention when you run into one. I watch how the best people work and then try to imitate them. That's how you learn a sport, or writing on the bias, and that's how you learn scholarship. Watch how the tennis player lines up her backhand. Watch how Bob Solow brings a personal tone into his scholarly writing. Keep your eyes open for hot tips.

Or hot anti-tips, watching the way the dopes do it. Some years ago, for example, I sent 50 pages of confidential comments on her paper to a historical demographer, reckoned a friend, who did not thank me but instead got angry. Bush league. She treated me with hostility even when I was being legally harassed by my sister about my gender change, while the other women academics at the Social Science History Association were supporting me warmly (they threw a party for me with balloons reading "It's a girl!"). Similarly, I replied at length once to a request by a well-known experimental economist to criticize a draft, ending by telling him he needed to read more. He got angry, too, like a bush leaguer.

Watch the major leaguers. From the world historian at Chicago, William McNeill, whose office was across the hall from mine, I learned that you should never complain about teaching. He combined his teaching with his research, as we all should—anyone who can't learn a lot about economics from teaching Economics 1 is intellectually dead. McNeill said it this way:

> A university promotes scholarship less through the leisure it confers upon faculty and students than through the routines of classroom performance that require student and teacher to have something to say at a fixed point in time, ready or not. By compelling initial formulations of a given subject matter in this way, ideas are literally

forced into existence, to whither or to flourish under subsequent examination as the case may be. (1980, vii)

From Milton Friedman I learned how to keep theory connected with fact, by asking myself every time I could remember it Milton's most terrifying seminar question, "How do you know?" Milton is always ready to listen to some fool's answer. At the first cocktail party I attended at Chicago as an assistant professor in 1968 I was holding forth to a group including Milton on the monopoly of professional sports, the existence of which I had learned from reading Milton's writings. He asked mildly: "How do you know? How do you know that professional sports is a monopoly?" Gak. Jessum. I dunno. . . . Milton told me so.

The problem is that it's hard to arrange to be around world-class scholars every day, right? After all, most of us are not at MIT, and even those who are there don't chat daily with Paul Samuelson or Peter Temin or Franklin Fisher, right?

Wrong. You can learn from writings, without a presence, whether you are in Cambridge, Massachusetts, or at the North Pole, if you give it a serious try. This entails, though, actually doing the reading, which most economists do not do enough of. Books, especially. I am often depressed by how few books economists have in their houses. An economist who thinks that economics, "like physics" (as he'll always say, without knowing the first thing about how physics actually operates as a science), requires one merely to read the latest articles is not going to be much of an economist. (It should be noted that most fields even in physics are not "like physics" in this sense and that, anyway, the best physicists have famously wide interests. The definition of a string quartet at the Institute for Advanced Study at Princeton is: three physicists and a mathematician.) I learned most about how to work, more even than from the actual presence of Fogel or Gerschenkron or Meyer or my parents, by reading books. I learned to pay attention to Bill McNeill by being a colleague, true, but I learned the idea about teaching from one of his books. Milton (Friedman, and for that matter the poet John) has taught me much more in print than in person.

There's an enormous literature on How to Cherish Your Flame, in as much detail and specificity as you could want. You've just got to read beyond the *Journal of Economic Theory*. If you're going to be anything but a routine scholar, you need to learn that people outside of economics are not all misled dolts. You can learn from them, if you'll just start buying and reading their books. Listen up.

An important example for me was the essay by the American sociologist C. Wright Mills (I do not recommend his views on economics) "On Intellectual Craftsmanship." It is an appendix to a collection of his essays called *The Sociological Imagination* and tells in detail how one fine scholar went about his work. Books on writing are good places to learn about flame cherishing, my own (*Economical Writing,* 2d ed., 1999) or others (Howard Becker, another great sociologist, wrote *Writing for Social Scientists* [1986] and *Tricks of the Trade: How to Think about Your Research While Doing It* [1998]) . After all, a scholar is a writer. For a while I was reading style books the way other people read econometrics books. Writing paragraphs well is just as important as inverting matrixes well. More. The *Paris Review* interviews of creative writers are the very type of flame-cherishing literature. They've been published now in successive collections, a half-dozen or so. Jay Woodruff has edited an amazing book of five interviews with the likes of Joyce Carol Oates and Robert Coles on how successive drafts change: *A Piece of Work: Five Writers Discuss Their Revisions* (1993).

Another good source of flame-cherishing advice is the academic biography. I read them compulsively. You need to know how other brain workers have lived their lives. The *Autobiography* of Edward Gibbon (1796) tells how to write *The Decline and Fall of the Roman Empire. The Education of Henry Adams* (1907) tells how to continue to educate oneself into old age. I especially like mathematical (auto)biography, such as S. M. Ulam, *Adventures of a Mathematician* (1976; as a child, I knew his younger brother Adam); Paul Halmos, *I Want to Be a Mathematician: An Automathography* (1985); and Constance Reid's books *Hilbert* and *Courant,* though you have to watch out in all of them for an uncritically worshipful attitude toward math. For economics read James Buchanan's autobiography, *Better than Plowing* (1992). The two volumes edited by J. A. Kaegel, *Recollections of Eminent Economists,* collected from pieces in the *Banca Nazionale del Lavoro Review,* should be perused by everyone interested in economics, though they show that not all economists are gifted in telling what happened to them beyond their resume.

The wider point is that the key to scholarly creativity is to combine your life and your work. That's how to cherish the flame: make the passions of your life a part of your work and your work a passion of your life. My best articles and books have come out of passions in my life—to mention a few examples, irritation with the stockbroking industry after it had enticed my mother to lose two little fortunes (*If You're So Smart*); or concern about lofty sneering at the Midwestern bourgeoisie ("Bourgeois

Virtue"); or the experience of gender change (*The Vices of Economists;* or, more directly, *Crossing: A Memoir;* I have in mind a book to be called *Differences* that will attack the idea that differences between significant and insignificant coefficients, or blacks and whites, or men and women, are given by nature without regard to the human significance of the difference). The autobiography by the psychologist Jerome Bruner, *In Search of Mind,* contrasts two models of intellectual life: "Alfred Kroeber [the anthropologist] once told me that the difference between him and Clyde Kluckhohn [another anthropologist] is that Clyde wanted to weave everything he knew into one tapestry—anthropology, psychoanalysis, classics. He, Kroeber, was quite content to let them live on their own" (1983, 77). I favor the unifying, civilizing Kluckhohn model (although Kroeber was hardly a barbarian). We should bring everything we know into our economics and into our lives.

Rule 6

Watch Your Words
and the Work
They Do

The Rhetoric of
Economics, Revisited

A postscript to a new edition of one of my books.

I just finished, now in the summer of 1997, writing a second edition of a book first published in 1985 (good Lord: 12 years ago), *The Rhetoric of Economics*. The new edition will be out in January 1998 from the University of Wisconsin. Yes, it makes a lovely gift for the Chinese New Year. Please, for the year of the Pig or the Stockbroker or whatever it is in China, buy copies for all your friends. The University of Wisconsin Press. 2537 Daniels Street. Madison. 53718. Cheap.

I didn't change the book much, illustrating my Law of Academic Productivity: Never publish only once. (George Stigler was once challenged by a newspaper reporter to explain why he, George, "only" had 80 or so items on his CV while his colleague Harry Johnson—who was very generous in supplying permissions to republish for new journals that wanted his weight—had hundreds and hundreds. George said, "Because my articles are all different.") Mainly, I changed the arrangement, putting the philosophical chapters that once opened it into the back and starting with many, many chapters showing over and over again that economics uses metaphors and stories and devices of style. For example, I added a chapter on the rhetoric of Ronald Coase. The book keeps the practice of doing rhetorical analyses mainly of economists I admire, to lean against the presumption that to find "rhetoric" is to find something bad. A lot of people thought the book was philosophical (the *Journal of Economic Literature* piece in 1983 that people imagine covers the essential content of the book was only the philosophical chapters 1–3 of the old edition). Actually, the book was and is rhetorical, not philosophical. It shows that economics has a wordcraft, a way of persuading itself, up to and including the madness of statistical significance (which gets a lot of attention in both editions but is better placed in the new one to show that real scientific issues hinge on this notion of rhetoric).

Well, has it worked? Since the first edition have economists paid attention?

No. Most economists have reckoned from the title of the book that Aunt Deirdre "advocates" rhetoric, as "against" mathematics. Or else maybe she is ripping aside a veil, showing economics to be Not Science, Merely Literature. (The dichotomies of modernism—such as art versus science—are deeply ingrained.) Or maybe she's just nuts. After all, late in 1995 we got another piece of evidence "consistent with" that Hypothesis, her cra-a-a-a-zy change of gender. The economists just didn't get it. At Indiana University they still hand out Milton's 1953 essay on positive economics on the first day to the first-year graduate students. *Oy.*

True, the book was widely and favorably noticed. There were around 50 reviews. I hope you saw this and were impressed. But even its friends kept getting it wrong in ways that let them go on as before. A wonderful review by Bob Heilbroner in the *New York Review of Books,* for example, said, This is nice, but after all it's just about Style, not Substance. Oh, Bob, Bob. When am I going to persuade you that style is substance, you master stylist? Bob Solow from another ideological direction had the same idea and evokes from me the same response. Oh, Bob, Bob. The number of economist who have understood the book and then acted on the understanding in print is to my knowledge small: Arjo Klamer first (he in fact discovered the point independently in his Ph.D. dissertation at Duke); Jack Amariglio, John Davis, Jerry Evensky, Willie Henderson, Don Lavoie, Hans Lind, William Milberg. Not a mainstream neoclassical establishment figure among them. And, anyway, not many of any description.

I am calm about this. Really, I am. I strike some people as arrogant, though more so in my former gender than now, I hope. But really I am as modest a lady as anyone could wish, very sweet and unassuming. I would never assume in particular that people who do not read my books or do not understand them or do not agree with them are fools and knaves. Cheap, yes. Disrespectful of the Chinese New Year, without a doubt. But not fools and knaves. People haven't agreed with me as a soft Marxist, as a social engineering transport economist, as a quantitative economic historian, as a Chicago School economist, as a neoinstitutionalist, as a libertarian, as a global monetarist, as a free-market feminist. No wonder they don't agree with me as a rhetorician of science.

Of course, like most people I do suppose that those folks are wrong and I am right. (And in sober truth—can I confide in you as a friend?—I *am* right.) But no matter. I learned the hard way, over and over and over again, that most people are not always open to persuasion to what's right. It's a pity that this is as true of your average professor carrying the *New York Times* as it is of your average Bubba carrying a six-pack, but there you are. It just goes to show that rhetoric is about something serious. As Schopenhauer once said: "It is quite natural that we should adopt a defensive and negative attitude towards every new opinion concerning something on which we have already an opinion of our own. For it forces its way as an enemy into the previously closed system of our own convictions, shatters the calm of mind we have attained through this system, demands renewed efforts of us and declares our former efforts to have been in vain" (1851 [1970], no. 19, 124). The late Thomas Kuhn said the same thing and showed it working in the rhetorical history of science.

I think the first edition and my subsequent writings made a space in economics for thinking about the conversation. But it's still a small space. Economists are still unaware of how they talk. I failed. Oh, well. Keep trying.

The results of the rhetorical unawareness of economists, I have realized more and more, are unspeakably sad. A lot of good work gets done in economics, new facts and new ideas. Economists are not stupid or lazy, not at all. I love the field. I belong to the mainstream and would float happily in it if it nowadays made a bit of sense. But the mainstream of normal science in economics, I'm afraid, has dried up and become instead a sandbox for a boys' game. It has become silly. Existence theorems, statistical significance. Qualitative, not quantitative, as Samuelson so ill-advisedly urged us to be in 1947. In practical terms what is published in academic journals of economics is so irrelevant to the way real scientific persuasion goes on, the finding of How Big, that I can by now only sit and moan quietly. Please, please, boys: let's get out of the sandbox. Let's start having a serious scientific rhetoric.

I once had a transatlantic flight seated beside a young economist who must qualify as the most barbarous scholar I have ever met. He told me that his scientific duty was to sit at his computer all day long. (Much as I do, I must admit, writing—but I've read a book or two.) What he meant is that he did not need to read anything or talk to any businessperson or even copy down government statistics. All he needed to do to be a modern economist was to run regression equations, searching for statistical significance, in standard data sets, already collected and committed to machine-readable form. Although I am pretty sure that the young man, now not quite so young, still has nothing but contempt for the values of actual science and scholarship that I vainly espouse in *The Rhetoric of Economics,* I do feel sorry for him and worry what will happen when he discovers that his life has been wasted. I look at the boys playing in the sandbox like a doting aunt and worry: Oh, boys, it is so foolish what you have allowed yourself to specialize in playing, this matter of "existence" of effect *X*; please, please, start caring about the world and its very interesting economy; you are going to feel very unhappy this evening when you go home and think over what you have accomplished.

It's not the man's fault that he is a barbarian. He was taught to be one in a fine graduate program by nameable modernist econometricians, positive economists, and methodologists with whom I am personally acquainted. By their fruits ye shall know them.

If I had my wish about how this second edition would be used, it would be that every graduate student in economics would read it and reflect—and flee an unscientific barbarism. In my day Koopmans's *Three Essays on the State of Economic Science* was The Book. It was, I realize now, an appalling production, outlining the fraudulent truce between econometrics and mathematical theory that has dominated economics since 1957. We all read it and thought it very fine. My book is partly an anti-Koopmans.

The cynical and perhaps realistic view is that nothing would actually change in economics if the graduate students read the second edition. Certainly, you should never underestimate the conservatism of science. Geologists fought for decades against plate tectonics (I was perhaps the last person in the United States to be educated in the old geology, by conservatives at Harvard contemptuous of the crazy notion that the continents fitted into each other). As George Stigler, America's leading vulgar Marxist, never tired of arguing, the status quo usually has lots of money and power to back it. A narrow, ignorant, antihumanistic, and unscientific economics is easier to run than anything better. Look at how popular the old way is with political scientists, for example.

But I think the cynical, Stiglerian or Marxist, view is wrong. If we will be who we are, take our courage and use it, we can change economics.

People sometimes ask me how my views of economics have changed since I became a woman. It's not been long, and I am, goodness knows, nothing like an expert at Being a Woman. In some important ways I never will be, alas. Still, I see some differences. The virtue of love, it seems to me, belongs in any serious science of economics and radically changes even the studies of prudence (a brilliant piece in the *Journal of Political Economy* in 1996 by Frey, Oberholzer-Gee, and Eichenberger made this point about sentiments of Not in My Backyard). The boys' games seem to me now to be even sillier than I had thought. A few other things, and more to come, I expect.

But what I mainly learned is that a life must be itself and, in a rich, free country like ours, it can be. People do not come into economics mainly because they like the sandbox games at present taking place in the field. Some do, but not most people. Most people want earnestly to change the world or to make a scientific contribution. To achieve such noble goals the first thing to do is to break through the phony rhetoric of modern economics and bring economics, that glorious conversation since Adam Smith, back into the conversation of humankind.

Please, my dears, please. And, anyway, buy and read my little book, to celebrate the New Year.

The Rhetoric of Economic Development and of P. T. Bauer

For a conference on Bauer's work, published in the Cato Journal *in spring–summer 1993. The papers referred to appear in the same edition.*

Peter Bauer has had at least the satisfaction of seeing his grimmest pre-diction come true. As he feared so long ago, economists have on balance delayed economic development. By their words.

I disagree, though, with the contrast announced in the title of one of Bauer's books on economic development, *Reality and Rhetoric.* The "reality," I say, is itself a matter of words. We cannot speak persuasively without being rhetorical, and by our rhetoric in economic development we make our worlds, North or South. The meaning of *rhetoric* here is its ancient and honorable one, not the meaning current since the seventeenth century, of rhetoric as ornament that "merely" fools or pleases the reader. On the contrary, rhetoric is the whole art of argument, from metaphor to mathematics.

As Bauer has been the first to understand, economic development is drenched, for example, with metaphor. He has remarked that the metaphor of the Third World was born with foreign aid and anticom-munism. And all we economists make a world of "production functions" and "human capital," embodied in mathematics, in places where lay-people see only factory workers and schoolhouses. As Deepak Lal observed in his paper at the conference, we are all rhetoricians, we scien-tists and policymakers together.

All this is obvious. The phrase *blindingly obvious* comes to mind. In this connection, however, Bauer notes with approval George Orwell's remark, "We have sunk so low that a statement of the obvious is the first duty of a thoughtful person." The obvious point I am making is that, for the study of economic development, words have consequences. By the mere act of speaking of equity versus efficiency, for instance, we import into the argument, as though it were uncontroversial, a utilitarian ethic. We are invited to think of tradeoffs between the one and the other, $U = U(Efficiency, Equity)$, in which *Efficiency* is the size of national income regardless of how it is achieved and *Equity* is measured by the distribution of income and not by the distribution of rights. This is not "wrong"; it is simply one style among many, some better than others.

The point is not that one form of speech in the discussion of equity during development is "reality" and the other "rhetoric." The point is that all forms of speech are rhetoric and no less right or wrong on that account. They are right and wrong on grounds other than rhetoricity, which all speech-with-a-purpose has. Of course, we ought to be conscious of *what* we speak, a philosophical reading *through* the text to what stands behind it. But we must also be conscious of *how* we speak, a rhetorical reading *on* the text, of what its surface tries to do.

Bauer notes, for instance, the danger in the metaphor of "nation building," a handsome neoclassical building in which political prisoners scream in the basement. The figure of a building, he notes, treats people as "lifeless bricks, to be moved by some master builder." Nation building is not "merely" a metaphor, "mere" ornamental rhetoric. It is a political argument put into a word.

Or think of the array of metaphors taken from sport, as in the "goal" of equity or the government as "referee." These are especially popular among Americans, who good-heartedly favor the notion of a game in which no one really gets hurt (in similar cases the Europeans will use metaphors of war and conquest). The ideal is team play, joining together to score a goal against the North or, in a more mellow way, to achieve a "personal goal." Whenever we hear that "we" should do such and such, we should watch for the team metaphor in action. The most that human frailty is likely to achieve along this line is Lester Thurow's book on *The Zero-Sum Solution: Building a World-Class American Economy* (1985). The book treats income and wealth as being extracted like football yardage from other people, especially Japanese people. As Karl Bruner pointed out in his comment to the conference, the image of income as a fixed manna from heaven to be shared is an argument persuasive to many, even to many economists. The zero-sum image has always been the main argument for mercantilism and now figures heavily in the talk of North and South.

The North, of course, is meant to feel guilty that by the grace of God it gets more of the manna than the South. Bauer has treated at length the use of the notion of "our" guilt as a justification for compulsory charity. The libertarian economist Murray Rothbard used to observe that American progressives around 1910 were disproportionately the sons and daughters of postmillenial Protestant clergymen. Clergymen and upper-middle-class intellectuals delight in the transformation of *mea culpa* into *nostra culpa,* prejudging in a word the weighty question of whether charity should be individual or social.

The word *problem,* likewise, answers a question before one thinks to ask it. Many reputable economists argue that the balance-of-payments problem is not a "problem" at all, in the sense of something requiring that "we" find "a solution." Yet everyone else is exercised about The Problem. The nineteenth century invented the talk of a "social problem," an "economic problem," and the like, problems for which finally the Great Geometer in Washington or London is to provide a solution, with compass and straightedge. The economic historian Max Hartwell speaks of the rhetoric of British parliamentary inquiries in the nineteenth century as defining problems where no one had seen them before. It is not done with mirrors; this or that condition does exist. But it *is* also done with words. Someone who has persuaded you to speak of inequality of income as a problem has accomplished the hardest part of her task.

The very word *development* is a metaphor, of course, limiting our thinking at the same time it makes thinking possible. *Economic growth* sounds better than *economic change* and *change* better than *losing existing jobs,* but they are translatable one into the other, implying different policies. Economists are not usually conscious of the difference the words make. A self-conscious metaphor has a different effect from an unselfconscious one. In his essay at the conference Mancur Olson compared a one-man boat, eight-man boat, and multi-oared galley. Because he uses the figure openly and self-consciously, the effect is merely communicative and ornamental. An explicit metaphor does not bite.

Metaphors are not the only rhetorical matters. Alan Walters made the point at the conference, as Bauer does in his book, that the audience for the main ideas of economics, as distinct from the technical gingerbread, is not the economics profession itself but the City or Whitehall or Fleet Street. Awareness of the audience has characterized rhetorical theory since Aristotle. The theory of rhetoric itself uses a metaphor of a speaker before the Athenian Assembly, which has proven a useful way of finding out what is going on in a country report by the IMF or in a technical article on trade policy. The Greeks had it right: the study of rhetoric is not a way of attacking a speech, necessarily, but is always a way of understanding it, reading on the surface of the text.

Consider in a rhetorical way, for instance, Alvin Rabushka's illuminating essay for the conference. I say at once that I agree with what Rabushka writes there. A rhetorical analysis, to repeat, is not a euphemism for debunking. But consider how the essay seeks to persuade. It appeals to a rhetoric of What The Facts Say. Rabushka knows that facts don't "say" anything unless human questions are posed to them, that the questions depend on the predispositions of the questioner, and that anyway the subset we call The Facts (out of the unbounded set of particular statements we might make about the universe) is our selection, not God's. Yet the move is effective. Hold up chart 1 and then chart 2 and then chart 3, appealing to what the logician so ill-advisedly call the "fallacy" of *post hoc ergo propter hoc*. Free countries, the charts say, do well. This is a fallacy, because after all it is not a syllogism. What the logicians call fallacies are what most of us call arguments, more or less appropriate to the matter at hand. That Hong Kong had a light-handed government (that is, not a light-fingered one) and then prospered does not have the demonstrative force that scientism seeks. But of course it partly and properly persuades. It should, while making room for possible points to the contrary.

Even "mere" style is an argument. The forthright character in the writings of Bauer and in the writings of George Ayittey does not please all audiences but makes an appeal to ethos, character. It announces that the writer tells it like it is. A more accommodating style would make an appeal to the ethos of moderation or of practicality. A style of mathematical precision would make still another ethical appeal. The euphemism of the development bureaucrat—"extra-budgetary revenues," for instance, a name for theft—soothes an audience worried that something might after all be said.

Development economics, in short, has a rich and unexamined and dangerous rhetoric.

The last word on rhetoric in economic development, though, should be accorded to Cato the Elder. Some 2,200 years ago he captured in a phrase how rhetoric, which is inevitable, must be used if it is to be good. There are no methodological protections against speaking falsely. We cannot ensure good results by mandating this or that model or metaphor.

The final protection, he argued, is human goodness. The arguer, said Cato, must be not merely a man (so Cato, when women had no voice at all) skilled at speaking, for this is a mere advocate, a showman. He must be a good man skilled at speaking, *vir bonus dicendi peritus.* Thus P. T. Bauer.

The Rhetoric
of Finance

For the New Palgrave Dictionary of Money and Finance *(1992).*

The rhetoric of finance is the language of the financial market and the language of its academic study.

One should understand *rhetoric* as speech with a purpose, that is, wordcraft. Dating from fifth-century Greece and still current in literary circles, the definition does not distinguish good purposes from bad. The rhetoric of finance is therefore not confined to misleading language used for bad purposes, as in the newspaper headline "Chancellor's Rhetoric on Bank Rate." The harmless tale of bulls and bears in the bond market is rhetoric, but so too is the forbidding majesty of the capital asset pricing model, because both are speech with a purpose; both are words, including mathematics and statistics, crafted well or poorly to persuade. A commission salesman hawking worthless house lots is using rhetoric, but so too is a CEO earnestly and honestly trying to persuade a banker to make a loan. To identify a piece of speech in finance as rhetoric is not to damn it but to identify it as part of wordcraft.

The jargon of the financial market is ripe for rhetorical study. Words weigh. Shakespeare imitates the financial jargon of his time in *The Merchant of Venice,* as when Salarino explains to Antonio why he is sad: "Your mind is tossing on the ocean; / There, where your argosies with portly sail . . . / Do overpeer the petty traffickers," the "argosies" being merchant ships of Raguza, bigger than mere local traffickers. To which Antonio replies, overconfidently it soon appears, that he is diversified: "My ventures are not in one bottom trusted, / Nor to one place; nor is my whole estate / Upon the fortune of this present year: / Therefore my merchandise makes me not sad." And throughout: *usance* for usury, *excess* for interest, *single bond* for a signature note, and *let the forfeit be nominated* (for an equal pound / Of your fair flesh).

The simplest literary criticism of financial markets would merely note such jargon, with perhaps a chuckle at its charm or pretense. Michael Johnson's book *Business Buzzwords: The Tough New Jargon of Modern Business* (1990) is such a compilation, from arbs to white knights. Jargon and the use of thrilling metaphors of sport and war are speech with a purpose. The purpose is usually to establish what the Greeks called an "ethos" worth listening to. Fluent use of financial jargon establishes its speaker as a member of a community of worthies or would-be worthies. The subdialect of Latinate or Greekifying words (disintermediation, prioritize, paradigm) even has a name in the financial world, *sonking*, that is, "scientification of knowledge." To know scientifically has a special worthiness in our culture, and it is no wonder that financial markets capitalize on its worth.

A step beyond chuckling is to note the use made of certain metaphors, such as war (raider, dawn raid, frag, take no prisoners, walking wounded, war room) or sport (team, player, track record, level playing field). The rhetorical tradition distinguishes "figures of speech" (jargon, repetition, rhyme, and the like) from "tropes" (which means just "turns" in Greek: metaphor, irony, narration, and the like). The tropes, are sometimes called "figures of thought" rather than merely of words. One chooses a theory by choosing a metaphor, revealed in one's language.

For example, Lester Thurow, although an economist trained in metaphors of demand curves and balance sheets, makes his argument in *The Zero-Sum Solution: Building a World-Class American Economy* (1985) and other of his works through a metaphor of American football. Thurow is annoyed that more of his fellow citizens do not see the world his way: "For a society which loves team sports . . . it is surprising that Americans won't recognize the same reality in the far more important international economic game" (107). "To play a competitive game is not to be a winner—every competitive game has its losers" (59), in the style of Vince Lombardi, the great coach, who is reputed to have said, "Winning isn't the most important thing; it's the only thing." The point is that Thurow's football trope is not innocent. Instead of trade as a sport in which everyone benefits, like aerobic dancing, the metaphor invites us to think of it as yardage extracted from one's trading partners. The path is short—a path taken by England and Germany, 1890–1914—from sporting metaphors to warring metaphors to the guns of August. Stories matter.

Yet stories, like metaphors, are necessary. If the literary world can teach the business world anything, it is this: to realize without shame, as the literary critic Peter Brooks put it, that "our lives are ceaselessly intertwined with narrative, with the stories that we tell and hear told, . . . all of which are reworked in that story of our own lives that we narrate to ourselves. . . . We live immersed in narrative" (1985, 3). As the critic Wayne Booth says: "We all live a great proportion of our lives in a surrender to stories. . . . Even the statisticians and accountants must in fact conduct their daily business largely in stories: the reports they receive from and give to superiors and subordinates; the accounts they deliver to tax lawyers; the anecdotes and parables they hear" (1988, 14–15).

It is obvious when expressed this way that participants in financial markets live their lives in metaphors and stories. The scientific study of finance, however, claims to reach beyond anecdote and parable to the dignity of science. The rhetoric of science since the seventeenth century has been that science is outside rhetoric. Such a rhetoric against rhetoric is mistaken. Look at the last sentence of the first edition of Eugene Fama and Merton Miller's classic, *The Theory of Finance* (1972): "We wish to suggest, however, that there is much evidence in support of the position that perfect markets models, like those developed in this book, have substantial value in describing real-world economic phenomena" (340). The closing statement in an oration, the "peroration," is presumably a place to arouse the reader to action. As is common in scientific rhetoric, however, Fama and Miller work against the presumption (as they habitually do in the book) by choosing qualified language: they wish only to "suggest"; there is "much evidence," not overwhelming; the assertion is merely a "position," not God's own plan for the world; models are plural, "like" other possible models, not unique, they admit freely; they have "developed" the models (that is, the metaphors), not announced them as Truth; the models, though merely models, have "substantial value," a modest claim; the models have value—merely *some* it is implied—in "describing real-world phenomena," which is pleasingly down-to-earth, but the models do not necessarily explain the world's deep meaning, merely its surface phenomena; after all, this is the real world, beyond the modestly relevant world of books. To end on such a modest note shows an ethos worth attending to—and giving a Nobel Prize for. With similar effect, the last paragraph of the two-page article in which Watson and Crick announced the structure of DNA was not given over to stirring calls to scientific action but thanks to the funding agencies. By being "unrhetorical" (an impossibility), Watson and Crick, and Fama and Miller, reinforced their reputations for sobriety, on which their scientific persuasiveness depends. It's rhetoric: not lies, but rhetoric, and worth watching.

It is perhaps no surprise to claim that a financial analyst or a financial economist is being literary when telling the story of the Federal Reserve Board last year or positing a "demand curve" (that startling metaphor) for pounds sterling. Plainly and routinely, 90 percent of what observers of the financial markets do is such story telling and metaphor using. But one can show in detail that even the purely academic remainder is affected by figures and tropes (McCloskey 1990, 1998). Stories, for example, end in a new state. In notably economic language the Bulgarian/French literary critic Tzvetan Todorov asserted that "the minimal complete plot consists of the transition from one equilibrium to another" (qtd. in Prince 1973, 31). Likewise, if a proffered economic story ends prematurely, an economist says "something's wrong: it's not an equilibrium." "Not an equilibrium" is the economist's way of saying that he disputes the ending proposed by some untutored person. Many of the disagreements inside economics turn on this sense of an ending.

To an eclectic Keynesian, raised on picaresque tales of economic surprise, the story idea "Oil prices went up in 1973, which caused inflation" is full of meaning, having the merits that stories are supposed to have. But to a monetarist, raised on the classical unities of money, it seems incomplete, no story at all, a flop. As the economist A. C. Harberger likes to say, it doesn't make the economics "sing." It ends too soon, halfway through the second act: a rise in oil prices without some corresponding fall elsewhere is "not an equilibrium." From the other side, the criticism of monetarism by Keynesians is likewise a criticism of the plot line, complaining of an ill-motivated beginning rather than a premature ending: Where on earth does the money you think is so important come from and why? The intellectual jargon is "exogenous": if you start the story in the middle, the money will be treated as though it is unrelated to, exogenous to, the rest of the action, even though it's not.

There is more than prettiness in such matters of plot. There is ethical weight. The historian Hayden White writes that "the demand for closure in the historical story is a demand . . . for moral reasoning" (1981, 20). A monetarist is not ethically satisfied until she has pinned the blame on the Federal Reserve or the Bank of England. Stories impart meaning, which is to say, worth.

The financial markets and their academic students, then, are immersed in rhetoric (cf. Klamer 1984). This is no bad thing, merely inevitable, and worth watching. Persuasive speech is rhetorical whether voiced by Pythagoras about right triangles or by Demosthenes about Philip of Macedon. Rhetoric, therefore, is more than an entertaining supplement to the study of financial markets. "I will buy with you, sell with you, talk with you, walk with you, and so following . . . . What news on the Rialto?"

Keynes Was a Sophist, and a Good Thing, Too

Eastern Economic Journal (spring 1996). I gave the piece at a conference in England, my first there as Deirdre.

Every economist should read Robert Skidelsky's biography of John Maynard Keynes (he's completed two volumes out of three projected)—even the numerous macroeconomists under age 40 who have not cracked *The General Theory of Employment, Interest and Money* and think themselves wiser because they have not. Skidelsky's opus is a great bedtime read, reminding you of what a sensationally good economist Keynes was, because he was more. And it makes you think about where economics is going. I guess no one will be surprised that the story of Keynes's life and thought makes me think about the "rhetoric" of economics. My thought is this: Keynes was a sophist, not a platonist (by which I mean here a follower of Plato and not the technical meaning in the history of philosophy). To read him as a platonist, as economists mostly have, makes him nearly impossible to understand.

You know the definition of *sophist* as a term of contempt. Plato himself established the contemptuous usage at the beginning of Western philosophy, and ever after the philosophers have defined themselves against sophistry. Thomas Hobbes, for instance, that founder of the Economic Way of Thinking a century before Smith, was eloquent in *Leviathan* and elsewhere against rhetoric and sophistry, such as the misuse of metaphor, and used many striking metaphors to combat its evil effects. *Sophistry* in Plato's sense means "mere verbal trickery," as against Really Knowing, that sort of thing a true philosopher knows. Admittedly, how exactly one would really know that one Really Knows is a detail the philosophers have not quite worked out, in 2,400 years of trying. But they are agreed that mere opinion (*doxa*) created by the exchange of words is to be sneered at.

The contrary view, that of the sophists themselves (including arguably Socrates himself, Plato's teacher), is that we humans must get along on exchanges of words and had better learn to exchange them well. Democracies and courts of law depend on an art of persuasion exercised in the here and now, not on a doctrine of Really Knowing established by an aristocracy with time on its hands. The sophists were, so to speak, professors of law. In later classical times the great Roman sophist Quintilian, following Cato the Elder, defined the ideal law student as the good man skilled at speaking. You don't have to believe this characterizes many law students, or economics students, to recognize it as an ideal, which recommends honest talk rather than dogmatic truth.

Recently, the words *sophist* and *rhetoric* have experienced a little rehabilitation. Some members of the National Communication Association have printed bumper stickers and T-shirts asking you to "Support Your Local Sophist." The historical sophists of ancient Greece have been reassessed in works such as W. K. C. Guthrie, *The Sophists* (1971), and G. B. Kerferd, *The Sophistic Movement* (1981). Sophisticated students of Greek philosophy no longer accept unthinkingly the philosopher's contempt for sophism. It is a plausible opinion (which Plato labored persuasively in his middle dialogues to undermine) that plausible opinion is all we humans have, even we human economists.

The original sophist was Protagoras, a fifth-century teacher whose writings are known only in fragments (and in Plato's dramatization in "The Protagoras"). Protagoras' most famous fragment declares that "humans are the measure of all things," a sentiment outrageous to the platonist mind, such as Francis Bacon's: "For it is a false assertion that the sense of man is the measure of all things. . . . The human understanding is like a false mirror, which, receiving rays irregularly, distorts and discolours the nature of things by mingling its own nature with it" (1620, xvi). The sophist rejects the metaphor of the mirror of Really Knowing (thus Rorty 1979) and substitutes instead a social and conversational metaphor for how we know. The most obvious modern sophists are therefore sociologists, psychologists, philosophers, and literary critics with a listen-talk understanding of how we come to know things, such as Jürgen Habermas, Michael Billig, Richard Rorty, and Wayne Booth. Economics, like every other part of Western culture, has two schools of thought, platonist and sophistic.

Keynes worked in the sophistic school. One piece of evidence, evident on every page of Skidelsky's biography, is Keynes's lifelong commitment to adversarial and sophistic styles of engagement. The most famous example is of course *The General Theory* itself, a dialogic book arguing against this or that, especially the allegedly classical economists, rather than stating axioms and deriving theorems as though no opponent were in view. Keynes was always an enthusiastic party politician, all his life a Left Liberal in the old British sense. He believed in politics in a way that Plato and the platonists do not, that is, he believed in democracy (though the democracy was of course to be guided by natural aristocrats like Maynard and his friends).

A sign of a sophist—a sign considered by platonists as the chief nuisance of sophism—is the ability to change one's mind. Keynes frequently changed his mind, about the desirability of free trade, to take a spectacular example. In economics it is rare that people change their minds. (It is rare in any field of life, come to think of it.) I suppose the modal number of mind changes in economics is zero. John Stuart Mill changed his mind once, toward socialism; George Stigler, by his own account once, as well, against it. Robert Fogel is an unusual case of an economist who changed his mind as much as Keynes did. Keynes gave a famous retort when someone complained about this sophism of his: "When I get new evidence I change my mind. What do you do?"

Well, so what? Suppose Keynes is better read as a sophist than a platonist. What does it matter? *Nu?*

This: Keynes is misunderstood by modern platonists. They keep trying to find his one Truth, keep trying to stuff him into a stable platonist theory. Right from the beginning platonist thinkers like Friedrich Hayek and J. R. Hicks could not grasp his method. His method was in fact "encompassing," as David Hendry puts it, that is, trying to see how opponents could have thought what they thought, and then encompassing their theories in one's own. The very title of *The General Theory* embodies this sophistic tactic. The joking form of the tactic is Stigler's spoof Conference Comment Number 4: "I can understand how Professor Jones is so misled, because until recently I was thinking along the same lines."

Keynes is one of a long if somewhat thin line of economic sophists as against the massed phalanx of economic platonists. Most economists have been platonists. The platonists believe that the one Truth is out there on the blackboard somewhere, or less commonly out there in the econometrics or in the experiment. That their program has failed repeatedly does not discourage them any more than it has discouraged platonists in philosophy these two and a half millenia past. They carry on seeking the one Immutable Truth for the Ages and scorn the practical sophists like Keynes making arguments that suffice unto the day.

The sophists believe with Keynes that truth, small *t* (to which Keynes was much if not perfectly attached), is always contingent, always arguable, always the result of a particular set of assumptions being true for now, not forever. General theories, Keynes said, are useless—this from the writer of one—unless they are applied.

Though as I have said it is a minority view, the sophistic tradition in economics is old. Adam Smith is an example. The very duality of his two books (yes, he wrote another one) drives the platonists to distraction. Platonists have a terrible time with Smith if they read both books, *The Wealth of Nations* and *The Theory of Moral Sentiments,* as unified Truth with a capital *T.* "All right, Professor Smith, what is it? Love or Money? You can't have it both ways." To which Smith replies, Why not? Situations vary, one alters the other, both are in constant dialogue, the Sacred and the Profane. If situations differ, I come to differing conclusions. What do you do? (The point is made brilliantly by Vivienne Brown in her book *Adam Smith's Discourse* [1994]).

Jeremy Bentham is the canonical example in economics and in modern Western thought of the opposite, a maker of Platonist/Cartesian/Comtean monologues. The monologue is the favored form of modern economics, exhibited in the works of Stigler, Becker, Lucas, and others.

But—I don't want you to draw the wrong conclusion from that last list—the Good Old Chicago tradition was sophistic. Friedman is the most obvious and famous example in economics. He resisted and resisted and resisted the axiomatic turn in modern economics, so damaging to changing one's mind or seeing two sides of an argument. His students Becker and Lucas then proceeded to give into it. Earlier there were sophists at Chicago, such as Frank Knight (who started at the University of Iowa) and Theodore Schultz (who started at Iowa State: Is a generalization, true for the age if not the ages, forming in your mind?). Nouvelle Chicago by contrast is unattractively platonist, as are many departments of economics nowadays.

In the old paperback version of his *Price Theory* Friedman explained why he had not formed the whole into a proper book, after 10 years of delay: "As an empirical economist . . . I cannot neglect the evidence that has accumulated in that decade. Clearly, I must reject the hypothesis that a fuller treatment is imminent." Maybe the empirical scientists in philosophy or economics should by now reject the hypothesis that platonism is someday going to work. Maybe we'd better get back to sophism, to real arguments for the real problems of the day. One way back is through that great economic sophist J. M. Keynes, compliments of Robert Skidelsky.

Rule 7

Learn to Write at Least Competently

Economical Writing:
An Executive Summary

Eastern Economic Journal *(fall 1999).*

The main cause of bad writing in economics is that economists don't read good writing. If economists would read Jane Austen or George Orwell, or even Adam Smith or J. M. Keynes or Thomas Schelling, in bulk, daily, habitually, they would improve. I'm always surprised by how few books economists read and how utilitarian their reading is. Look at their bookcases: empty of good books. I once met a young colleague in a second-hand bookstore in Iowa City and was delighted at this new evidence of intellectual life: "Buying some interesting books?" "No," he replied, as though the idea of buying books was strange, "selling some textbooks." It's a rare economist—an Alchian or a Hirschman or a Yeager—who reads seriously outside economics.

A subsidiary cause is that economists don't know the rules. I hope it's more than subsidiary, because about this second, subsidiary reason I can do something. I can teach the rules. Or so I keep hoping. Back in the 1970s I gave a course to graduate students at Chicago on how to write. Tom Borcherding, when he was editor of *Economic Inquiry,* encouraged me to make it into an article, which came out in 1985, and later I made the article into a little book, published by Macmillan (gobbled up by another publisher, orphaning the book: merger destroys the specific human capital of business relations, yes?). Now a new edition of the book, *Economical Writing,* has come out from Waveland Press. Moderately priced, it's *just* the thing for your students. If you assign papers, your students are going to need the little book. As William Strunk (of the indispensible Strunk and White, *The Elements of Style;* also Macmillan) used to say to his students at Cornell, "Get the little book! Get the little book!"

But you, I know, are a busy, busy person. You just haven't got time to read even a 90-page book on how to write. Not to speak of books by Jane Austen or Tom Schelling, Mark Twain or Joan Robinson, Margaret Atwood or Bob Solow. Not in bulk.

So I offer here for the professoriate an executive summary, in the spirit of the cassettes advertised in airline magazines that promise the essence of The Classics *and* The Year's Best Books on Business in 10 minutes a week. Think of it as a *Reader's Digest* article about the new edition. If there's enough demand I'll read it into a tape that you can plug into while you drive to work. $14.95 postage paid.

Here are some rules.

1. *Choose a reader and stick with her.* Changing your implied reader is in an economic sense inefficient. An article using the translog production function wastes motion if it rederives the elementary properties of a Cobb-Douglas production function. No one who has gotten so far into such an article will be innocent of Cobb-Douglas. The writing mixes up two mutually exclusive audiences.

2. *Avoid boilerplate.* Boilerplate in prose is all that is prefabricated and predictable. Little is getting accomplished with econometric chatter copied out of the textbook, rederivations of the necessary conditions for consumer equilibrium, and repetition of hackneyed formulations of a theory.

3. *Impenetrable theoretical utterances have prestige in economics but shouldn't.* The economist will write about the completeness of arbitrage in this way: "Consider two cities, *A* and *B,* trading an asset, *X.* If the prices of *X* are the same in market *A* and in market *B,* then arbitrage may be said to be complete." The clear way does not draw attention to its "theoretical" character at all: "New York and London in 1870 both

had markets for Union Pacific bonds. The question is, did the bonds sell for the same in both places?"

4. *The table of contents paragraph is an abomination to the Lord thy God:* "The outline of this paper is as follows." Don't, please, please, *for God's sake, don't!* Nine out of 10 readers skip to the substance, if they can find it. The few who pause on the paragraph are wasting their time. They can't understand the paragraph until, like the author, they have read the paper, at which point they don't need it. You will never see it in competent writing. Weak writers defend it as a "roadmap." They got the idea from Miss Jones: "Tell the reader what you're going to say. Say it. Say that you've said it." It's exceptionally bad advice. The person who made up this memorable phrasing of it is burning in Hell.

5. *Tables are writing.* The wretched tables in economics show how little economists care about expression. Titles and headings in tables should be as close to self-explanatory as possible. In headings of tables you should use words, not computer acronyms. Remember: you're trying to be clear, not Phony Scientific. A column labeled *LPDOM* requires a step of translation to get to the meaning: "Logarithm of the Domestic Price." You want people to understand your stuff, not to jump through mental hoops. The same things can be said of displayed equations. It's clearer (and no less scientific) to say "the regression was *Quantity of Grain* = 3.56 + 5.6 (*Price of Grain*) – 3.8 (*Real Income*)" than "the regression was Q = 3.56 + 5.6P – 3.8Y, where Q is quantity of grain, P its price, and Y real income." Anyone can retrieve the algebra from the words, but the reverse is pointlessly harder. The retrieval is hard even for professional mathematicians. The set theorist Halmos said: "The author had to code his thought in [symbols] (*I deny that anybody thinks in [such] terms),* and the reader has to decode" (38; italics added). Tables, graphs, diagrams, and displayed equations should elucidate the argument, not obscure it.

6. *Don't overload your sentences.* The novelist John Gardner suggested a clever rule: *Become self-conscious about how much you're putting into each part of a sentence.* An English sentence has, grammatically speaking, three parts: subject, verb, object. Thus: subject = *An English sentence;* verb = *has grammatically speaking (grammatically speaking* modifies the verb *has);* object = *three parts: subject, verb, object.* Vary your sentences, Gardner suggested, by how much you put into each, and in each sentence choose only *one* of the three parts for elaboration. In the sentence just finished the score is: subject absent but understood = *you;*

verb = *vary,* complexly modified by "how much you put into each"; object = *your sentences,* quite simple, though not as simple as the subject. A sentence with too much in all three of its parts can ruin a paragraph. (Gardner's Rule again: a complex subject ["A sentence with too much in all three of its parts"] connected to a simple verb ["can ruin"] and simple object ["a paragraph"].)

7. *Paragraphs should have a structure like (AB)(BC)(CD).* Note the linkages of repetition, one *B* connected with another, *C* with *C,* and so forth. Economists would call it "transitive" writing. To do it you must violate the schoolmarm's rule of not repeating words. Verily, you *must* repeat them, linking the sentences and using pronouns like *it* or *them* to relieve monotony. The linkages can be tied neatly, if not too often, by repeating words with the same root in different versions, as was just done with the verb *linking* in the previous sentence and the noun *linkages* in this (the figure is called in classical rhetoric "polyptoton"). There are other tricks of cohesion. They rely on repetition. (In this paragraph, for instance, the word *repetition* is repeated right to the end in various forms: *repetition, repeating, repeat, repeating, repetition.*)

8. *Avoid Elegant Variation.* A paper on economic development used in two pages all these: *industrialization, growing structural differentiation, economic and social development, social and economic development, development, economic growth, growth,* and *revolutionized means of production.* With some effort you can see in context that they all meant about the same thing. The writer simply liked the sound of the differences and had studied elegance too young.

9. A lot of people are confused about the colon (:) and the semicolon (;). The safest rule is that *the colon indicates an illustration to follow:* just like this. *The semicolon indicates a parallel remark;* it is (as here) an *additional* illustration. The semicolon (;) means roughly "and"; the colon (:) means roughly "to be specific." The semicolon is also used to mark off items in series when the items themselves are long. "Faith, hope, and charity" uses commas; but if each item were elaborated ("Charity, the greatest of these, the light of the world"; and similarly with each) you might use the semicolon (;) as a sort of supercomma. You can see that the semicolon is also a sort of period lite; you can hurry the pace a bit by splicing two sentences with a semicolon, as here. So the semicolon falls between comma and period. Remember the difference between colon and semicolon by noting that the semicolon contains both a comma and a period within it, a printed compromise.

10. *Weak writers these days use too many commas and use them by*

rule rather than by ear, probably because Miss Jones told them to. It's no rule of life, for instance, that "an if-clause always requires a comma after it" or "when a clause cannot stand alone it must be hedged with commas." In fact, such rules lead to a comma in nearly every sentence and a consequent slowing of pace. When applied too enthusiastically a rule-driven comma ends up separating subject from verb. (Notice that I *did* use a comma after "In fact" in the sentence before last but *not* after "When applied too enthusiastically" in the next. Stay tuned.) In revision the trick is to delete most commas before such clunks as *the,* as I just did after "In revision" and did a couple of sentences earlier after "When applied too enthusiastically"; I don't do it after "In fact" in the earlier sentence because the next word was not *the.* The *the* signals a new phrase well enough without the clunk of a comma.

11. *Cultivate the habit of mentally rearranging the order of words and phrases of every sentence you write.* Rules, as usual, govern the rewriting. One rule of arrangement is to avoid breaking, as in this clause, the flow with parenthetical remarks. Put the remark at the end if it's important and at the beginning if it's not.

12. The most important rule of rearrangement is that *the end of the sentence is the place of emphasis.* I wrote the sentence first as "The end of the sentence is the emphatic *location,*" which put the emphasis on the word *location.* The reader leaves the sentence with the last word ringing in her ears. I wanted, however, to emphasize the idea of emphasis, not the idea of location. So I rewrote it as ". . . is the place of *emphasis.*" You should examine every sentence to see whether the main idea comes at the end—or, second in emphasis, the beginning. Dump less important things in the middle, or in the trash. A corollary of the rule is that putting less important things at the end will weaken the sentence. It would be grammatical to write, "That putting trivial things at the end will weaken the sentence *is a corollary of the rule.*" Yet it shifts the emphasis to something already finished, *the rule.* The clearer way emphasizes the novelty, the idea of the weakened sentence, by putting it at the end.

13. *This-ism is becoming a plague.* These bad writers think this reader needs repeated reminders that it is this idea, not that one, which is being discussed. Circle the *this* and *these* in your draft: you'll be shocked at their number. The *this* points the reader back to the thing referred to, for no good reason. No writer wants her reader to look back, because looking back is looking away, interrupting the forward flow and leaving the reader looking for her place. The *this*es and *that*s are demonstrative pronouns on the way to becoming the definite article (*le* and *la* in French

came from Latin *ille* and *illa* = *that*; ancient Greek went through a similar development from Homeric to Attic). But we already have a definite
article. It's called *the* (derived from an Indo-European word meaning
that). Often the plain *the* will do fine and keep the reader reading. *Such*
often works. Consider repeating the word represented by *this*. Repetition, remember, brings clarity and unity to English. The rule is to query
every *this* or *these*. Take most of them out.

14. *Watch out for bad words.* If economic prose would drop *via*, *the
process of, intra, and/or, hypothesize,* and *respectively,* the gain in clarity
and grace would be big. If it would drop *at least minimal, process of,
thus, overall, basic,* and *factor,* the world would be saved. The best practice provides the standard. Virginia Woolf would not write *and/or* or
he/she because she wanted prose, not a diagram. Some others that I'm
sure Virginia would have disliked appear in my personal list of Bad
Words: *individuals, agents, structure, process of, existence of, time
frame, former, latter, very, for convenience, due to, via, in terms of,* and
a hundred more. How to know them? Read good books.

And meanwhile, *get the little book, get the little book.*

Why Write Well?

A reply to a friendly comment by the George Mason University economist Jack High on my long paper published in Economic Inquiry *(the paper became "the little book,"* Economical Writing*).*

Jack High's comment resembles what soldiers call "friendly fire"—shells from one's own artillery that accidentally fall on one's own front line. He praises the details of my essay but disagrees with its broader themes. I'm a little worried that the offensive he and I both want to start will not get started if the shells fall short.

I have to agree with him that a lot of bad writing does get published. After all, that's why I give all that advice on how to write better. I also have to agree that good writing is expensive—though he in turn agrees with me that on balance the high cost to writers and editors of better writing would be more than balanced by the lower cost to readers on the other side of the social account. Hemingway said, "Easy writing makes hard reading." The market failure comes at the retail stage, at the journal editors. If six nameable editors of journals in economics started acting as agents for the readers, as is their duty—listen up, Orley—the social and private cost of writing would become equal.

Editors have good reason to avoid their duty. As editor of the *Journal of Economic History* for five and half years, I faced a lot of bad writing, in a journal that gets better than average writing submitted to it. At first I did spend, in Jack's words, "the enormous amount of time it would take an editor to transform every piece into respectable prose." What killed my enthusiasm after a while was that most authors were outraged by my suggestions for making their writing better. Evsey Domar, after I had spent three days translating his piece into English, did not speak to me for a year. His was only the worst case of many of looking the gift horse squarely in the mouth. As I say in the article, most economists have a bush league attitude toward revision, unlike the major leaguers in journalism or literature. The major leaguers like criticism, because they can

pick out the good parts of it and make their stuff better. The bush leaguers think that if you criticize their illiteracies you don't love them.

So there's a market failure. The high value that readers put on economic writing they can understand does not get transmitted back to the
manufacturer. But I still maintain, contrary to High, that even in the
presence of market failure it might be advantageous as an empirical matter for an economist to write better. That is, good writing is not valued as
highly as it should be yet nonetheless might be valued highly enough that
an economist would do well to supply it.

Not all economists would, of course. Some people have such a comparative disadvantage in writing that they should go into some other line.
But economists learn mathematics and statistics and economic reasoning,
often against the strict dictates of comparative advantage, judging from
results. Likewise, most of them could learn to write a lot better, too, if
they worked at it.

The argument is that better writing gets read (it's not the only or
even the main argument, of course: the main argument is that you *should*
write clearly; that it's *bad* not to, just as it would be bad to mess up your
math). Many economists get more attention than their creativity or pen-
etration as economists warrants because they are good at mathematics.
I'm saying that the same holds for writing, that the coefficient is interestingly large. Turn over in your mind the following sample of good and
bad writers: George Stigler, Oliver Williamson, Paul Samuelson, Robert
Solow, Robert Mundell, John Maynard Keynes, Francis Edgeworth.
Control as you will. The partial derivative on style is large. How many
mute, inglorious Muths exist out there whose pathbreaking but incom-
prehensible article was *not* rediscovered 10 years after it was written?

It sounds cute to an economist's ear to say that obscurity is
profitable. The story is told of a French historian, notorious for his
wretched French style, whose book was translated with great effort into
utterly lucid English. He read the translation and concluded with a sneer
that "it does not capture *ma profundité.*" "Profundity" my foot. The
profunditeurs are seen through more often than they realize.

Suppose it is true, though, that in fact, as Jack claims, "an economist
trying to publish will misallocate his resources if he takes 'Economical
Writing' too much to heart." Suppose I am wrong that for most economists an investment in better writing would pay off well. Suppose it is
advantageous to write badly.

I repeat in reply that, anyway, writing badly is unethical. It is unethical to write badly when at small cost you can do better, and it is espe-

cially unethical to cultivate obscurity to get some material benefit. High agrees with this in the end, promising the careful writer of economics "rewards in utils, not in prestige or pages published." I would go further. I would say, with Socrates in the *Gorgias* (478E), that it is better to suffer evil (lack of promotion) than to perpetrate it (writing in the Official Style for selfish advantage): "Happiest therefore is he who has no vice in his soul, since we found this to be the greatest of all evils."

Most economists will be uncomfortable with such an argument. Our scientific civilization is uncomfortable with ethical discourse, dismissing it as "preaching" (so different, you see, from the preaching that goes on in handbooks of scientific method). But good science is after all a matter of goodness. It's a matter of not lying; of not being a fake; of listening to others; of being courteous to ideas.

Some economists, worse scientists on this account, believe that they must be unethical in order to be true to their prudence-only model of man. They believe that because an economic man would do it they should do it too. The belief justifies much unethical behavior in economic scholarship, such as choosing to say something in 28 vague words when you could say it in 14 clear ones. It's time that we outgrew this yuppie way of looking at the good. Whatever the economic man may think, we know that the good is not merely what is profitable.

So I stick to my guns and hope that Jack High's friendly fire is not misunderstood. I think good writing might be privately profitable; he is not so sure. We agree, however, on the main issue of the war: even if it were not profitable to write as well as you can, it is the ethical way of scientific life.

Yes, Competence Is Profitable, Now That You Ask; But Why Ask?

A reply published in Economic Inquiry *in October 1992 in response to an unfriendly comment by David Laband and Christopher Taylor.*

It must have been around 1968, in the coffee room of the Social Science Building at Chicago, that Milton Friedman and the late George Stigler had a jovial and public conversation about being economists, a conversation which made a big impression on me. Milton was lamenting the stupidity of tariffs, and George broke in, from a foot above, saying something as follows:

George: Milton, you're such a preacher! If people want free trade, they'll get it. If they don't want it, no amount of jaw-boning by economists will change their minds.

Milton: Ah: that's where we differ, George. We both admire markets, but you think they've already worked.

George: And why not? People are self-interested, and they vote their pocketbooks—that's enough market for me. They bought tariffs. Tariffs must be what they want.

Milton: No: they pursue their interests but often do not know what their interests are. People need education. The average citizen has no idea that a tariff hurts him.

George: Education! Try educating a lobbyist for the textile industry.

Milton: As I said, that's where we differ: I'm a teacher, and think that people do *some* things because they are ignorant.

George: And I'm a scientist, an economic scientist: people do what they do because they are wise."

Laband and Taylor are Stiglerites. They believe with Dr. Pangloss that we are in the best of all possible worlds. The Friedmanites, which is my own tribe, believe that we *could* be in it if we would only stop to think. The Stiglerites assume rationality; the Friedmanites teach it. The Stiglerites want to praise the world, the Friedmanites to change it. The Stiglerites detest policy: what is, is. The Friedmanites embrace it: what might be, can be. The Stiglerites are pessimistic, in the manner of the master. The Friedmanites are optimistic.

David Laband and Christopher Taylor have a pessimistic and Stiglerite explanation of why they have not learned to write competently. They defend themselves against advice such as I give in the original paper in *Economic Inquiry* by saying that it is "presumptuous of anyone to claim unique knowledge of the marginal benefit to authors of investment in better presentation."

If the investment we were talking about were oil drilling, I'd agree with their economics. I've written a book called *If You're So Smart* that makes a similar point about economic experts going around offering advice. But the investment in question—here is where Laband and Taylor go wrong—is economic education. Laband, Taylor, and I are economic educators. In the educational industry we are the oil drillers, the company geologists, the experts. We educate our student roughnecks in the craft, teaching them because we *do* know better (or else we should not be standing up there TuTh 10:55–12:10). Part of the craft, Laband and Taylor agree, is "attending to elements of presentation."

So the initial mistake in their paper is economic. They think that, because some advice is silly and misinformed, all advice must be, even advice from teachers to students. Stiglerites tend to drive themselves into such extreme skepticism. No one of course can actually live as an extreme skeptic. I'd like to see what Laband and Taylor say to a student who thinks that markets are bad for us—do they agree mildly that it's just a matter of opinion and that the student is entitled to his mistaken view?

Another Stigler story. George opposed requirements in the graduate curriculum at Chicago. Around 1970 he killed off the requirement in the history of thought, which was his own field, and tried repeatedly to kill off economic history (when I left the faculty in 1980 Sherwin Rosen, I am told, instantly proposed what George had advocated, and it passed).

George's argument, which is heard in many other departments of economics, was that the graduate students should be free to choose (pay attention, Milton). After all, they are just like consumers.

What George, and Laband and Taylor, never answered was the Teacher's Point, which Milton made in the original faculty meeting about the history of thought requirement. We are teachers, he said. We *do* know better. Graduate students, because they are not educated already (that's why they are students), often make bad decisions about their curricula. (If Laband and Taylor looked back over the decisions they made as graduate students, they would probably agree; I certainly am appalled at my own curricular decisions as a graduate student, such as not going up to MIT to listen to Bob Solow or dropping a course by Gottfried Haberler at Harvard because he talked funny [I should talk about talking funny!] or spurning a course by the great Simon Kuznets because it was "just data collecting.")

To put it economically, the product at Chicago was the Ph.D. student. If the student took a pattern of courses that left him an ill-educated dolt, then all other Chicago Ph.D.s would suffer from his reputation. The faculty collectively, not the student individually, should decide on the qualities of the product. To do otherwise would have been to shirk entrepreneurial and managerial—and pedagogic and scientific—responsibility.

My paper [and the little book of 1986, now 2000] was 98 percent teaching, Friedmanite. I was trying to change the tastes of the producers and consumers of economic writing. That's called teaching. More than that, I was trying to change their ethical attitude toward writing. That's teaching, too. I said so in my response to Jack High, which Laband and Taylor apparently did not read.

Had they read the response they would know that they have misidentified my theme. They focus all their attention on the 2 percent of the paper that claimed that good writing is selfishly good for you (only part of the 2 percent, by the way, was the careerist argument that Laband and Taylor focus on; the rest was the argument of Socrates and other teachers that being good is—selfishly—good for your soul). Laband and Taylor think my "general theme" was that bad writing hurts the pocketbook.

But if I were making chiefly such a Stiglerite point in a Stiglerite world, what would be the point of writing the article? Economists do not have to be warned off using out-of-date statistical methods or studying topics that are not currently fashionable or failing to use constrained-maximization arguments as much as possible, any more than citizens need to be warned off protective tariffs if they do in fact vote their pocketbooks in selfish wisdom. The rewards and punishments in such a world are plain.

But a Stiglerite economics explains too much. If it were correct, then we would now be in the best of all possible worlds with respect to the uses of econometrics, say, or the standing of this or that piece of economic theory. The producers of economic scholarship would already have adjusted to the demands of economic readers. By the Laband and Taylor argument there would be no economic persuasion, no place to teach people to do better, as Laband and Taylor might themselves want to be taught to do better in, say, the use of statistical significance or specification searches or entry-and-exit arguments.

Arguments about What Is to Be Done are the guts of science. Economists of taste—for instance, Zvi Griliches, Kenneth Arrow, Edward Leamer, Gordon Tullock, Robert Solow, Robert Lucas, Axel Leijonhufvud, Albert Hirschman, James Buchanan, Lawrence Summers—argue that economists should write well. Or they argue that economists should do more empirical work. Or they argue that economists should examine the quality of their data more thoroughly; or that they should be consistent in their assumptions about rationality; or that they should be literate in the history of their craft; or that they should not use statistical significance as the equivalent of economic significance. And, having taught such general arguments, they teach that economists should believe X or disbelieve Y about the economy. They do not suppose that on all these margins the optimal adjustments have always already been made.

Close down the graduate schools, Laband and Taylor imply. Fire the editors of journals. Dismiss the referees. Let the consumers decide in their ignorance what they want to consume. Quality decisions are unnecessary in a capitalist paradise. Put every quality on the market—economists who know price theory, for example, and economists who do not, Chicago Ph.D.s who know there was a past to economics and those who do not—and see what people buy.

I dunno. As a libertarian myself, I admit that their vision (they do not know they have it; that's the trouble with not knowing the history of the craft) is tempting. But Milton and I reckon we are at present in a second-best world, in which people need some education in responsibility before they are ready for the Coming of the Messiah of the market. We disagree with George, who believed that the Coming had already come and that George Stigler was its John the Baptist.

My main purpose was not to establish the actual marginal product or the perceived marginal product of better writing. I know my colleagues do not put a high value on writing well. That was why I felt moved to teach them, as one might try to teach them to use fixed-point theorems correctly or to recognize that the Federal Reserve is speaking to an audience. I wanted and still want to change my colleagues' minds—not by appeals to self-interest, chiefly, but by appeals to professional responsibility. Laband and Taylor do not want to argue about professional responsibility. They want to argue about profit.

They make a distinction between "personal" and "professional" ethics in writing. Apparently, as people they would like to work on their writing, but, heh, they've got careers to run. They end up asserting boldly that they and other economists are and should be governed by "profit, broadly speaking." Greed is good. They give an example toward the end of the paper about the decision at the margin between exhibiting some pointless econometrics or spending time on the prose to gain "adherents" (the point is made earlier, too, four times). They ask, "Is the economist a fool or irresponsible for not making such a substitution?"

Why of course he is a fool and irresponsible. He is unethical not to work on the prose, as he would be unethical not to work on the quality of the data or on the correct use of statistical tests. He is uncraftsmanly, unscholarly, unscientific. Comparative advantage, naturally, should be consulted. But everyone should try out every margin. Most economists, as Laband and Taylor show in their own writing, do not know the first thing about writing and therefore have no idea what better science they can do by taking care in it. (For example, most economists, and Laband and Taylor, though they quote Walter Salant on the matter, do not know that phrases like *knowledge claim production function* are German-like mud.) It would be as though economists did not know some obviously relevant tool such as statistical decision theory (actually, most economists do not).

That was my point, the usual one in scientific discussions: do better. Not perfectly, but better. Science is difficult to do right. Forget about whether it is profitable, broadly or narrowly speaking, to cheat. Standards of scientific responsibility constrain profit making. It may be profitable to fake your data, but it's irresponsible. It may be profitable to write with a trowel, but it's irresponsible.

To put the point another way, Laband and Taylor have a yuppie's idea of scientific responsibility. If the "market" demands it, pornography or not, print it. If one's career can be advanced, do it. Defect. This is why economics departments are hard to administer. About a quarter of the people in most economics departments think that being an economist means never having to think about responsibility. They think that the right behavior in the face of a group responsibility is to defect from it. (A classic experiment found that most people cooperated in prisoner's dilemma games more than optimally, being properly socialized. Which do you suppose was the only group tested that followed the economist's model of irresponsible defection?)

So a reply in Stiglerite fashion to Laband and Taylor would be lacking in point. The main point of my article was what should be done in a fully responsible economic science, not the testing of the profitability of what is actually, irresponsibly done.

But, as I said, I'm a Friedmanite optimist and believe in the efficacy of teaching, so let's teach. Price theory first.

Their price theory says that the market is superior to "a biased observer's criteria" of stylistic merit. Not in most price theory. The set of prices thrown up by a market are no more "biased" than a single observer's valuations, as one would understand if one understood the theory of index numbers.

Their price theory justifies the use of computer programs on style by noting that, "since [the programs] are marketed to would-be writers, the presumption would have to be that there has been some attempt to capture relevant aspects of style in these measurement techniques. Otherwise, it seems unlikely that they would survive and flourish in the marketplace." Not in most price theory. The demands of would-be writers, who by assumption do not know what they are doing, are not enough to ensure that the company captures relevant aspects of style. Laband and Taylor would on the same basis recommend that you listen to the late-night pitch for making a million on property deals, which must somehow capture relevant aspects of buying low and selling high. It has survived and flourished. That there is a sucker—or a first-year graduate student—born every minute does not figure in their price theory.

Their price theory explains that the crummy style in economics has developed "to (presumably) communicate efficiently." Not in most price theory. Mind games and cheating, the use of obscurity to claim profundity, the appeal to fashion and status, the fear of straight talk, or simple and correctable ignorance of the elements of style can all explain bad writing: in a word, defection. One wonders what scientific world Laband and Taylor inhabit and whether they have heard of the prisoner's dilemma.

They claim toward the end of the paper that "the evidence suggests that economists communicate efficiently." *Their* evidence says nothing of the kind; *the* evidence of one's senses points the other way. I wonder if Laband and Taylor have ever sweated through a paper for an hour or two, discovering at length the five-cent point buried under the five-dollar words. I wonder if the average economist regards the style of the *American Economic Review* as an aid to her understanding of the science. The daily waste of our scientific time is not "efficient."

I am especially surprised that Laband and Taylor think that more math always makes for more "cost-effective forms of communication." People will say such a thing, because they want math department values to win over engineering and physics department values (McCloskey 1994, chaps. 9–13), but no one actually believes it, except the small group of people who can read mathematics faster than English. Many professional mathematicians don't like symbolic nonsense and say so. Stanislaw Ulam, complaining along with many other mathematicians about the raising of the symbolic ante in the style of Nicholas Bourbaki, wrote: "I am turned off when I see only formulas and symbols, and little text. It is too laborious for me to look at such pages, not knowing what to concentrate on" (1976, 275f). Laband and Taylor like market arguments. Well, so do I. Here's an issue that actually can be settled by one: ask the members of the American Economic Association whether they agree with Ulam or with Laband and Taylor.

The "theory" in the Laband and Taylor paper, then, is feeble, a rewriting of the marginal conditions copied out from elementary textbooks, and misunderstood. I'm afraid their "empirical work" is at the same level, firmly in the lower tail of modern economics. Let's teach.

What's mainly wrong in the use of econometrics in the profession is that it is not used for serious inquiry but for reaffirming what everyone, especially the authors, already know (Cooley and Leroy 1981). Laband and Taylor, for example, labor with their econometric machinery to deliver up the mouse of a result that the *Wall Street Journal* is better written than the *Journal of Political Economy*. "Economists' writing varies according to the intended audience." Uh-huh.

They use a crude instrument to detect good and bad writing. They pick a few indicators that will be easiest to quantify and then make a proxy argument: "Writers displaying excellence on one margin of clarity [average words per sentence] would exhibit excellence on other margins of clarity." Well, maybe, and maybe not. I don't know in what metric the marginal argument could be tested. No one will be surprised that according to their results their instrument doesn't seem to measure anything: that's their main finding, according to their own (mistaken) notion that fit is importance, that the instrument fails.

The one test of validity they offer suggests that there is something wrong with the instrument. They run the instrument on journals of English (I could have supplied them with a better choice of journals). The English professors do no better. Something is screwy. What conclusion do they draw? That the discriminatory power of the instrument is low? That the test has low power? Back to the drawing board? By no means. They conclude that English professors write no worse than economists. Uh-huh.

The one econometric mistake they do confess to openly and fully is omitted variables, so it would be boorish of me to emphasize the point. But, briefly, what is learned from the statistical "failure" of a misspecified model? We can do our econometrics more intelligently than that. With omitted variables the coefficients of the included ones are not even consistent. (It's hard to tell from their ill-written table, but it appears, by the way, that most of the style variables they pick from my list have the correct sign, though I can't tell how big the effects are because they don't give units. I suspect I am reading it correctly, because Laband and Taylor would have said so if the signs were wrong. Like failing to give units of the variables, sign testing is part of the routine of bottom-tail econometrics).

I was not providing material for a mechanical test of the profit to be had from being scientifically responsible. I was trying, as Milton did, to teach people who want to write better, out of a given sense of scientific responsibility. And I was trying to arouse shame in the hearts of people open to being ashamed about their scientific incompetence. But if for some reason you wanted to perform the test that Laband and Taylor want to perform, you would want data that were valid. One would think the valid way of collecting the data would have occurred to Laband and Taylor. The valid way is to put unidentified examples of prose in front of (1) expert judges of writing and (2) average readers of professional articles and then ask them to grade the writing, with perhaps a little quiz on reading comprehension appended. That's what one does implicitly in concluding that Robert Solow writes better than, say, Deirdre McCloskey (a test by Art Diamond using the sort of mechanical criteria Laband and Taylor used—though using them much more intelligently— concluded that the best writer of economics was . . . D. N. McCloskey; I rest my case against mechanical criteria). And it is the procedure in competent studies of readability. Using sentence length because it is easy to calculate is not much of an argument for collecting the wrong data, though usual in economics: look for the keys under the lamppost because the light is better there.

Toward the end of their paper it becomes clear that Laband and Taylor mix up *effectiveness* and *clarity*. Effectiveness means getting your way; clarity means trying to make things easier on your readers. I have no doubt that the most-cited economists are "effective," by definition. But Hitler was effective. Nixon was effective. (And let's be fair to radical Republicans: Clinton was effective, too.) Lying can be effective. Being pointlessly obscure can be effective. Repeating marginal arguments copied out of elementary books over and over again can be effective, at least in some circles. Claiming the character of a Technical Thinker by misusing statistical significance can be effective, at least with an audience that does not understand statistical theory.

The ethical problem at the core of the Laband and Taylor paper is that they cannot imagine that being effective, regardless, is not a complete guide to scientific responsibility in an imperfect world. They are utilitarians, as many economists are, which in the simple form Laband and Taylor espouse it is the religion of barbarians, the enemies of good science.

In my response to Jack High I called his paper "friendly fire." Laband and Taylor's paper is unfriendly fire, sure enough, not from my side. Fortunately, though, their shells are aimed straight upward and drop back on the gunners who shot them.

Rule 8
Don't Specialize without Intellectual Trade

Kelly Green Golf Shoes and the Intellectual Range from *M* to *N*

Eastern Economic Journal *(summer 1995)*.

As Bruno Frey among others has shown (1984), academic economics in the United States is narrow. I'm going to preach against the narrowness, of course, or else I would have called it "admirable rigor and focus" or "desirable specialization of the intellect" or "the shoemaker sticking to his last."

Economists disdain learning. They want lawyers and political scientists and sociologists to pay attention to economics but will not listen in turn. Few economists read anything beyond the latest news from their special field. By contrast a real scholar feels shamefully ignorant. She knows she is only like a girl playing on the seashore, diverting herself now and then finding a smoother pebble or a prettier shell than ordinary, whilst the great ocean of truth lies all undiscovered before her. The real scholar knows that if she has seen further it is by standing on the shoulders of giants. Economists are not scholars. They are specialists.

When an economist is told she is narrow, her reflex is to offer bad economics about "specialization." No one can read everything; so I specialize in two preprints a month from Princeton. The word *specialization* is used now routinely by deans defending normal science against challenge: leave the Department of Economics alone to do what everyone else in economics does, the deans say, because that's called specialization. We need specialization if the academy is to be productive. We deans, whether from English or economics, are tough, businesslike characters, you understand. After all, the extent of the market is limited by the division of labor. Uh. Or is it the other way around?

The problem is that no one in academic administration knows about the second, essential part of Smith's theorem, the market. Smith said, specialize *and then trade* in the market. "Shoemaker, stick to your last" is good advice *only if the shoemaker makes shoes that people want to buy.* If he's piling up kelly green golfing shoes with chartreuse tassels in his backyard unsold, or more exactly "sold" only to other shoemakers, the advice is bad. It's the advice a specialized economics has been following for some time now.

The odd thing about the way the advice has worked out in practice is that it has yielded a drearily uniform economics. You would think that specialization would result in some special economics, the way the University of Texas once specialized in institutional economics or UCLA specialized in property rights economics. The trouble seems to be that everyone has the same idea of what we should be specializing in. The kelly green golfing shoe of economics, on which all the best shoemakers agree, is microfoundations of overlapping generations in a game theoretic model with human capital and informational asymmetry. To attach a justly honored name to the shoe, it's The Samuelson, a nifty number, kelly green with those chartreuse tassels, only $49.95 a pair piled in the backyard of your local shoemaker. Economics departments like Washington and Virginia that once were special have become routine in this Samuelsonian way.

There are a few, but very few, exceptions to the specialization in Samuelsonian economics. The University of Massachusetts still could be said to specialize in Marxist economics and parts of NYU, George Mason, and Auburn in Austrian economics (though at NYU and George Mason the Austrians are under attack). But the few divergences that have survived the inquisition ordered by Cambridge, Mass. make everyone uncomfortable, and when an assistant professor in an alternative tradition comes up for promotion you will find the other, mainstream, and ignorant people in the department wondering sagely if it's a good idea for a young person to be reading Hegel or studying economic history or doing any of those other non-Samuelsonian things. (That's how they are trying to kill off the Austrian program at NYU.)

It's a pity, this insistence that we all specialize in being a pale imitation of MIT circa 1980. I know a department with some good economists in it but economists terrified that they will not be seen as conventionally competent in the Samuelsonian specialization, who refused to promote a leading young feminist economist in their midst. *Feminist* economist! My Lord, how's *that* going to be brought into a model of constrained maximization?! They were unmoved by the evident truth that she was the best-known economist in the department and was encouraging economics in others of an entirely new sort. No novelties, please: we're specialists. As Harry Truman almost put it, a specialist is someone who doesn't want to learn anything new, because if he did he wouldn't be a specialist. A couple of years later the journal the woman had started was named one of the best new journals in the world.

A good example of the narrowing of economics by specialization, paradoxically, is the *Journal of Economic Perspectives.* It was founded as the third, popular journal of the American Economic Association in the early 1980s with Joe Stiglitz at the helm (Joe persuaded me to join the original board of associate editors, a decision I almost immediately regretted; a couple of years later we parted amicably). In 1994 and 1995 the *JEP* was the subject of controversy within the association, causing some stormy sessions of the Executive Committee in Washington and San Francisco.

The accusation was leveled that the *Journal* does not encourage contributions outside the mainstream, slighting post-Keynesian or Marxist or Austrian or institutionalist or feminist economics. It's specialized, the critics complain, in Samuelsonian economics. A member of the editorial board (not the working associate editors but the big-name folks above that level) put it this way: "All *The Journal of Economic Perspectives* lacks are . . . economic perspectives." Defenders of the *Journal,* on the other side, see such criticism as evil politics. One member of the Executive Committee said with some irritation that to run the journal differently would be to make it into "a political rag."

On the face of it the harsh complaints of the critics don't seem persuasive. People of the intelligence and integrity of the main editors—Joe

Stiglitz, to begin with, and Carl Shapiro and, most recently, Alan Auerbach—are not common. On all sides it is agreed that they have tried with all their considerable energies to run the journal for the members as readers. Surely with such intentions we can rest easy, can't we?

No. A closer look reveals some nasty if unintended consequences of the way the *Journal* was conceived and run. For reasons that are not clear it was decided from the outset that the *Journal* would not be run on market principles. Maybe it's somewhat clear, come to think of it. When you're producing kelly green golfing shoes the market doesn't look like a producer-friendly institution. Anyway, instead of inviting submissions from all comers and then selecting the liveliest and best written, the associate editors commission articles. The profession is still confused about this policy and still submits unsolicited about 100 articles a year—90 percent of which are thrown out by an assistant editor before being seen by anyone else.

The critics claimed that such central planning has not worked any better in the *JEP* than it did in Poland. If the politburo running the show were diverse, maybe the result would be better. Maybe the market test would be applied to the golf shoes. The senior coeditors declared in their published report to the Executive Committee in January 1995 that "the journal has . . . a diverse group of editors . . . [offering] differing perspectives." But this is mistaken. The editorial board underrepresents women (of course), and, of the 17 members plus the editor and coeditor in early 1995, not one was at an institution in the South or the Mountain States or the Northwest or southern California; two were in the Midwest (Hal Varian before he decamped to Berkeley; and Jim Heckman—though he was identified as from Yale, he had by that time moved back to Chicago). All except Varian and Heckman and the 5 northern Californians came from the Northeast, north of Virginia, east of Pennsylvania. The *JEP* is the *Journal of Northeastern Economic Perspectives:* 12 out of 19. Or of *Ivy League Perspectives:* 9 of the 19. Or *Private Institution Perspectives:* 13 of the 19. Or of *Berkeley Perspectives:* an embarrassing 3–4 with Varian. The numbers say, "Mainstream economists from elite institutions within the City edition of the *New York Times* [heh: except you hep cats in the Bay Area] are what we economists are."

The critics, you see, are bitter about the questionable representation, because they think it reflects a provinciality common in American academic life. Coasties find it hard to grasp why there's something wrong with running intellectual life entirely from zip code 02139 or 18540. [Before I moved in 2000 to the University of Illinois at Chicago I regularly received mail from Harvard and Princeton colleagues addressed to "the University of Iowa, Ames, Iowa." We sold a T-shirt on the same theme, "University of Iowa, Idaho City, Ohio."]

Of course, it's possible for a geographically narrow group of associate editors to represent wide interests, beyond kelly green. Edmund Burke made this argument in the late eighteenth century about the unreformed British Parliament. Mechanical representation of the sort one finds on university committees does not always work well.

But in the case of the *Journal of Economic Perspectives* the lack of representation does not work at all. It results in a mainly Samuelsonian specialization. If associate editors consisting of We Guys at Berkeley and Cornell produced a magazine that in fact covered a wide range of topics from differing perspectives, no reasonable person would complain. But, say the critics, it does not. It's kelly green all the way.

In their report the editors claimed that the *Journal* covers "a wide range of topics: from economics in the laboratory to rejected classic articles by leading economists; from core theory to allocation of resources in the presence of indivisibilities; from universal banking to the sale of spectrum rights; and more." That the editors view a range "from core theory to the allocation of resources in the presence of indivisibilities" as "wide" shows what the problem is. As a mainstream economist myself, I am not horrified, outraged, stunned by the contents. I view universal banking and the sale of spectrum rights as mildly interesting topics. On the other hand I do not find myself being stretched to new economic perspectives, Right or Left, Austrian or feminist, quantitative or literary. For instance, the editors claim to exhibit "a range of approaches to econometrics" but appear by this to mean additional estimation methods that the falling cost of computation will make obsolete in two years. No calibrated simulation. No serious talk about errors in variables. No exploration of novel sources for economic facts. (And no criticism of economics as a field beyond the monotonous, specious, and dangerous articles reducing scholarship to the "reputation" of journals.)

I was, like many members of the Association who thought about it, opposed to the founding of the *Journal,* as I told Joe Stiglitz at the time. I believed it would let the *American Economic Review* off the hook in matters of intelligibility and general interest (it has). As a matter of fact, in some circles the *JEP* was viewed at its founding precisely as a protective belt for the *AER.* The view persists. As it was expressed to me by an eminent senior member of our profession, "the *Journal of Economic Perspectives* is a stupid journal for stupid people" (I quote exactly). In his view it was intended to be so. It was *not* in his view (a view seconded by other eminent people at the time) *really* meant to be the journal of economic "perspectives." A wink and a sneer. Above all protect the notion that kelly green is the hottest fashion idea since supply and demand.

To put it briefly, the *Journal,* like the typical, and narrow, American department of economics these days, ranges all the way from *M* to *N.* If one stands close to such a range one can become convinced that it is wide. But it does not stretch to Israel Kirzner or Barbara Bergmann or Jim Buchanan or Tom Weisskopf. It does not get beyond kelly green golf shoes, valued because other shoemakers insist that we specialize in making them.

The situation reminds me of a retort Harry Johnson, notorious for his sharp tongue, made to George Borts, back in the 1970s when both were editors, George of the *American Economic Review,* Harry of the *Journal of Political Economy.* George: "Harry, you must have the same problem at the *JPE* that we have here at the *AER:* we get more good articles than we know what to do with!" Harry: "Then why don't you publish a few?" A corresponding joke about the market for the few assistant professors nowadays whose idea of an intellectual life extends beyond the kelly green of modern economics is: "We get more assistant professors with ideas for *new* specializations in economics than we know what to do with." "Then why don't you hire a few?"

The Invisible College
and the Death
of Learning

For the magazine of higher education Change *(Nov.–Dec. 1991).*

In the 1960s the sociologist of science Derek Price used the phrase *Invisible College* to describe the old-boy network of Big Science. Since then the rest of academic life has caught up to the social structure of physics, scattering old boys and old girls around the globe in each special field. The result has been damaging to the visible college and, in the end, damaging to science and scholarship. The experiment since the 1950s with turning intellectual life over to specialists has not worked, at least in the fields I know, especially economics.

The *visible* college consists of the fellow economists down the hall and beyond them, in the next building, the noneconomists in French and chemistry. The Invisible College, by contrast, is the group of expert specialists in one's narrowly defined field, such as medieval English agricultural history or the geomorphology of glaciers. The fellow experts live in faraway places like Bologna or College Park. In field after field they have come to govern the enterprise. Hiring, curriculum, promotion, and the rest have come to be decided by people in the special fields, not by one's literal colleagues.

Some time ago an economist at a distinguished university (all right: the University of Chicago) was serving on a committee to choose the best Ph.D. thesis in the social sciences that year. He came to the meeting and announced with a decisive air that the thesis from the Department of Economics was, in fact, the best and should get the prize. The Invisible College had pronounced its verdict that the thesis was What's Hot Right Now in a special field of economics. His colleagues in anthropology and sociology wanted to know why it was such a good thesis—not that they doubted it, understand; they just wanted to hear the case. No soap. "You can't judge the thesis," declared the economist, "because you are not expert economists. Just accept what I say." The colleagues politely demurred. The economist resigned in a huff from the committee, and the department of economics at that university (all right, as I said, Chicago) stopped submitting entries to the competition. It's damned if it's going to be judged by the merely visible college.

The takeover of the visible college is not all bad, of course. In the 1960s some actual and visible colleges needed new standards. Those of a fellow specialist in labor economics or Dante studies may not be God's own, but at least they are an improvement over the cocktail party standards that most of the American professoriate then lived by. The visible college needed a kick in the rear, to get it serious about evaluating colleagues.

On the scientific front, too, the experiment in extreme specialization has not been all bad. Indeed, if you believed the shills for Big Science, you'd believe that the new specialization has been all to the good. An economics rhetoric is called on to justify it: don't you believe in specialization? To this an actual economist would reply: specialization is bad when it reaches diminishing returns and useless if it does not entail trade after specialization. Talking to a colleague across the hall in the same subfield of engineering will be a fine thing exactly up to the point at which one could learn more from talking to a colleague in mathematics or English across the college quad.

And the results of specialization have to be of some *use:* they have to be worth trading with others. Economics cannot be justified "for its own sake" or "just for fun." It's not art, and it's not chess problems. The judgment of when to speak to visible colleagues depends on how one values the products of specialization. The Invisible College claims boldly that each of its products is worthwhile, by virtue of being "tested in the market." All serious talk therefore should be with other experts, since that is what's "in demand." Another economic metaphor. But the economics is again defective. The "demand" is created by the Invisible College itself, by an agreement to honor expertise, however useless, so long as the other experts keep quiet about the uselessness of one's own expertise. The average article in economics, for example, is read by fewer than a half-dozen people. It would be as though Chrysler sold its cars only to Chrysler employees yet claimed boldly to be a viable enterprise.

What a college does nowadays is determined increasingly by

whether or not an Invisible College exists to value it. The notion that a literal, on-site colleague should be able to read one's work is in many fields unthinkable. The dean's committee will weigh publication lists and try its hand at the hermeneutics of recommendation letters. But it will not read the work. Even inside most departments the notion of reading has died. Where it lives on, as in departments of history, it is under attack from administrators looking for Prussian neatness in filling forms.

The economic outcome of such market-driven promotions and hirings is, to be sure, neat, like identical bunks in an army barracks. If you want your college to look like every other college, then do not read your colleagues' work. Hire on the basis of reputation and ranking. Rely on "the market." Departments at different colleges will then hire people from the same Invisible College and get identical bunks neatly made.

The market uniformity has happened in economics because economists are besotted with the market metaphor, though as I say bizarrely misunderstood to mean uniformity. The same looks to be happening in history. With each new call for vacuous letters of recommendation—in 1991 one university in Pennsylvania (all right: the University of Pittsburgh) required 40 of them, taking what amounts to a public opinion poll with bad statistical properties—and with each new call for "building on excellence" (which is to say, building on the fields judged excellent by the Invisible College) the uniformity grows.

The uniformity would be good if it actually yielded excellence. What it yields in bulk is normal science, routine literary study, publishable social science, fundable engineering. It yields more specialization from the Invisible College. The rule adopted recently at Yale that only N pieces (where N is small) can be considered in a promotion would at least reduce the bulk of the dull-normal science. But the Invisible College would still be the only reader.

The professors and administrators who value specialization and sneer at interdisciplinary work think that they are being tough and economistic. But they are not understanding the economics. They are being soft and noneconomistic.

For one thing, looking to the market to acquire one's standards is the strategy of the follower, not of the entrepreneur. Henry Ford made his sort of car—not someone else's—and was willing to make it in any color, so long as it was black. True, following is necessary in the economy of intellect as much as in the economy of cars. But it does not lead to real breakthroughs. The dynamism of capitalism depends on leaders, what the economic historian Jonathan Hughes called "the vital few." American academic life is becoming by contrast a herd, tended by deans of animal husbandry.

Good economics knows that specialization is not in itself good. The blessed Adam Smith (not to speak of Marx) was eloquent about the damage that specialization per se does to the human spirit. What is good about specialization is that it allows more consumption, through trade. As Smith declared: "Consumption is the sole end and purpose of all production; and the interest of the producer ought to be attended to, only as far as it may be necessary for promoting that of the consumer." By all means, shoemaker, stick to your last—*but then trade.*

Intellectual trade is the use of other people's work for our own enlightenment. If we actually read each other's work and let it affect our own, we are well and truly following the economic model of free trade. That's the tough-minded economics. It's what is accomplished by interdisciplinary work—such as biochemistry or social history—if the work is something more than polite acknowledgment of the other's expertise, insulated from disturbing one's own.

Though most of the advances of science and scholarship have come from such trade, the Invisible College does not approve. People outside geology offer continental drift for sale, people outside engineering offer chaos theory for sale (in both cases, oddly, it was a meteorologist who was selling to the unwilling buyers), and it takes decades for the departments in question to open their markets. The protectionists in the Invisible College make the Japanese look like free traders. The trade goes on in some real and visible colleges but mainly as a black market off the books.

The economic incentives are against the trade. One is paid by the present departments, not by the departments that would result in 20 years if intellectual problems were approached cooperatively. The deans, because of the incentives they face, routinely neglect their main job, which is investing in what comfortable departmental monopolies wish to drive out of business—an approach to technical philosophy, for example, that the existing department does not like; or the collaboration of a biologist with a geographer that does not match the National Institutes of Health's cellular idea of biology.

Nobody is looking after the trade that makes for advances in science and scholarship. The central administrators worry about the next budget and the next lawsuit or the next and better administrative job for themselves, not about making new trade. The charitable foundations, which might have led the way, have settled for normal science and consensus politics, not to speak of a regionalist prejudice that judges anyone outside the BoWash corridor a hopeless hick. No one, I should hope, expects the states or federal government to help (though it is notorious in science that the NSF is more innovative than, say, the Rockefeller Foundation). With few exceptions even the science journalists view their job as the selling of normal science and get their prestige from cheering the present hierarchy.

And the expert faculty, who could change it by starting to talk to their colleagues, lie low. Most never crack a book outside their subdisciplines and never talk seriously to colleagues in medicine or theology. They follow the economic model once popular in Albania, specializing in oxcarts and moldy wheat. Albania at length saw the light. But American academic life continues to have whole departments of oxcarts.

The argument is not against specialization, understand, but against the failure at last to trade. It applies to arguments as much as to subjects. Failure to trade is going to limit you. Classicists loathe quantitative arguments for poetic structure; physicists flee in terror from economic evaluation of space telescopes; economists will not listen to science based on questionnaires. The reply to such unproductive specialization in argument is again economic. Constraints hurt, like carrying a sack of cement in the 100-yard dash. We will do better with fewer arguments constrained to priori to be unspeakable.

Ruling out fewer arguments entails less sneering in academic life, less ignoring of chemists by physicists or of sociologists by economists or of statisticians by mathematicians. Considering that other scholars read different books and lead different lives, it would be economically remarkable, a violation of economic principle, if nothing could be learned from trading with them. Just as differences in tastes or endowments are grounds for trade, disagreements about the cause of crime or the nature of capitalism are grounds for serious conversation.

The bad economic outcomes can be reversed if we are willing to trade in earnest. A college would again be something more than a shared problem of parking. If colleagues would read each other's work, authors would start to write for a set of colleagues beyond the cospecialist in Edinburgh. If appointments and promotions came under the eye of administrators who cared about trade, the departments would pay less heed to the Invisible College. If joint and team teaching were made something other than an overload disdained by all departments, the professors would teach themselves along with the students. If the professors looked for the unities in their intellectual lives—such as their common interest in sound argument, a "rhetoric of inquiry," as they say at the University of

Iowa—they would integrate the curriculum instead of pretending that the students do it.

When Daniel Coit Gilman, the president of Johns Hopkins a century ago, was asked why the place had so much intellectual vigor, he replied: "We take each other's courses." Not in the Invisible College, you don't.

The unacknowledged crisis in academic life is an Albanian closing of borders. We need academics who take seriously the conversation of the academy, not additional inarticulate experts from the Invisible College. It's a matter of economics. Economists themselves should not be so arrogantly pleased with their expertise. But neither, on strictly economic grounds, should their colleagues across the quad be pleased with their own. Specialize, yes. But trade.

Rule 9
Read More Widely

Economics: Art or Science or Who Cares?

Eastern Economic Journal *(winter 1994)*.

Cambridge University Press published in 1994 *Knowledge and Persuasion in Economics*. Nice book. The blurb, which I did not see before publication, begins, "Is economics an art or a science?" That's the standard question that editors, journalists, and many economists like to ask about economics. Let's get this straight. Art or science? Entertainment or business? OK. Now we can talk.

As often in weak thinking, what's mainly wrong with Art versus Science is the question itself. Here are three pieces of news about the question from the frontier of science studies, a field revolutionized since the 1960s.

The first news is that the "art-science" distinction beloved by late-nineteenth-century British writers is hard to defend. No one who has looked closely at the matter since 1970 has found seams in the universe that distinguish art from science. The linguist Solomon Marcus, for example, wrote a paper in 1974 called "Fifty-two Oppositions between Scientific and Poetic Communication," in which he tried to drive a wedge between what gets written in the *Economic Journal* and what gets written in *Poetry*. No go. Both use metaphors. Both are rational and irrational, explicable and ineffable, persuasive and expressive. Marcus did what amounts to an analysis of variance and found as much variation within as between science and (poetic) art.

The physicist Tullio Regge remarked to Primo Levi, the chemist and writer, "I liked the sentence in which you say that the periodic table is poetry, and besides it even rhymes" (Levi and Regge 1992, 9). Levi responded, "The expression is paradoxical, but the rhymes are actually there. . . . To discern or create a symmetry, 'put something in its proper place,' is a mental adventure common to the poet and the scientist" (9–10). Attempts to distinguish art and science do not seem to work, though from the best workers. The late Thomas Kuhn noted truly that "we have only begun to discover the benefits of seeing science and art as one" (1977, 343). But then he tried out a distinction anyway. He argued that beauty in science (a differential equation with startlingly simple solutions, say) is an input into the solution of a technical problem, whereas in art the solution of a technical problem (*contraposto* in representing a standing figure, say) is an input into the beauty. Maybe. Yet at different levels of the art and science you find different inputs and outputs. An economic scientist will work like an artist at a technical problem to achieve beauty; but then the beauty at another level will become an input into a technical problem. One might stand better amazed, as a physicist did of mathematics, about the unreasonable effectiveness of aesthetic standards in science. So: art and science are not separate realms.

The second piece of news from the front lines of science studies is that modern English has a notably weird definition of *science*. We English speakers over the past century and a half have come to use *science* in a peculiar way, as in British academic usage—arts and sciences, the "arts" of literature and philosophy as against the "sciences" of chemistry and geology. A historical geologist in English is a scientist; a political historian is not. The usage would puzzle an Italian mother boasting of her studious little boy, *mio scienziato,* my learned one. She does not mean that he is a physicist. Italian uses the science word to mean simply "systematic inquiry" (as does French, Spanish, German, Dutch, Icelandic, Swedish, Norwegian, Gaelic, Polish, Hindi, Hebrew, Hungarian, Finnish, Turkish, Korean, Tamil, Japanese, and every other language I have inquired unsystematically into). Only English, and in fact only the English since the mid-nineteenth century, has made physical and biological science (definition 5b in the old *Oxford English Dictionary*) into, as the *Supplement* and the *New Oxford* describe it, "the dominant sense in ordinary use." The first citation is from the *Dublin Review* of 1867: "We shall . . . use the word 'science' in the sense which Englishmen so commonly give to it; as expressing physical and experimental science, to the exclusion of theological and metaphysical." The Italian half of the *Cambridge Italian Dictionary* warns of English *scientific* that *nell'uso comune non si referisce ai principi filosofici classici:* that is, in the common English use, by contrast with Italian, the science word does not admit knowledge learned outside the laboratory or observatory. In other tongues the word means "something more systematic than casual journalism." *Wissenschaft* means just "systematic inquiry," and so the German word for the arts and humanities contains the science word: *Geisteswissenschaften.* In English *spirit science* sounds just weird.

The non-English and the English pre-nineteenth-century sense is used, for instance, by Doctor Johnson in 1775 about part of his trip to the Western Isles: "Of Fort George I shall not attempt to give any account. I cannot delineate it *scientifically,* and a *loose and popular description* is of use only when the imagination is to be amused." The most famous declaration of the new and narrower sense of the word, with its implied scorn for art (and for biology, geology, economics, history, and, come to mention it, most fields of physics and chemistry), is Kelvin's in 1883: "When you cannot measure it, when you cannot express it in numbers, your knowledge is of a meagre and unsatisfactory kind. It may be the beginning of knowledge, but you have scarcely in your thoughts advanced to the state of *science.*" Alfred Marshall, in some ways an old-fashioned guy, was still in 1895 using the older, Johnsonian sense. To describe one blade of the supply-and-demand scissors dominating the other "is to be excused only so long as it claims to be merely a popular and not a strictly *scientific* account of what happened" (bk. 5, v. 3, l. 7). The English definition was won by Kelvin. So: *science* is special mainly for English speakers.

The third piece of news from the new science studies is that scientists are . . . are you ready for a shock?? . . . *just like other people!*

Good Lord, what next?! The finding comes from a new method, applied since 1970 or so, the method of studying science by studying not what philosophers say about scientists but by *studying the scientists and their scientific activities.* Shocking. The new studies of science claim that in answering the question "What is Science (contrasted with Art)?" we should *not* depend on philosophers or philosopher wannabes among physicists and economists but *actually look at what the scientists (and artists) do.* Cra-a-a-zy.

Scientists are people. They are not the machines for accumulating data that you find in Baconian philosophy, nor are they the romantic heroes seeking falsification that you hear of in Popperian philosophy. They are men and women trying to figure things out and then trying to persuade each other. In other words, science even in the narrow and modern English sense cannot be "demarcated" from other serious persuasive activities, such as law courts or family discussions. The warmed-over positivism that focuses on demarcation, still popular in economics many decades past its time, turns out to have little to do with laboratory life or how experiments end.

These new "social studies of science" are mainly British. An older line in the study of science is mainly American, the intellectual children of the Columbia sociologist Robert K. Merton, who does not wholly approve of the newer clan (though Merton told me once that he's a "social constructivist," too). The old clan concerned itself mainly with schools and influences and used biography as its method. By contrast the Britishers and their American allies (with a stray French person or two) call themselves the Children of Thomas Kuhn, especially the Kuhn of his early book on Copernicus or his collection of essays in 1977, *The Essential Tension* (not the Kuhn of *The Structure of Scientific Revolutions*, which has surprisingly little influence in science studies). Their method is anthropology and close reading.

Another way to state the lineage of the Kuhnian clan is to mention three names: Fleck, Polanyi, and Kuhn. It's a test of whether an alleged expert on science actually knows about science studies to ask her whether she's read these three. Fleck before World War II (1935 [1979]), Polanyi after it (1946, 1962, 1966), and Kuhn from 1959 on remade the study of science. All three were trained as scientists in the English sense and could therefore engage in participant observation with some credibility. The first two were internationally known in their sciences, and Kuhn, trained as a particle physicist, was internationally known as a historian. As the philosopher Paul Feyerabend observed: "Fleck, Polanyi and then Kuhn were (after a long time) the first thinkers to compare . . . school philosophy with its alleged object—science—and to show its illusionary character. This did not improve matters. Philosophers did not return to history" (Feyerabend 1987, 282), continuing to stoutly ignore Fleck, Polanyi, and Kuhn. No facts, please: we're philosophers.

All right, then, what's the payoff for economics? Since I'm an economist, I won't say. If I were so smart as to know the future of the science, I'd be rich. But if you believe that knowing what you are doing is a good idea, then you'll want to listen to the new studies of science, the Clan of Kuhn. Even some pretty smart scientists do *not* believe that knowing what you are doing is a good idea—witness statistical significance in economics or witness recent assaults on science studies themselves by outraged scientists like Victor Weisskopf (Tom's dad, by the way). When I told an eminent experimental economist about the findings of science studies he got angry and started shouting at me. Some people don't like to get reading lists.

But if you do like reading, the reading list here is a way of seeing science as art and seeing art as science, together, the way people once did and the way non-English speakers still do. It's a way to get started thinking how a participant-observer or a literary critic of economics might think about the field. Especially, it's a way round the silly question, a question no one thought to ask before the late Romantics and which after a century and a half without coherent answer should perhaps be retired, "Field X: Art or Science?"

Further Reading: Getting Started in the New Studies of Science

Feyerabend, Paul. 1987. *Farewell to Reason*. New York: Verso. Don't be misled by the terrifying title.

Fleck, Ludwik. 1935 (1979). *Genesis and Development of a Scientific Fact*. T. J. Trenn and R. K. Merton, eds. Foreword by Thomas Kuhn. Chicago: University of Chicago Press. A biologist asks, "How did a disease get to be called one?" (Note that Merton edited it.)

Keller, Evelyn Fox. 1983. *A Feeling for the Organism: The Life and Work of Barbara McClintock*. New York: Free Press. Think that feminism has nothing to do with *science?* Think again.

Kuhn, Thomas. 1977. *The Essential Tension: Selected Studies in Scientific Tradition and Change*. Chicago: University of Chicago Press. Read this, not *The Structure of Scientific Revolutions*.

Lakatos, Imre. 1976. *Proofs and Refutations: The Logic of Mathematical Discovery*. Cambridge: Cambridge University Press. But math is different, right? Wrong. Don't read his other books: in this one, his D. Phil. Dissertation, he got it right.

Levi, Primo, and Tullio Regge. 1992. *Conversations*. Trans. R. Rosenthal. Harmondsworth: Penguin. One wishes Regge, a typical physicist too sure of himself, had let the chemist Levi talk more.

Mulkay, Michael. 1985. *The Word and the World: Explorations in the Form of Sociological Analysis*. London: Allen and Unwin. One of a score of British sociologists of science (some other names to watch for are Trevor Pinch, Harry Collins, or the Frenchman Bruno Latour) who write close studies of science in action. This one is about oxidative phosphorylation and the problem of stoichiometry. Yeah.

Nelson, John, Allan Megill, and D. N. McCloskey, eds. 1987. *The Rhetoric of the Human Sciences: Language and Argument in Scholarship and Public Affairs.* Rhetoric of the Human Sciences. Madison: University of Wisconsin Press. The "rhetoric of inquiry" introduced here is what the science studies people do, often without realizing it.

Polanyi, Michael. 1962. *Personal Knowledge: Towards a Post-Critical Philosophy.* Chicago: University of Chicago Press.

———. 1966. *The Tacit Dimension.* Garden City, N.J.: Doubleday. A briefer version.

Selzer, John L., ed. 1993. *Understanding Scientific Prose.* Madison: University of Wisconsin Press. Rhetoric of the Human Sciences. On Gould and Lewontin on the spandrels of San Marco.

Reading I've Liked
in the Humanities

Eastern Economic Journal *(summer 1994).*

When I told the economic historian Bob Fogel that since about 1980 I've been doing reading in the humanities, he asked me amiably whether I had "become a mystic." Bob, who did get the Nobel Prize I predicted he would when this piece was first published, whose brother was a professor of English, and who is a widely cultivated man, was nonetheless using the mental categories of 1955. In 1955, at the high point of Two-Culture thinking, you were either a scientist or a touchie-feelie. You could be rational, scientific, empirical; or, alternatively, you could be into Zen and emotion. Scientist or mystic. That was it.

The mental categories of 1955 are well summarized in a fact of geography. The world capital of rationality since about 1955 has been the RAND Corporation, which is located in the world capital of irrationality since about 1955, Santa Monica. (The "Randians" in another sense, followers of Ayn Rand, also have had their headquarters there since about 1955, I am told; the coincidence is enchanting). The RAND people have gotten along all right with the City, called in the old days "The People's Republic of Santa Monica." The getting along is another part of the categories of 1955. In 1955 you would choose up sides, scientism or humanism, physics or Tao, but then you were not supposed to bother the other people or make them read your stuff. The ideal was an amiable lack of contact or understanding, which Fogel was reflecting. Humanities? You mean "mysticism." Hey, man, whatever turns you on.

Bob is mistaken about this (though not about much else—well, maybe also about the wheat market in England in the seventeenth century being closed to European prices; and how to react to someone who's changing gender). The mistake is to believe that "the humanities" have nothing to do with "the sciences," of which economics is of course an example. A dean of research at a large university came to Iowa some years ago and said in her speech that the social sciences, of course, take up where the physical and biological sciences run out of explanations, and then the humanities take up where the social sciences run out. In her mind, and in Bob Fogel's, the three are arranged in lexicographic order, from most to least rational.

The dean's economics is not persuasive. Like most economists, I view lexicographic orderings as themselves irrational. It's unlikely that what humanists do has no connection with the sciences except the crumb-gathering, the dealing with the ineffable, that the dean had in mind. It seems more likely that an economist could learn a thing or two from an English professor, and vice versa. Trade is advantageous between people with different factor proportions. Millions of intelligent people have signaled with big investments in Homer and Shakespeare and Hegel that they have found a lot in them. You can't know whether the humanities have something to say to you unless you try them, and pretty seriously, too.

I'd like to induce you to try. You can't know your intellectual budget constraint before investigating the market.

Clifton Fadiman, a literary man of the 1930s and 1940s, published in 1942 an anthology called *Reading I've Liked.* In the introduction he tells how as a book-loving boy he experimented one summer *not* reading: "I felt I had grown too dependent upon other people's ideas. The only way I could perceive to cure myself of this dependence was to abjure other people's ideas completely." He reports that "the effect is purgative," that is, the mind "for a time seems vacant. Then gradually it fills up again, . . . with the few clear ideas." I would suggest that we economists have run Fadiman's boyish experiment far too long, out to the point of diminishing returns, spending entire decades without reading a book. Maybe that's why our ideas are so clear, and few. Time to read.

My proposal is that you join me in learning a thing or two from the English professors. The most boot camp way of doing this is to start right now taking college courses in English, religion, communication, philosophy, languages, film studies, feminist criticism. Go ahead. Pick one and start. The English poet Auden remarked that one could start reading anywhere in the history of poetry, and, if you kept reading whatever seemed the next relevant piece of it, you would arrive at the end with the same wide picture.

One way is to start with language courses, especially for reading literature rather than for ordering breakfast in Mexico City. A dean in a college in Connecticut, a sociologist I think, was asked why at age 40 he had started taking courses in Latin, a dead language with no possible use for business. You can't even ask anyone the time of day in it, unless you're in the Vatican City. He said: "I was 40 years old and was ashamed I could not read the language of European learning." An economist owes it to her noble profession to be a learned person.

One does not need to be a professor to start taking courses, since American life is saturated with colleges. But it's so easy if you're already on a college campus that it's strange it doesn't happen more. Why don't the professors of English take from time to time a course in physics or the professors of economics a course in philosophy? Tom Sargent for many years—I don't know if he has kept it up recently—did not let a term go by without taking another math course. My hat's off to him. Dick Posner, law professor, federal appellate judge, and cofounder of law and economics, learned Greek as an adult. Two hats off.

But if you want to keep it secret for a while, until you are hardened to charges of mysticism and are emotionally prepared for German vocabulary quizzes every Friday, the other route is reading on your own. I mixed the strategies, in middle age studying Latin a good deal, with smatterings of Greek and Italian, and at the same time reading English and translated literature I should have read decades ago. You can disguise yourself in dark glasses and a wig, procure a copy of Thomas Mann's *Buddenbrooks* in another town, and read it on the sly, perhaps hidden between covers of an *American Economic Review*.

At a conference on law and society I noted that Armen Alchian had brought Johnson's *Journey to the Western Islands of Scotland* (1775). The book had nothing to do with the conference (although I ask any economist who has read it whether she doesn't see in Johnson a fellow measurer and social *scientist* before the name). During the breaks he would beaver away at it. In 1968 Steve Cheung told me that when Armen wanted to know about the history of law he read the two big volumes, 1,379 pages, of Pollock and Maitland's classic, *The History of English Law before the Time of Edward I* (2d ed., 1898). He liked it. Any economist would, since Maitland, the chief author, did not know economics technically but was so smart that he could reinvent it on the spot while discussing the Saxon law of murder. So when Armen finished he started over and read it again. Armen's a scholar. So should you be.

What to read? In a way its obvious—on the whole, no fiction or poetry from last year, since we won't know for decades whether it's worth reading. We do know about Jane Austen (see if you don't find eco-

nomic man, and especially economic woman, in her minor characters),
Defoe (*Robinson Crusoe* is the type of bourgeois myth), and Dickens (I
assign *Hard Times* to my course on the Industrial Revolution: it's
appallingly bad history and economics but for that reason useful in
teaching).

The trick is to exploit survivorship. There's a reason that books last.
The old and famous books are old and famous because the growth from
reading them has proven to be high. My mentor, the economic historian
Alexander Gerschenkron, read *War and Peace* (in Russian) six times,
four of the times in a pair of readings. When he got to the end of the book
he did not want to leave its world. So, like Alchian with Pollock and
Maitland, he turned back to the first page and read it again. Stop looking
at the *New York Times* best-seller list, a list mainly of transient rubbish
(*The Bridges of Madison County* [written by a fellow Iowan and acade-
mic] broke all records on it: need I say more?). Start with the Bible and
Don Quixote and get to work, or rather to pleasure, or rather to Z-good
production.

It can be disorienting, though, and discouraging to simply leap into
the world of Horace or the Bhagavad Gita. All credit to those who take
the leap unaided, but another route to the same end is recent books in the
humanities, that is, books *about* the books worth reading. It's how I got
started. The suggestion violates my rule against recent books, I admit,
but has the advantage that the people speaking come from (roughly) the
same culture and can give you a reason to leap.

You may have heard, though, from the deep literary thinkers at the
New York Times and the *Wall Street Journal* that recent books in the
humanities are deconstructionist, politically correct, jargon filled, red
under the bed, and in other ways ignorable. All right. If you want to
remain as ignorant as the editorial writers, let them shortcut your education right here. But if you take the view that most things believed by editorial writers are wrong, such as that foreign trade "creates" or
"destroys" jobs or that companies will end up paying 80 percent of health
insurance costs if the law specifies that they will, regardless of economic
incidence, then stick around.

Here are 21 accessible books to choose from in beginning your study
of the humanities. The list reflects of course my tastes, or rather my igno-
rances (which, come to think of it, are economically the same). I'm a dun-
derhead at classical music, a nitwit at painting, so be warned. I confine
the list to books you can pick up and read with understanding without
already being a literary person. You can't start with Kenneth Burke, the

great American critic, any more than you can start with Samuelson's *Foundations* (1947), as against *Economics* (1948).

Reading I've Liked: Twenty-one Recent Books in the Humanities Which You'll Like, Too

Austin, J. L. *How to Do Things with Words,* 2d ed. Cambridge, Mass.: Harvard University Press, 1975. A great little book, spawning libraries on "speech acts" (a good follow up is Sandy Petrey, *Speech Acts and Literary Theory* [New York: Routledge, 1990]).

Berger, John. *Ways of Seeing.* London: BBC and Penguin, 1972. An easy way to start reading this Marxist but penetrating historian of painting.

Booth, Wayne C. *Modern Dogma and the Rhetoric of Assent.* Chicago: University of Chicago Press, 1974. A readable use of modern rhetoric, philosophy, and literature.

————. *The Company We Keep: An Ethics of Fiction.* Berkeley: University of California Press, 1988. How stories make ethical judgments. You see I admire Booth. In the professorial line he's what I want to be if I ever grow up—a female Wayne Booth.

Brolin, Brent C. *The Failure of Modern Architecture.* New York: Van Nostrand Reinhold, 1976. Ever wonder why downtown Dallas reminds you of the Arrow-Debreu Theorem?

Feyerabend, Paul. *Against Method.* London: NLB, 1975. Read this, and you will never read science the same way again.

Fish, Stanley. *Doing What Comes Naturally: Change, Rhetoric, and the Practice of Theory in Literary and Legal Studies.* Durham, N.C.: Duke University Press, 1989. The bête noire of anti-deconstructionist journalists turns out to be a sensible, readable, and amusing critic, here of law and literature.

Frye, Northrop. *The Educated Imagination.* Bloomington: Indiana University Press, 1964. Text of six radio talks by the Canadian critic. As *College English* said, "Read this book."

Gombrich, E. H. *Art and Illusion: A Study in the Psychology of Pictorial Representation.* Princeton: Princeton University Press, 1960. You can see that I do not keep current in art criticism; a stunningly good book, shaming our narrowness.

Goodman, Nelson. *Ways of Worldmaking.* Indianapolis: Hackett, 1978. A philosopher who was once a professional art dealer shows that we make worlds with our words of art.

Jonsen, Albert R., and Stephen Toulmin. *The Abuse of Casuistry: A History of Moral Reasoning.* Berkeley: University of California Press, 1988. Ethical theory is more than warmed over Kant and Bentham, contrary to what you might think from the journal *Economics and Philosophy.*

Kennedy, George A. *New Testament Interpretation through Rhetorical Criticism.* Chapel Hill: University of North Carolina Press, 1984. The best short introduction to what one sort of "criticism" might mean, applied to a familiar text.

Lakoff, George, and Mark Johnson. *Metaphors We Live By.* Chicago: University of Chicago Press, 1980. By a linguist and a philosopher, explaining why models are metaphors.

Lodge, David. *After Bakhtin: Essays on Fiction and Criticism*. London and New York: Routledge, 1990. The same David Lodge who writes fine novels that get turned into TV series was until recently a professor of English who writes front-line but highly readable criticism.

Passmore, John. *A Hundred Years of Philosophy*. Harmondsworth: Penguin, 1966. Brings you up to speed in modern philosophy; his *Recent Philosophers* (1985) continues in the same format.

Putnam, Hilary. *Realism with a Human Face*, ed. James Conant. Cambridge, Mass.: Harvard University Press, 1990. Lucid essays in modern philosophy, such as "Beyond the Fact/Value Split" and "The Craving for Objectivity."

Rorty, Richard. *The Consequences of Pragmatism (Essays 1972–1980)*. Minneapolis: University of Minnesota Press, 1982. An enchanting postmodern.

Smith, Barbara Herrnstein. *Contingencies of Value*. Cambridge, Mass.: Harvard University Press, 1988. One of a handful of literary people thinking in other than Marxist terms about economics and literature.

Todorov, Tzvetan. *The Poetics of Prose*. Ithaca: Cornell University Press 1977. Even a Bulgarian-French literary critic can be a model of perspicuity.

Tronto, Joan. *Moral Boundaries: A Political Argument for an Ethic of Care*. New York: Routledge, 1993. A political philosopher shows that Adam Smith was a feminist.

White, James Boyd. *When Words Lose Their Meaning: Constitutions and Reconstitutions of Language, Character, and Community*. Chicago: University of Chicago Press, 1984. White is a professor of law and of English at Michigan, adjunct in the Department of Classics, and believes that we economists have picked up the wrong end of the human stick.

Such writers are pros, on the level of Fogel, Arrow, Coase, Friedman, Becker, Tobin. I'll wager that you can't read any of the books without deciding that the humanities are worth looking into, big time. The next step would be to read other books by the people here you find most interesting then explore the less transparent but still instructive ones (Alasdair MacIntyre, Hayden White, and, yes, Kenneth Burke). None of this is nursery school stuff (Berger's is a TV script and comes the closest). You have to pay attention. But like comparable books in economics (Olson's *Logic of Collective Action,* Hirschman's *Exit, Voice and Loyalty,* Schelling's *Micromotives and Microbehavior,* Frank's *Choosing the Right Pond*), if you pay attention you learn a lot, even a lot that is relevant to economics. I promise.

Rule 10
Learn Price Theory, Which Is No Easy Task

Schelling's Five Truths
of Economics

Eastern Economic Journal *(summer 1992).*

A long while ago I was at a conference in Sweden, in a splendid hotel far up the lakes from Stockholm, during a warm summer like an Ingmar Bergman movie. A number of American economists I admire were at the conference, the economic historians Douglass North and Bob Fogel, for example, and Tom Schelling. As an undergraduate in the early 1960s I had *not* taken Schelling's pioneering course in game theory. Students are like that, tasteless, because they are ignorant. The list of courses from great economists that I ignorantly spurned is long and embarrassing: Galbraith's course on industrial structure, Leontief's course in graduate price theory, Kuznets's course in national income statistics, Haberler's course in international trade, Solow's course up the street at MIT in anything at all. It's why I am not laissez-faire in matters of curriculum. By definition and by empirical test the student/consumers are too ignorant to select optimally.

Anyway, I was acquainted with Schelling but had never been his student. So I had not heard his amazing proposition about economics and accounting.

At the Swedish conference he told the story of a visit to Yale in the 1950s of Peter Bauer, already then a distinguished economist whose opinions were to be believed. Bauer asserted mysteriously that an economist knew only five things—that is, really, truly knew, as against what one might be willing to publish in the *American Economic Review* or think vaguely plausible when the moon was new. Schelling, a nervous assistant professor at the time, did not get around to asking Bauer which five things he was thinking of, so had to reconstruct them himself.

Schelling figured out that what economists really, truly know, and noneconomists do not, are matters of accounting. (1) The national accounts add up, national product equaling national income. (2) The balance of foreign payments adds up, too. (3) The money supply is "created" by a system of banks in which each holds as a reserve only a fraction of the money deposited with it (this one was discovered by Chester Phillips of the University of Iowa in the 1920s). The fourth and fifth of the Truths consist of a couple of demographic truths of accounting, which might be illustrated with the growth of the unmarried population by exactly two when a husband and wife get a divorce.

These are the few things an economist would be willing to stand before God and declare to be True. Learning to think like an economist, Schelling argues, consists in good part of learning to speak such bits of accounting logic. As Adam Smith said in the first sentence of *An Inquiry into the Nature and Causes of the Wealth of Nations,* where he announced the Truth that national income equals national product equals national expenditure, "The annual labour of every nation is the fund which originally supplies it with all the necessaries and conveniences of life which it annually consumes."

Schelling's proposition is not likely to thrill most economists. They reckon they are quite a lot smarter than their colleagues in the Department of Accounting, who do not deal with Deep Behavioral Propositions such as $Q_D = D(P)$ or Max U s.t. $B = 0$. The trend in academic accounting, actually, is to remake the field into economics of the Max U sort. Like political scientists and some sociologists, the accountants are econowannabes.

But when you get inside an economic argument you are likely to bump into accounting. Schelling himself provides an example in his eye-opening little book, *Micromotives and Macrobehavior* (1978). To quote the blurb:

brake lights flash, cars slow down, traffic crawls. An accident has occurred in one of the *outbound* lanes. Why is it the *citybound* traffic jams up? Drivers have reduced their speed to get a glimpse of the wreckage on the other side of the divider. Each driver pays ten seconds for his own look and nine minutes, fifty seconds for the curiosity of the drivers ahead of him.

Schelling's argument is crucial to understanding the externalities of congestion. The behavioral premises are trivial. So is the accounting: each driver pays for the cumulated time spent by each person ahead of him in the queue. But the economics is startling, first-rate stuff, one way that economics makes progress.

Schelling and I are claiming that if you examine important economic arguments you will find 9 times out of 10 an accounting identity overlooked by the man in the street or even by the economist in the study. Take Marty Feldstein's point about the way Social Security pushes the saving rate down. Any economist knows there's something in it. Set aside the controversy about the magnitude of the effect. Surely we as economists know—really, truly know, if we know anything—that private saving for one's old age is fungible with public saving for the same purpose. Maybe it's not perfectly fungible, but no economist worthy of the name will assume unthinkingly that the presence of Social Security has *no* effect of reducing people's saving for their old age. It's right there in the accounting. A pension from the government is an asset, too.

The identical point is involved in the long-running controversy over the burden of the government debt. (By the way, why didn't economists complain about its treatment in political discussions around 1990? The men and women in the street, and in Congress, didn't get the accounting even roughly straight.) Bob Barro's point long ago was that if the public had an ounce of accounting common sense it would see that the interest on a government bond is matched by some nasty liabilities down the road called "taxes." That's what the empirical dispute is about: Do people have an ounce of accounting sense?

It's hard to find an economic argument of any importance that is not dominated by a more or less tricky point in accounting. At any rate the point will be tricky enough to elude most economists until some other economist notices it.

The first generation of economists with formal training in graphical analysis thought that they could prove on a blackboard that society would be better off if we prevented speculators from smoothing prices.

The consumers preferred varying prices in good and bad years, in the way that people prefer sales in clothing stores: they buy more when the price is low and gain on balance from the varying price. The proposition was taken seriously, a new theorem. Then Paul Samuelson pointed out that the accounting was wrong. To be sure, if some "outside Santa Claus," as Samuelson put it, could be found to buy high and sell low, against his self-interest, then the consumers for their part would be enriched by varying prices. But if you do the accounting correctly the enrichment of the consumers is more than outweighed by the impoverishment of producers and speculators. For the consolidated accounts, stable prices are better.

In the same spirit and at about the same time it was announced that income taxes could be proved on a blackboard to be superior to excise taxes. Such were the products of the first generation of formalists in economics. (It makes you wonder about the next generation of formalists in economics or the next or the next.) Almost immediately, however, I. M. D. Little and Milton Friedman, separately, made the point that the accounting was wrong. The alleged superiority, it turned out, came from assuming that the society could violate its budget constraint. Another outside Santa Claus shot down by an accountant.

Everywhere you look in economics you find a balance sheet or an income statement or a convention about the value of housewives' time staring you in the face. Seeing the burden of inflation, for example, depends on a close accounting. It is not the case, as the newspapers assert, that everyone is hurt by inflation. A crude accounting, to get started, would note that every dollar expended in higher prices ends up as a dollar on the income side. So much for people being hurt on average. But wait, said Phillip Cagan: the account is still not quite complete; look at the balance sheets, too. The holder of dollar bills is hurt by inflation, even if he is better off on some other account. Early and late, it was an accounting argument.

The untangling of mistaken or incomplete accounting has been one of the chief activities of late-twentieth-century economists. The IS-LM curves, for instance, were invented in 1939 by Hicks as a rough-and-ready summary of Keynes's theory of national income. But the idea is defective accounting, as Hicks himself was later to point out: it mixes up capital accounts in the LM curve with income-expenditure accounts in the IS curve, as it had to if it were going to represent Keynes's muddled insight. The theorists of macroeconomics spent much of the next 60 years attempting to repair the accounting.

Likewise, Ronald Coase's "theorem" of 1960 was merely a careful accounting of the costs and benefits from pollution. His point is routinely misunderstood to be that if property can move around easily then it will get into the hands of the people who value it the most; if not, not. Such a proposition should be called, rather, Adam Smith's or Edgeworth's or Arrow's Theorem and is the opposite of what Coase thinks the world is like. Coase's real contribution, as he has argued from his first professional papers to his last, was the accounting framework imposed, in explicit contrast to an earlier accounting by Pigou and Samuelson. Coase says, in effect: "You have been accustomed to accounting the smokestacks as the 'cause' of pollution, and therefore assuming automatically that they deserve to pay fines. Has it occurred to you that one might just as well account the breathers of the polluted air as *the* cause? And that leaving the pollution on the breathers might lead to the cheapest avoidance of the evil, when indeed it should be viewed on balance in the social accounts as an evil?"

The notion of "human capital," invented by Theodore Schultz, is nothing more than an agreement to account human skills the same way that plant and machinery is accounted. In 1946 Schultz spent a term based at Auburn University interviewing Alabama farmers in the neighborhood. One day he interviewed an old and poor farm couple and was struck by how contented they seemed. Why are you so contented, he asked, though poor? They answered: You're wrong, Professor. We're not poor. We've used up our farm to educate four children through college, remaking fertile land and well-stocked hog pens into knowledge of law and Latin. You can see that we're rich. The parents had informed Schultz that the *physical* capital, which economists think they understand, is in some sense like the *human* capital of education. The sense is accounting.

We economists spurn accounting—another course I never took. But we end up reinventing it. Maybe we should study the subject a little, or at least make our students learn it. After all, it's what we Really, Truly Know.

The Natural

My very first column in the Eastern Economic Journal *(spring 1992). Hal Hochman invented the genre.*

A while ago I spent a couple of days in Colorado Springs with Richard Bower, another economist. We were assigned to do a routine review of the undergraduate program in economics at Colorado College. One benefit of such an assignment is that the reviewers talk and think about programs for a concentrated day or two. If you suppose that professors think about teaching programs every day, on the job, you are mistaken. Two days of talk put some things into focus.

I had not met Bower before. One intellectual generation older than me, he got an MBA from Columbia (1956) and a Ph.D. from Cornell (1962) and has taught for a long time at Dartmouth's business school. He specializes in public utility economics and the teaching of price theory. He's a lively, articulate man, who graduated from Kenyon College in 1949 during its last glory days as an American literary center and has taught at Colorado College itself. That is to say, he understands and commends the liberal arts.

But—why always the *but* when economics meets the liberal arts?— Richard Bower is an economist right down to his wing-tip shoes. He knows Sophocles and Shakespeare all right, but (there it is again) he believes in economics. Not all economists do, of course. Bower does, as do I and perhaps 20 percent of the profession. Give the Bowers or the McCloskeys any social situation, from insider trading to an obstreperous teenage child, and they look to economics for an answer, or at least for a start.

People who "believe in economics" tend to agree on who the best economists are. They admire economists like Armen Alchian, Ronald Coase, Gary Becker, Gordon Tullock, Leland Yeager, economists often as not unknown or misunderstood by the unbelieving mainstream of the profession. Bower, like me, is a believing economist. It's like being a believing Christian. ("In more ways than one," you can hear the unbelievers say; ye of little faith).

So Bower and I agree on economics. Our agreement makes puzzling our one disagreement about teaching it. Bower thinks that we can teach economics to undergraduates. I disagree. I have concluded reluctantly, after ruminating on it for a long time, that we can't.

We can teach *about* economics, which is itself a good thing. The undergraduate program in English literature teaches about literature, not how to do it. No one complains or should. The undergraduate program in art history teaches about painting, not how to do it. I claim the case of economics is similar. Majoring in economics can teach about economics but not how to do it.

We economists, especially the true believers, hold up as an ideal of economic education at any level that the students should begin to "think like economists" (see Siegfried et al. 1991). No one, least of all Bower or me, would deny that thinking like a (Good Old Chicago School) economist is splendid. Bower summarizes the thinking in a triad: a thought of maximization, a thought of equilibrium (see maximization), and a thought of interaction (see equilibrium and maximization). He's right (though Tom Schelling and I would add a thought of accounting identity). After such thinking like an economist has become one's way of looking out at the world, nothing could be more splendid, or easier. What *do* you want? All right, then, what are your constraints? Fine. Anything else? How about those other guys? And does net wealth still equal assets minus liabilities?

But this splendid, easy way of thinking, in case you have not noticed, is extremely difficult to teach. Undergraduates uniformly complain about intermediate micro, which we economists uniformly recognize as the guts of the field, where we Think like Economists. The kids hate it. And they don't learn much. Show me the A+ undergraduate who can formulate and solve a problem in micro, applicable to an actual economy, that is something other than a toy problem copied out from the book. Compare what a first-rate undergraduate engineer or historian can do, and weep.

I hope, forlornly, that the difficulty lies in our teaching methods (Bower thinks it does). Good science after all is interesting and teachable. If we can just get, say, Hal Varian, bless him, to stop writing those formalist economics texts and if we can get some real, business school case studies with economic content into the curriculum, the students will catch on and start thinking like economists.

It sounds good. But I've tried and tried and tried it—going so far as to write an intermediate textbook with case studies by the hundreds. The book has its fans (and one fan club), but we all agree that in the present version it is Too Difficult. Why is that? Because it tries to teach people to think like economists—not to copy out fourth-rate applied math or to get a feel for the politics of the economy or to learn *about* economics but to think the way Robert Solow does or Milton Friedman does.

I have to conclude from this and other experiences that thinking like an economist is too difficult to be a realistic goal for teaching. I have taught economics since 1968, and I tell you that it is the rare, gifted graduate student who learns to think like an economist while still in one of our courses (sometimes it comes to them when doing their dissertations), and to actually think like an economist at age 19 it takes a genius undergraduate (Sandy Grossman, say, who was an undergraduate when I came to Chicago in 1968; or David Romer, to whom I taught price theory). Most of the economists who catch on do so long after graduate school, while teaching classes or advising governments. That's when I learned to think like an economist, early in teaching, and I'd be surprised if your experience is not the same.

Let me sharpen the thought. I think economics, like philosophy, cannot be taught to 19-year-olds. It's an old person's field. Nineteen-year-olds are most of them romantics, capable of memorizing and emoting but not capable of thinking coldly, calculating in the cost-and-benefit way. Look, for example, at how irrational they are a few years later when getting advice on postgraduate study. A 19-year-old has intimations of immortality, comes directly from a socialized economy (called a family), and has no feel on his pulse for those tragedies of adult life that economists call scarcity and choice. You can teach a 19-year-old boy from a suburban, middle-class family all the math he can grasp, all the history he can read, all the Latin he can stand. But you cannot teach him a philosophical subject. For that he has to be, say, 25; or, better, 45. Or female.

Why, then, does Bower disagree? Why does he think that we can teach a young person how to think like an economist? We had to go home from Colorado Springs before I could work it out with him, but I have an inkling. I think Bower is what I call a Natural. A Natural understands economics the first time he hears it. The rest of us need repetitions at higher and higher levels, like a spiral staircase. The Natural does not; he gets the point at the bottom. Naturally, a Natural like Bower assumes that everyone else finds it just as easy, because it's natural.

Most economists are non-Naturals, like me, who learned the cynicism of the field after a hard slog. Heh, I'm not stupid. But I'm not a Natural. When I was 25, having studied economics for 6 years, I grasped suddenly that prices are for allocation, not fairness. When I was 28, an assistant professor with Steve Cheung as an office mate, I grasped that prices are only one possible system of allocation (violence and queuing are others) but socially the cheapest. When I was in my thirties I could spot this stuff for myself in actual markets. The Naturals can already at 19.

Looking over the Naturals I have known, I see two types. One, reasonably common in the profession, is the Prudent Natural—that is, a man (all of them in my acquaintance are male) who has a personality mimicking *Homo economicus*. (I don't mean that the Natural is all nasty; some of the most charming and loyal men I know are Naturals.) His personality makes it easy for him to figure out why economic man would behave in such a nonromantic, non-late-adolescent way. Many of the people I know who are like that did very well in their first economics course and went on to become professors of law: from my college class I can think of two right off the bat. Bower points out rightly that many physicians are Natural economists.

The other and vanishingly rare type is the Sympathetic Natural, a young person who can understand economics because she has mature powers of imagining herself in the shoes of other people, even of economic man. She is like the very few at 19 who can write good fiction (as against poetry, which is romantic), the Flannery O'Connors of economics. These people go on to become economics professors or successful novelists. I know for sure only one, an economic historian of my acquaintance, and he died.

My point is this: 99 percent of our students are not Naturals. We should stop pretending that we are dealing with such people, the Sandy Grossmans or Flannery O'Connors. Our undergraduates, and most of our graduate students, can learn a lot *about* economics that they can use in life. But unless they join us in that slog up the spiral staircase they are not going to think like economists. Perhaps we should redirect our energies, teaching them economic facts and stories, say, or inspiring them for later study, unlikely to be economic. We could do a lot with economic "criticism," thought of in the way the English department would.

Dick Bower thinks like an economist, but he is wrong about economic education. What we both want, alas, is not in the production set.

Why Economics
Should Not Be Taught
in High School

*I was commissioned to write this for the American Textbook
Council, for its* Social Studies Review, *in the fall of 1991.*

Each stage of education has to make up for the methods of the earlier
one. The methods are not wrong. It is right for students in elementary
school to learn that, as Woody Allen says, 80 percent of success is showing up on time. So our sixth-graders do well if they show up and pay
attention. But by high school they have learned to their dismay that
showing up is not enough and that a successful student has to memorize
things at home, too. French irregular verbs do not get into one's head
without some pounding, as my daughter found out in the ninth grade. So
our college-bound twelfth-graders have become demon memorizers, or
else they are not college bound.

The job in college, however, is to understand. College teachers have
to work hard to drive out the notion that learning means highlighting the
textbook. Learning is *under*standing, subordinating yourself to a field of
study, making yourself into a disciple of good thinkers in chemistry or
English or sociology. It is not the dumping of miscellaneous facts into
your head as so much "content," though of course you have to keep exercising those earlier tricks of showing up on time and memorizing the periodic table. Then graduate school has to turn the students around again,
getting them to criticize what before they were meant only to understand.
Now they must "overstand," as the literary critic Wayne Booth put it.
Then in life, age 30, the former students must create what they were earlier meant only to criticize. And later, age 40, they must synthesize what
they were earlier meant only to create. And age 50 they must judge what
they were earlier only meant to synthesize. (I'm waiting with dismay to

find out what's expected at age 60.) It's wearing, and is one reason why success at one level of education or life correlates so poorly with success at the next.

The trouble is, I only started understanding economics in my second year of graduate school, about the same time I learned to criticize the subject. I didn't really grasp how to criticize it until I was a young assistant professor, expected to create it. I don't think it's because I was especially dense. Some few people understand economic arguments the first time they hear them, in high school or early college. Most of us, though, don't. Economic education, I've said, is like a spiral staircase, going over and over at a higher and higher level the same ground—scarcity, supply and demand, rational choice, entry and exit, aggregate behavior. At the Nth repetition one suddenly arrives on the right floor, the "Aha!" effect. I remember studying for my qualifying exams in the second year of graduate school, going over for the $N + 1$th time the rationale for the price system. I was reading an essay by Edward Mishan, who wrote the trot for graduate students in those days, when it suddenly hit me what this stuff was all about. "Aha!" said I to no one in particular, "Prices are good because *they allocate scarce resources,* not because they are fair!" Two years earlier I had done well in a graduate course taken while I was a college senior because I had mouthed those very words on an exam, answering a question about traffic flow. But at that stage I was still memorizing, not understanding, much less overstanding. As John Dewey used to say, I didn't feel it on my pulse. Something we think we are teaching to our twelfth-graders or freshmen took in my case years and years of repetition to sink in. The economist Alain Enthoven noted once that professional economists use daily the arguments they heard in their very first economics course. But they didn't make the arguments their own until a Ph.D. degree gave them a vested interest.

Now why is this? As I say, I was not especially dense. Most economists will tell you similar stories.

What turned me from being a history major to being an economics major early in college was a push and a pull. The push was taking a couple of courses in my declared major of history, from Frank Freidel and William Langer. Their courses made it clear that history requires one to know something, in fact quite a lot, and therefore entails many hours of tedious reading. This is not what I had bargained for. Nor did I like history's postponement of synthesis. Just as I wanted a Marxist formula right away for politics, I wanted a formula right away for history. If Freidel or Langer (both great scholars) had been one of the leftist professors equipped with formulas that so many of my contemporaries later became, I would have stayed with history, becoming in the end, I suppose, a leftist professor. As it was, I later became through economics a professor of history and then of English, too, but a decidedly conservative one.

The pull was a book that has made hundreds of economists: Robert Heilbroner's *The Worldly Philosophers,* first published in 1953, now in its Nth edition. Again there is a political irony here, since Heilbroner is a man of the Left. I read him in the summer after my freshman year and instantly decided to major in economics. The book is a beautifully written set of brief lives of economists from Adam Smith to Hayek and Galbraith, giving the young reader the impression of understanding economics—not economics as she is taught but economics as perhaps she ought to be taught.

For Heilbroner's book teaches by way of personality and story, Marx and his boils scribbling in the British museum, Keynes and his ballet dancer. Unhappily, by contrast, economics is in fact taught to high schoolers and undergraduates by precept and theory. Here, the teacher intones, is the general formulation of the law of demand. Here are a few examples. Here is the definition of *elasticity.* Here is a useless application of it, a mostly useless idea. Only someone made passionate in another way could love such a subject.

I think the trouble with economics as a high school course or for that matter as a college course is that it does not draw on the passions of young people. The miser in literature is an old man. This can be said of many subjects: philosophy and pragmatic politics are for old folks, too. Young people can emote, as I did about Vietnam and Civil Rights. Young people can memorize, as I did poetry and song lyrics. Young people can follow enthusiastically, as I did the doctrines of socialism and then the doctrines of social engineering and then the doctrines of the free market. Can young people study a philosophical subject in its own terms? I don't think so.

Heilbroner was right to call economists "the worldly philosophers." Economists are more interested than most philosophers in such worldly things as the futures market in onions or the appointment of Susan Phillips of Iowa to the Federal Reserve Board. But philosophers they are, trying to achieve insight by sheer thinking. Many economists have other strings to their bow, such as social history or social engineering. But in most economic music the philosophical string carries the tune.

Why, then, was I slow to understand this philosophical subject? The answer, I suggest tentatively, is that philosophical subjects cannot be taught directly to people below 25 years of age. My colleagues in philosophy would probably agree. They would be appalled if state legislatures were to mandate courses in philosophy (don't laugh: ethics is a branch of philosophy, and, startlingly, some legislators think it efficacious to make it a course, another "skill"). I know how little I learned from a philosophy course in my freshman year: merely to respect the names and lives of Socrates, Plato, Aristotle, Augustine, Aquinas, Kant, Hegel, and Kierkegaard. That's all, in a pretty good student at Harvard College (I wish it had been Radcliffe) who did most of the reading in a course taught by world-famous philosophers and their earnest graduate students. But I was 19. You cannot expect a 19-year-old to understand philosophy beyond a certain factual recall, one damned doctrine after another.

The same, I am afraid, is true of economics. This bad news, notice, is coming from someone who teaches freshman regularly, who has written numerous textbooks in economics, and who wants the whole world to learn the subject.

The trouble with teaching economics philosophically is that a 16- or a 19-year-old does not have the experience of life to make the philosophy speak to her. It's just words, not wise reflections on her life. Economically speaking, she hasn't had a life. She has lived mainly in a socialist economy, namely, her birth household, centrally planned by her parents, depending on loyalty rather than exit. She therefore has no conception of how markets organize production. Though she probably works at a market job (too many of our students do, mainly to pay for their silly automobiles), she does so without that sense of urgency that comes over a person with a child to support. She does not have any economic history under her belt—no experience of the Reagan Recession or the Carter Inflation or even much of the Clinton Boom, not to speak of the Great Depression or the German Hyperinflation. Elder hostellers make better learners of economics.

One can teach economics, on the other hand, politically. As long as it draws on the extreme passions that young people can feel, as in my own self-education, the program works. But because it has to be radical to be attractive it is impossible to do in a high school and not easy in a college. Most parents do not thrill to seeing their pleasantly quiescent teenagers turned into radicals of Left or Right, no matter how much insight into society comes along with it. They get the school board or the board of regents to stop it.

The only way to teach economics to young people, I reckon, is by indirection. Put the economics in the background of more experiential courses in history or home economics or literature. (I am compiling an anthology called *Reading the Economy,* literature with economic subjects, such as Frost's "Mending Wall"). The formal methods can be learned, but they will be forgotten immediately—as the college professor finds that high school economics is forgotten—because they do not refer to anything in the student's life.

My conclusion will sound like an appeal for "relevance" of the 1960s type. In practical terms it is something like the opposite. Relevance of the middle sort does not work. What works is the supreme irrelevance of literature and history, on the one hand, or the entire relevance of home economics and auto mechanics, on the other. Don't mess with Mr. In-Between. At the extremes you can teach economics, by indirection.

Colleagues of mine in Communication Studies have worried about the mechanistic way that high school debating programs have developed, teaching the debaters to talk fast and superficially. The problem seems to be that the programs ask students to become passionate about subjects whose obvious relevance is in fact obvious only to the middle-aged: In 1960 should we abolish nuclear weapons? In 1995 should we finance the reform of the Soviet economy? I suggest they return to an ancient pedagogy in rhetoric and use frankly fictional texts as the year's subject. Imagine many thousands of high school debaters spending the year asking, "Was the wrath of Achilles justified?" Glorious.

Economics should be taught through a similarly tacit dimension (as Michael Polanyi the crystallographer and philosopher would have put it). Let the students learn about life in its rounded form, whether in history or in the shop, then at age 25 show them the wonders of an economic point of view thought of as philosophy, as it is now. Alfred Marshall, the economist responsible for much of modern economics, defined economics over a century ago as "the study of mankind in the ordinary business of life." The students need some ordinary business before they turn to its study. That's why for most of us the lessons of economics do not take hold until youth has lost its flower.

Rule 11
Don't Be Silly about Statistical "Significance"

The Loss Function
Has Been Mislaid

*This first attempt to get the point across to the economics
profession appeared in the* American Economic Review *in the May
(conference) issue of 1985. It had been presented to the conference
in December to a large audience. I repeated and amplified its
argument in chapters 8 and 9 of the first edition of* The Rhetoric of
Economics *(1985); then with more evidence in chapters 7 and 8 of
the second edition (1998). And again and again. Nothing has
changed.*

Roughly three-quarters of the contributors to the *American Economic
Review* misuse the test of significance. They use it to persuade themselves
that a variable is important. But the test can only affirm a likelihood of
excessive skepticism in the face of errors arising from too small a sample
at conventional levels of "significance" along an arbitrary scale of largeness and smallness. The test does *not* tell the economist whether a fitted

coefficient is large or small in an economically significant sense. It does *not* say whether the effect "exists" or not.

My criticism is distinct from the criticism that in a world of publication-counting deans there is an incentive for economists to mine the data, giggling uncomfortably when caught. Economists, being professional cynics, are much amused by data mining and significance fishing (Tullock 1959; Ames and Reiter 1961; Feige 1975; Leamer 1978; Mayer 1980; Lovell 1983; Denton 1985).

Neither criticism—my "new" one or the old one that the data is mined—is controversial or arcane. Statisticians, psychometricians, sociometricians, econometricians, and other metrical folk have understood them both since the 1920s and 1930s (see Arrow 1960; Griliches 1976). Both should be parts of the statistical education of an economist, yet almost none of the texts in econometrics mention them.

For example the usual test of purchasing power parity (see J. R. Zecher and myself 1984) fits prices at home (P^*), allowing for the exchange rate, $e: P = \alpha + \beta(eP^*) + \varepsilon$. The equation can be in levels or rates of change. If the coefficient β is statistically significantly different from 1.0 the hypothesis of purchasing power parity is rejected; if not, not. The test seems to tell about substantive significance without any tiresome inquiry into how true a hypothesis must be in order to be true. The table of Student's-t will tell.

But this is idiotic. A number is large or small relative only to some standard. Forty degrees of frost is paralyzingly cold by the standard of Virginia, a normal day by the standard of Saskatoon in January, and a heat wave in the standard of most interstellar gas. A *New Yorker* cartoon showed water faucets labeled "Hot (A Relative Concept)" and "Cold (A Relative Concept)." Nothing is large-in-itself. It is large (or yellow, rich, cold, stable, well-integrated, prudent, free, rising, monopolistic) relative to something to which it can be interestingly compared. The remark "But how large is large?" is one of those seminar standbys, applying to any paper, like "Have you considered simultaneity bias?" or "Are there unexploited opportunities for entry?" It's usually a good question, inheriting some of its excellence from its father in thought, the mind-stunning "So What?" (And its Jewish mother: "So What Else Is New?"). You say the coefficient is 0.85 with a standard error of 0.07? So? In Yiddish, *nu?*

The literature does not discuss how near the slope of β has to be to 1.0 to be able to say that purchasing power parity succeeds or fails. It does not answer how large is large. The only standard offered is statistical significance, that is, how surprising it would be to be the observed sample would be if the hypothesis of $\beta = 1.0$ were in fact exactly true given the level at which one has arbitrarily decided to register surprise and given that one is going to pretend that sampling is the only source of error.

But "exactly" true is not relevant for most economic purposes. What is relevant is merely that β is in the neighborhood of 1.0, where "the neighborhood" is defined by why it is relevant—for policy, for academic reputation, for the progress of knowledge. The question requires thought about the loss function. One begins to think that the neighborhood of small loss in the case of purchasing power parity might be large. And, even outside it, one begins to think $\beta = 0.1$, say, would still be economically significant, constraining prices at home; or that even a coefficient of -7854.86 would belie closed economy models of inflation.

The usual test does not discuss standards. It gives them up in favor of irrelevant talk about the probability of a Type I error in view of the logic of random sampling and the arbitrarily chosen level of significance and the arbitrary scaling of important differences. Most economists appear to have forgotten how narrow is the question that a statistical test of significance answers. It tells the intrepid investigator how likely it is that, *because of the small size of the sample she has,* she will make a mistake of excessive skepticism in rejecting a true hypothesis (in this case $\beta = 1.0$), all this assuming for some reason that the deviation picked out by some conventional level of significance is *economically* significant. Not much is being "tested" here. The test warns her about a certain narrow kind of foolishness, arbitrarily scaled.

The elementary but neglected point I am making is that statistical tests of significance are merely about one sort of unbiased errors in sampling. The standard error of the sample, after all, is just $\sigma/N^{1/2}$. Except in the limiting case of literally zero correlation, if the sample were large enough, all the coefficients would be significantly different from everything. The inverse of the square root of an extremely large number is very small. Any social scientist with large samples has had such logic impressed on her by events. A psychologist, Paul Meehl, for instance, reported a sample of 55,000 Minnesota high school seniors that "reveal statistically significant relationships in 91 percent of pair-wise associations among a congeries of 45 miscellaneous variables such as sex, birth order, religious preference, . . . dancing, interest in woodwork. . . . The majority of variables exhibited significant relationships with all but three of the others, often at a very high confidence level" (1967, 259).

The large sample case makes clear the irrelevance of statistical significance to the main scientific question: So what? In the usual test of purchasing power parity, a sample size of a million yielding a very tight estimate that $\beta = 0.999$, "significantly" different from 1.0, could be produced under the usual procedures as evidence that the theory had "failed." Common sense, presumably, would rescue the investigator from asserting that, if $\beta = 0.999$, with a standard error of .00000001, we should abandon purchasing power parity or run our models of the American economy without the world price level. Similar common sense should be applied to findings that $\beta = .80$ or 1.30 with sample sizes of 30. It is not.

The point can be put most sharply by supposing that we knew the coefficient to be, say, 0.85. Suppose God told us. God does not play dice with the universe, and Hers is no merely probabilistic assurance. Would the scientific task be finished? No, it would not. We would still need to decide, by some criterion of why it matters (a human, not a divine, concern), whether 0.85 is high enough to affirm the theory. *No mechanical procedure can relieve us of this responsibility.* Nor is it a decision that should be made privately, as a matter of "mere opinion." It is the most important scientific decision, and it should be made out in the open. The test of significance doesn't make it.

The grotesque overuse of statistical significance came largely from its name. Surely, it insinuated, we serious scientists should be interested first of all in "significant" coefficients: the wise and good would not wish to waste time on trivialities. The appeal was part of the rhetoric of statistics. The British inventors of statistics, educated in Latin and Greek, were skillful in naming their ideas. As William Kruskal, an American statistician of note, has argued:

> Suppose that Sir R. A. Fisher—a master of public relations—had not taken over from ordinary English such evocative words as "sufficient," "efficient," and "consistent" and made them into precisely defined terms of statistical theory. He might, after all, have used utterly dull terms for those properties of estimators, call them characteristics A, B, and C. . . . Would his work have had the same smashing influence that it did? I think not, or at least not as rapidly. (1978, 98)

As the word *significance* spread to less sophisticated research workers the job of undoing the rhetorical damage began. The earliest paper I have found making "my" point was written in 1919. Attacks on the mechanical use of significance became early a commonplace in statistical education. By 1939, for example, a *Statistical Dictionary of Terms and Symbols* of no great intellectual pretensions was putting the point utterly plainly: "A significant difference is not necessarily large, since, in large samples, even a [substantively] small difference may prove to be a [statistically] significant difference. Further, the existence of a [statistically] significant difference may or may not be of practical significance" (Kurtz and Edgerton 1939, "Significant Difference"). M. G. Kendall and A. Stuart's *Advanced Theory of Statistics* explicitly recognized the mischief in the rhetoric, recommending the phrase *size of the test* in preference to *significance level* (1951, 163n); the sociometricians Denton Morrison and Ramon Henkel (whose book, *The Significance Test Controversy* [1970], is the best reading on the subject) suggest that *significance test* be replaced by the less portentous "sample error decision procedure" (198).

In the 1930s Jerzy Neyman and E. S. Pearson, and then more explicitly Abraham Wald, argued that actual statistical decisions should depend on substantive, not merely statistical significance. As Wald wrote in 1939:

> The question as to how the form of the weight [i.e., loss] function W(.) should be determined, is not a mathematical or statistical one. The statistician who wants to test certain hypotheses must first determine the relative importance of all possible errors, which will entirely depend on the special purposes of his investigation. (302)

Economists have ignored Wald's economical logic, with the result that almost no textbooks in econometrics mention that the goodness or badness of hypothesis cannot be decided on merely statistical grounds.

It is not easy, then, to justify the use of probabilistic models to answer nonprobabilistic questions. You might retort that good economists don't make such a mistake. But they do, as you can see from their best practice, the *American Economic Review*. From the 50 full-length papers using regression analysis in the four regular issues of 1981, 1982, and 1983 I took a random sample of 10 for close scrutiny. Since the purpose is to criticize a socially accepted practice, not to embarrass individual writers, I withhold the names.

Of the 10 papers only 2 do not admit experimenting with the regressions, sometimes with hundreds of different specifications. None propose to alter their levels of significance. Only 2 of the 10 do not use a sign test in conjunction with a significance test: "the variable has a statistically significant coefficient and the right (or expected) sign." No statistical theory lies behind the practice, although it seems sensible enough—a beginning, indeed, of looking beyond statistical significance to the size of the coefficient. One of the papers uses a sample of convenience so convenient that it looks like a universe, about which sampling theory can tell nothing: all counties in Alabama, Mississippi, North Carolina, and South Carolina. Four of the 10 use true samples, such as the opinions of 6,000 Swedes on the current and expected rate of inflation. The only doubt here is the disproportion of effort in dealing with sampling errors when others are probably more serious. At $N = 6,000$ we can surely dismiss Student and attend to bias. As Edward Leamer remarked, "when the sampling uncertainty . . . gets small compared to the misspecification uncertainty . . . it is time to look for other forms of evidence, experiments, or nonexperiments" (1983, 33). The other 5 papers use time-series. One can only ask quietly and pass on: from what universe is a time-series a random sample, and, if there is such a universe, is it one we wish to know about?

The most important question is whether the economists in the sample mix up statistical and substantive significance. Even on purely statistical grounds the news is not good. Only one of the papers mentions the word *power,* though all mention *significance.* Statisticians routinely advise examining the power function, but economists do not follow the advice. Some follow its spirit, avoiding the excessive gullibility of the Type II error by treating the machinery of hypothesis testing with a certain reserve. Most do not. Only 3 of the 10 do not jump with abandon from statistical to substantive significance. The very language, though mostly formulaic, sometimes exposes the underlying attitude. One paper slipped into using the phrase *statistically important.*

Seven of the papers, then, let statistical significance do the work of substantive significance. Usually this is accomplished by a fallacy of equivocation. The result on page 10 (statistically) significant turns up as (economically) significant on page 20. In the worst cases there is no attempt to show how large the effects are or whether the statistical tests of their largeness are powerful or what standard of largeness one should use. In four of the seven papers with significant errors in the use of significance there is some discussion of how large a coefficient would need to be to be large, but even these let statistical significance do most of the work. And even in the three papers that recognize the distinction and apply it consistently there is flirtation with intellectual disaster. The siren song of significance is a hazard to navigation.

If we do not wish to leave science to chance we must rethink the use of statistical significance in economics. Econometrics courses should teach the relevant decision theory, as judging from results they appear not now to do. It would help if the standard statistical programs did not generate t-statistics in such profusion. The programs might be written to ask: "Do you really have a probability sample?" "Have you considered power?" and, above all, "By what standard would you judge a fitted coefficient large or small?" Or perhaps they could merely say, printed in bold capitals beside each equation, "SO WHAT ELSE IS NEW?" Or just "NU?"

Why Economic Historians Should Drop Statistical Significance and Seek Oomph

I wrote this for the Newsletter of the Cliometrics Society *in November 1986. You can see that I was beginning to get impatient.*

A long time ago, when we were both young, Dwight Perkins, the eminent China specialist at Harvard, served as examiner in econometrics for my Ph.D. oral examinations. The memory embarrasses us both, I am sure: that I claimed to be examinable in the field and that he claimed to be an examiner in it. At the time, though, my main embarrassment was that he asked me a simple question about the interpretation of statistical significance. I muffed it. Like most economists, I had a cloudy idea of what exactly statistical significance was claiming. In later years, following Dwight, I have taken to asking economic historians who use the notion of statistical significance whether they know what they are doing. Most don't, and the other economists and calculators are no better. I have recently become a nuisance at historical conferences and in referee reports about statistical significance. The profession deserves an explanation.

Step back for a minute and think through what a significant coefficient means. It means that the *sampling* problem has been solved, or at any rate solved well enough to satisfy conventional standards. (The great statistician John W. Tukey gave some reasons for doubting the conventional standards in "Sunset Salvo," *American Statistician* [Feb. 1986]: 72–76.) In other words, *the sample is large enough to ensure that if you took another sample it would give the same result, roughly (by some announced but arbitrary standard of "roughly").* The sampling standard deviation, which is the population's standard deviation divided by the square root of the sample size, has been driven down to some nice, low figure. As John Venn put it in 1888, at a time when our procedures were a mere twinkle in the statistician's eye, the coefficient (or the mean or the difference between two means or the estimated variance or the R-squared or whatever other statistic we are examining) would probably be "permanent." We would probably come up with the same estimate again.

But a permanent coefficient is not necessarily an important coefficient. It could well be that unusually high corn yields in little Iowa would raise the income of the United States a little and that a proper regression analysis of income on the Iowa corn yields would show this. A large enough sample of years would make the relationship register at any conventional level you happen to like and would make it keep on registering in successive samples. (Never mind what "successive samples" of *years* could possibly mean: that's another problem with statistical significance, a philosophical one I put aside.) The coefficient would be statistically significant. *Yet that it registers at some level of significance and would keep on registering does not mean that it is important. Statistically significant* does not mean "substantively significant." It just doesn't.

What matters is oomph. Oomph is what we seek. A variable has oomph when its coefficient is large, its variance high, and its character exogenous. A small coefficient on an endogenous variable that does not move around can be statistically significant, but it is not worth remembering. Oomph is what we mean when we talk about money being "important" for explaining the price level or about capital being important for explaining income per person. The Iowa corn yield certainly does affect average national income but has little oomph because the coefficient is low. Likewise, the existence of oxygen in the atmosphere certainly does affect combustion, but it does not vary enough from this city block to the next to give it oomph in an explanation of why a particular house burned down. The stock of money in the hands of Iowa Citians certainly does "determine" statistically speaking their expenditures, but because it is endogenous it has no oomph.

Statistical significance, which now guides a large part of the intellectual life of economists and sociologists and psychologists and educationists and population biologists and medical scientists, has nothing to do with oomph. It implies, to repeat, that you have acquired some control (the degree of control measured by the arbitrary significance level: .05, .01, .001, and the like) over *sampling* error as a source of doubt, given the null (arbitrary itself, a zero or 1.0 when a coefficient of 0.5 would still be *substantively* significant). Sampling error, though, is seldom the main source of doubt. The main source of doubt is whether a variables matters or whether it matters to such-and-such a degree: what matters is whether foreign prices affected American prices under the gold standard *significantly* (that is, with oomph) or whether American wages affected migration from Europe significantly or whether social security wealth affected capital accumulation significantly. *Statistical* significance will not reveal this substantive significance, this blessed oomph. The point is not controversial. It is elementary, but an elementary point that a lot of people don't know.

The best way to see the point is to suppose that you really do know what the coefficient is. For sure. God has told you, with no nonsense about confidence intervals: sampling error is zero. The *t*-statistic is infinite. Well, then: Has the variable got oomph?

Go ahead, my dear friends. Tell me. Does it? It's *significant,* in the way statisticians talk. All right, but is it important for history or economics?

You don't yet know. To find out you have to ask and answer other questions, having nothing to do with statistical significance, such as whether the coefficient is large (how large? Large enough to matter in some conversation of scholars or policymakers); or whether the variable could vary enough to produce effects you consider important. For most scientific questions the answer "across successive samples that have a nice, random character the coefficient would be permanent (or statistically significant, given an undefended standard of .05 or .01 imposed on an unexamined scale of important differences)" is only mildly interesting.

"Mildly interesting" is not the same as "not interesting at all." Not quite. Occasionally an economist will have a genuine sample and because of its small size will have a genuine worry about the sampling problem. But dealing with the worry should come after deciding that the variable has oomph, not before. And, by the way, usually our statistical problems have nothing to do with sampling error. They have to do, for example, with bias (see Leamer's "Let's Take the Con Out of Econometrics").

At this point I need to treat some objections.

[The Regressor, a thin young man with sandy hair, sharp nose, and a superior attitude, is confident, even arrogant, in the time-honored way of economists. He knows a thing or two about statistical theory. He says to himself: Who is this dope? A mere economic historian, who learned econometrics in the 1960s, for God's sake, not a tough-guy, up-to-the-minute econometrician like me. Smirking from on high, the Regressor replies:] "Statistical significance is an approximate test of what you call 'oomph.'"

Educate me. Tell me how the permanence of an estimate over successive samples tells how important the variable is. To be sure, large coefficients will ceteris paribus have larger statistical significance. But why not look directly at the size of the coefficient and ask directly whether it is large enough to matter? Why be approximate and irrelevant when you can be precise and relevant?

"Don't be silly: the *t*-test is an indirect measure of 'large enough to matter.'"

Why put the coefficient through an irrelevant transformation? The calculation of statistical significance fools people into thinking they've solved the central intellectual problem of any science, namely, how important a variable is. But the calculation can't do it. It must be done *by us:* the regression is material for a decision, but *we* must decide how large is large. Tables of *t* tell us how large is large only (1) given the arbitrary (that is, power-ignoring) choice of significance level; and (2) given an arbitrary scale along which the bigness of the numbers is measured; and (3) with respect to the permanence in sampling, alone. They do not tell us where to set the null hypothesis for the test; this is a question of substance, not of statistics. The test does not tell us how large is large with respect to the economic argument in question.

[He looks a little worried, but not much:] "What are you talking about? Significance is merely a term-by-term version of fit, R^2. Don't you believe in fit-within-my-present-sample as a measure of importance?"

No, of course not, and neither should you. *So what* if fit is "close" for variable X? The oomph is a scientific or policy question and cannot be answered unless one *uses* the statistics instead of merely staying inside them. Arthur Goldberger gives an example of a regression of health against weight and height. Suppose in the sample the variable *Height* proves to fit extremely well, with a narrow confidence interval (at conventional levels of significance). What would you think of a doctor who looked at this and then said to you, "Your problem is not that you are overweight—the coefficient on *Weight* is not conventionally significantly different from zero. Your problem is that you are too short"?

[He pauses to think for a while. He is beginning to get worried:] "But statistical significance provides a good initial hurdle for the variables. They should at least be statistically significant. Those that survive can be tested later for what you call oomph."

No. There's no reason to make a necessary hurdle out of a merely desirable quality—the quality, remember, of appearing to be permanent within such-and-such bounds, at least so far as sampling error is the problem, as it usually is not, and at least at the level of significance chosen, which is supposed to be a question for scientific discussion and decision but usually is not. Following the "first-let-it-be-statistically-significant" criterion would be like choosing academic colleagues "first" on the basis of their geniality. Geniality is a desirable quality, Lord knows, but not so desirable that it should head a list of lexicographically ordered "priorities." The procedure would make it impossible to hire a brilliant person with a slightly sub-par amount of geniality. Such a rule would ruin most good departments of economics. Anyway, we economists know, for all the talk of "priorities" in public discourse, that lexicographical orderings are irrational. Either you believe in Max U, as you claim to, or you do not. If you do, you must use a loss function right in the estimation procedure. The irrationality of first-statistical-significance is of course greater when the "later testing" for other qualities is not in fact carried out. In actual middle-brow econometric practice it seldom is. Most economists (three for every one who does not, Ziliak and I later learned [1996]) pack up their statistical package and go home as soon as they find significant results "consistent with the hypothesis." They should be testing for oomph, then test, in the rare cases in which they really seem to have a sampling problem and know their loss function, for Type I error.

[Beads of sweat appear on his forehead.] "But everyone does it. It must have some survival value in producing good economics. And someone who knows more about statistics than I do must have decided that it is a good practice. After all, the econometrics textbooks and the canned programs and all the papers in the journals are filled with it."

The argument here is from authority. Arguments from authority are not always wrong, though this one seems to be. I do not know why economists and quantitative historians have misread their statistics books. It would make a good paper on the rhetoric of econometrics to trace the literature back to the authoritative turnings. (The reliance on significance in dropping variables is not usually recommended in so many words by textbooks but in practice has figured heavily, in proportion as computation, following Moore's Law, has become cheaper.) I can only quote authorities in reply and note that the authorities are of the best sort. I refer, for instance, to the article by William Kruskal (past president of the American Statistical Association, etc., etc.), "Statistical Significance" in the *International Encyclopedia of Statistics* (1978; and an earlier version in the *International Encyclopedia of the Social Sciences* [1968]; or the first edition of the elementary book, *Statistics* (esp. 501, A-23), by David Freedman, Robert Pisani, and Roger Purves (well-known statisticians, youngish turks, etc., etc.; [I note with sadness that later editions of the book have de-emphasized the point, perhaps for marketing reasons]). The point has been well-known among thinking statisticians since 1919. Only 5 percent of economists, significant at the 0.01 level, seem to be aware of it (a short list would include some specialist econometricians such as Griliches and Leamer, though surprisingly not all of them, and a few gifted amateurs such as Arrow and Mayer; I learned it from the UC Davis economist Eric Gustafson).

[He loosens his tie, sweat dripping from his nose.] "But there's nothing else to do. I want to use statistical procedures. What do you propose to substitute? How will I fill my days?"

Fill them with statistical calculations that are to the point. Find out what people consider to be a large coefficient and then see if your data show it. Do sensitivity analysis. Simulate. Bend over backwards to see how robust your argument is. Encompass your opponent's model with yours, showing how his results follow as special cases of yours. Take collecting "data" seriously (the word means "givens" in Latin: we should prefer *capta*, things *taken*). There's plenty of useful econometric work to be done (see Sims and Leamer, for example, among econometricians, and Mosteller, Tukey, Hogg, *et alli* among statisticians) that does not rely on the misuse of statistical significance.

[He is quaking nervously and his palms are wet. But presently a lightbulb goes on over his head. You can see it starting to glow. A new smirk spreads over his face:] "Oh, to hell with you. Self-interest is the only guide to scientific behavior. As long as editors keep publishing articles that misuse statistical significance, I'm going to keep on submitting them. I've got a career to run."

Shame on you. Your argument is unethical. The custom of forbidding talk about ethics is strong among economists, some of whom think like you that the model of prudence-only behavior is in fact a set of suggestions about how to behave. But there are no two ways about it: it's unethical to lie, and for a scholar it's a mortal sin. That 95 percent of editors fall into the group of economists who do not know the difference between statistical and substantive significance does not justify someone who *does* know the difference (and now you do) in going on pretending he does not. Scholarship that depends on convenient lies will not last.

Unfortunately, since the 1940s, and especially after the fall of computation costs in the 1970s, economists have substituted statistical significance for oomph. This means that all their results are wrong. They have added and dropped variables, made judgments in the conclusion about importance, carried on all their statistical work on the erroneous premise that statistical testing is the same thing as scientific testing, absent a loss function (which is the only way to connect sampling error with scientific oomph).

To put it sharply, it is gradually becoming plain that all the econometric work since the 1940s has to be done over again. All of it. This is good news for young economists: make your reputation, kids, by rerunning the classic pieces of statistical inference in the discipline (though I note, by the way, that the pieces of statistical inference that have mattered in the scientific long run are surprisingly few) and not relying on loss-functionless statistical significance to tell you how big is big.

Economic historians are well placed to do better. We capture our own data and therefore know that errors in variables are no joke. The intellectual traditions of cliometrics favor self-doubt, which in turn favors counting that statistical theorists call "robust." Above all, we are trying to answer substantive historical questions about particular events, not trying to "test" more or less vague hypotheses about Economic Behavior. Economic historians can lead economists into the promised land of considered oomph.

The Bankruptcy of Statistical Significance

Another try, this time in the Eastern Economic Journal *(summer 1992).*

Kenneth Arrow just visited the University of Iowa. My colleagues and I ate dinner with him at the local Italian place and went to his talk afterward, on why public higher education should not be free. The encounter reminded me why Arrow is widely considered the best American economist of his generation. He got an M.A. degree in mathematics as a youth, but nonetheless the man somehow learned to be an *echt* economist, no mechanic. One sign was that his main argument against subsidizing research by giving money for undergraduate education is an accounting argument, namely, that after all only 1 percent of our graduates go on to graduate school. The other sign of being a true economist was that he was willing to talk economics right through the meal.

I brought the conversation round to statistical significance—that standby of gracious dinner conversation among economists—and reminded him that in 1959 he wrote a paper in an obscure festschrift (for Harold Hotelling, widely considered the best American economist of *his* generation) saying that statistical significance is useless. Arrow corrected me: he had not said that it is useless, merely grossly unbalanced if one does not speak also of the *power* of the test. But, I replied, we never do speak of power. "Yes," said Arrow, "I agree. Statistical significance in its usual form is indefensible."

Then he said something surprising. I was the only person, he claimed, to pick up on his 1959 article, in a little squib in the *American Economic Review* in 1985 called "The Loss Function Has Been Mislaid" (one of the many titles after Bob Gordon's original classic of empirical economics, "$45 Billion of U.S. Private Investment Has Been Mislaid," *AER* [1969]). What's so surprising? This: the best economist of his generation says, in effect, "Folks: your main method for running empirical work is *indefensible,*" proving so beyond rational objection, and yet practically no one pays attention.

Maybe it was the obscurity of the outlet, but I don't think so. The same message, with nearly the same quality of messenger, making one or another devastating criticism of statistical significance, has been delivered again and again and again in places anything but obscure: Edward Leamer's "Let's Take the Con Out of Econometrics" in the 1983 *AER* is one instance; Tom Mayer's "Selecting Economic Hypotheses by Goodness of Fit" in the 1975 *Economic Journal* is another; Gordon Tullock's one-page blast in the *Journal of the American Statistical Association* back in 1959 is another. And when you start looking into it you find people making the same crushing points over and over again, across the sciences. A famous psychologist, who gloried in the name of Edwin Boring, made the central point in the *Psychological Bulletin* of 1919 in a paper called "Mathematical versus Substantive Significance." A great statistician, William Kruskal, reminded us of it in his article on "Statistical Significance" in the old *International Encyclopedia of the Social Sciences* (1968). Another great statistician, John Tukey, in his "Sunset Salvo" in the 1986 *American Statistician,* likewise attacked the gross misuse of significance levels. For that matter, the original article of 1933 on which modern statistics is built, by Neyman and Pearson in the *Philosophical Transactions of the Royal Society,* part A, makes the point with an example of a criminal conviction (296). Among economists Ed Feige, Zvi Griliches, Knox Lovell, Frank Denton, and many others have demolished statistical significance in public for all to see.

Yet no one sees. Most recently the man from whose book I learned econometrics back in the 1960s, Arthur Goldberger, has again made clear that something is deeply wrong with the economic use of statistical significance, on page 240 of his excellent new textbook (he cites my *AER* piece). But I'll be amazed if anything changes. Statistical significance is bankrupt, its assets valueless, its liabilities growing by the minute; but the creditors have simply decided to keep on pretending that checks signed "S. Significance" are worth banking on. The result has been a scientific inflation, a regular bubble.

A coefficient roughly permanent from sample to sample is not necessarily an important coefficient. *That's the main point.* Forget all your cynical, if true, jokes about trolling through the data for the significant coefficients. Sure, statistical significance doesn't mean what it claims to mean if, as one naive student admitted to his thesis committee, you have run fully 200 different specifications of the same economic idea. But set that point aside. The main point—which would remain true of the most virginal classical regression on an absolutely fresh cross-section, a literal and unbiased sample from a well-behaved universe, with perfect specification, complete agreement on the Type I error, full treatment of the power function, and an honesty in handling the data to the standard of Mother Theresa and George Washington combined—is that a coefficient of, say, 1.3567 on X is not *scientifically* significant unless it is interestingly big or small or close to 1.00 or different from zero or in the neighborhood of 1.8923 or whatever by *scientific* standards. The coefficient of 1.3567 might be statistically significantly different from, say, zero at the .000000000001 level of significance (and would in fact be so if the sample size were large enough). *Yet its permanence, speaking of sampling variability, at just about 1.357 does not make it important.* If the question asked by putting X in the regression is scientifically unimportant, what does it matter if the answer is permanent? *Statistically significant* does *not* mean "substantively significant." The two significances have nothing to do with each other. That's *nothing*.

What matters, to use a technical term, is oomph. *Statistical significance has nothing whatever to do with oomph.* A variable can have oomph without statistical significance (for example, for unique events, such as the Potato Famine in explaining Irish migration) or statistical significance without oomph (if the sample size is large enough). They are not connected unless one uses a loss function, which tells how much oomph is given or taken by this or that variation in the variable.

So what? Here's what. None of the econometrics that decides whether variable X is important by using statistical significance has been correct, for all these years.

Some will say: but only bad economists do such bad things. Ho, ho. Look at the latest issue of the *AER* or any other journal of economics. I will present a $100 check to anyone who can show to the satisfaction of a panel of world-class statisticians (I get to choose them, but trust me) that more than a small fraction (a third, say, to be sure of my bet) of the empirical papers do anything but grossly confuse statistical with scientific significance. (Stephen Ziliak and I later tested this assertion on all 182 of the empirical articles in the *AER* in the 1980s and found that 70 percent of the papers did not mention *any* other criterion of importance or oomph beyond statistical significance and that 96 percent misused statistical significance, even if some of these 96 percent [namely, 96 − 70 = 26 percent of the whole] recognized that something beyond Student's-*t* should figure in a scientific life. See our article in the *Journal of Economic Literature* for March 1996; or the second edition of *The Rhetoric of Economics* [1998, chaps. 7 and 8]).

Want to make yourself unpopular with your colleagues? Xerox this piece and put it in their mailboxes. Worse, go read the literature against statistical significance and start asking your colleagues if they know what they are doing. And here's a question to ponder. Eminent statisticians and many econometricians have declared statistical significance to be bankrupt; some have been saying so since 1919; in the 1960s even the much-despised psychologists and sociologists recognized the problem in the Significance Test Controversy, revived in psychology in the late 1990s. Yet scientific practice does not change at all. Not at all. Econometrics courses ignore a devastating criticism of their main method. The textbooks go on miseducating the students. What's going on? Ethical failure in the profession? Careerism gone mad?

I dunno. Go figure. But, when figuring, don't use statistical significance.

The Insignificance of Statistical Significance

One of my Scientific American *columns (Apr. 1995). Many requests for reprints. Still no change.*

Economists, astrophysicists, sociologists, geologists, medical researchers spend a lot of time looking at experiments that God has already performed. If God had not arranged things so that some stars were young and some were old, the astrophysicists would not know much about stellar evolution. Likewise, if God had not arranged things so that the minimum wage varied relative to the average wage for unskilled labor from decade to decade and state to state, economists would have a hard time convincing anyone that the minimum wage puts poor people out of work.

Economists and astrophysicists come to their knowledge by finding regularities of some kind in the world; one crucial part of their task is figuring out whether particular correlations point to an important law or to mere coincidence. As a matter of fact, economists are having a hard time convincing people that the minimum wage contributes to unemployment because recent studies show no "statistically significant" effect on jobs. When Congress takes up the issue, as it periodically does, the livelihoods of thousands of people hang in the scientific balance. And not just the livelihoods of economists themselves.

But just what does that phrase *statistically significant* mean, and what does it have to do with the debate? Go back two centuries, to Pierre Simon, the Marquis de Laplace, the first person to apply the notion of statistical significance to a serious scientific problem. In 1773 Laplace wanted to know where comets came from. He reasoned that if they originated inside the solar system they would orbit in the same plane as the planets, whereas if they came from the far reaches of space their paths would have no correlation with those of the planets. Laplace checked the motions of the last 12 comets to be discovered and firmly rejected the hypothesis that comets came from inside the solar system. If the comets were of local origin, one of them might still by chance travel at some weird angle to the place. But the odds of getting two anomalies would be lower, of three lower yet—the probability, so to speak, of rolling snake eyes three times in a row. This was a very smart idea.

In the succeeding two centuries statisticians have refined Laplace's smart, simple idea into this "statistical significance" (it was so named by Francis Edgeworth in the 1880s) and developed an arsenal of formulas which they claim tell them whether the phenomena researchers observe are caused by sampling error (accidentally picking unrepresentative subjects) or "real" effects. The gold standard for most studies is the "95 percent confidence level," which indicates (users of statistics believe) odds of merely one in 20 that a result arises from chance. Medical researchers use it to decide whether half an aspirin a day keeps the cardiologist away. Economists use it to test whether the minimum wage has a "significant" effect on employment.

Gradually, however, it has dawned on a few scientists that something is screwy. An obvious problem is that with so many people doing so many studies, some of them are going to run into that 1-in-20 chance. By chance.

But another mistake is more elementary, and much, much more important. It is that scientists care about whether a result is statistically significant, *but they should care much more about whether it is meaningful*—whether is has, to use a technical term, oomph.

Sadly, many scientists believe that statistical significance measures oomph. If an answer meets the 95 percent confidence criteria, it must be *important*; if it doesn't, it isn't.

Brrringgg! *Wrong!*

A well-known refutation of the notion that statistical significance tells you about oomph came in the study that established the lifesaving effect of aspirin in men who had already had a heart attack. Researchers stopped the experiment before their numbers reached conventional levels of merely statistical significance because the effect of a half an aspirin a day was so obvious that they considered it unethical to go on giving placebos. *New Yorker* cartoon: drawing of a tombstone with the inscription, "John Jones, Member, Placebo Group."

Is the confusion of substantive with statistical significance Laplace's fault? No. He was right about comets because the relevant scale for measuring the oomph in orbits was obvious. But the scale for measuring the effects of aspirin or of changes in the minimum wage is not so obvious: you may get statistically impeccable answers that make little difference to anyone or "insignificant" one's that are absolutely crucial. For example, if astronomers calculated that a certain asteroid were likely to hit the earth 10 years from now and exterminate all life, it would not matter if the sampling probabilities were such that the chance was remote. Even a remote chance of the end of the world is worth worrying about, spending a big share of earth's income to send a spaceship out to deflect it, say.

The confusion is evident now in the debate among economists about the minimum wage. David Card and Alan B. Krueger of Princeton University have used tests of statistical significance (and, more admirably, new data) to argue there is no convincing evidence that the minimum wage has a strong effect. Most other economists disagree, because of other evidence of long-standing and robustness (such as downward-sloping demand curves for labor). But because both sides are muddled about the difference between oomph and statistical significance the disagreement is not likely to get resolved in time to help Congress.

Economic physician, heal thyself. Get over the madness of statistical significance.

Rule 12
And Don't Be Silly about *A*-Prime, *C*-Prime "Proofs" in Economics, Either

The *A*-Prime/ *C*-Prime Theorem

My first attempt to make the point (Eastern Economic Journal [spring 1993]). The next year I published Knowledge and Persuasion in Economics, *chapters 9–13 of which give the rhetorical argument in full.*

I am pleased to announce a theorem about theorems that describes tolerably well how half of economics has developed since Samuelson began. It goes like this:

The *A*-Prime/*C*-Prime Theorem

For each and every set of assumptions *A* implying a conclusion *C*, there exists a set of alternative assumptions, *A′*, arbitrarily close to *A*, such that *A′* implies an alternative conclusion, *C′*, arbitrarily far from *C*.

Take free trade as an example. Suppose that the first set of assumptions, *A*, are competition, convexity, full employment, and so forth, which lead to the blackboard conclusion, *C*, that "the North American Free Trade Agreement is swell for the American economy." Imagine a paper drawing such a conclusion published at time *t* (sorry: I just can't express myself without mathematics). You know as well as I do what will happen before time *t* + *1*: a paper will be published showing that, on the contrary, if the assumptions are jiggered a bit, to *A′*, by introducing, say, a nonconvexity in the *i*th industry, then the old conclusion falls, and *C′* is erected in its stead: "the North American Free Trade Agreement is rotten for the American economy." If you don't like nonconvexity (which covers a lot of ground), try transaction costs or macroeconomic considerations or the dynamic specifications or failures of expectation.

Look at the figure presented here. It says that if you change the assumptions a little (the economic theorems in question *don't provide a standard for how little*) then the conclusions, if you're clever about it, can change as much as you want:

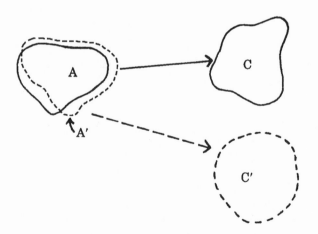

A small change in assumptions can always be found
that leads to a large change in conclusions.

Ask yourself whether the *A*-Prime/*C*-Prime Theorem doesn't pretty well describe half the contents of economics journals nowadays. (It described them in olden days, too, right back to Plato, but that's another story.) The figure of a half comes from Wassily Leontief's (1982) observation that half the contents of the leading economics journals around 1982 were purely theoretical, the same percentage as in sociology, and by contrast with the mere 10 percent in the leading journals of chemistry and physics. It's worse by now.

Take, for example, rational expectations. Professor L of Chicago proves on a blackboard that certain assumptions A lead to the conclusion C that the public can figure out what the government is up to, and so the government can't fool all of the people all of the time. A implies C. Some months later Professor F of Harvard proves that if you alter the assumptions A by what looks like a tiny bit, making them into A', the conclusion changes to C'. The efficacy of government policy, and the foolishness of the public, is gloriously reinstated. But the theorem can be applied as many times as the scholarly audience can stand it, and is. Professors X, Y, and Z now spring forward to prove other theorems about the formation of expectations and the efficacy of policy. Within a few years the air is thick with A', A'', A''' and their corresponding Cs.

Or take game theory "applied" to industrial organization and read Franklin Fisher's devastating summary in an article in the *Bell Journal* in 1989. Notice that even then game theory had 130 solution concepts and counting, A^{130}, and notice that finite games unravel and that infinite games have infinite numbers of solutions, C^{∞}. End of game theory. Or take, if your tastes run to necrophilia, abstract general equilibrium. Or macroeconomic theory. Or econometric theory. Or the theory of international trade. Or the burden of the debt. Or the revivals of growth theory innocent of economic history. Or the many misreadings of the Coase Theorem (someday the people writing on Coase might want to read a little Coase). Or this or that rediscovery of monopolistic competition (someday they might want to read a little Chamberlain). The *A*-Prime/*C*-Prime Theorem says that if these subjects stay on the blackboard, as they all do, then they are doomed to wander through A, A', A'', A''' without limit.

What's going on? Why do economists persist in believing, against their science, that intellectual free lunches are to be had daily on the blackboard? The answer I think is that economics has adopted the intellectual values of the math department instead of the physics department. (Again the love of Greek mathematics is nothing new: it too goes back to Plato.)

In other words, economics, surprisingly, is more mathematical than physics. I'm not saying that economists know more math than physicists do, which is false. The average physicist is a stunningly better applied mathematician than the average economist. I'm saying, rather, what's true, that economists have adopted the intellectual values of the math department. By contrast, the physicists, unlike mathematicians and economists, are not in love with blackboard proof.

The contrast comes out in the new Sante Fe Institute, founded by Kenneth Arrow and a famous physicist to help economics imitate physics. In 1989 *Science* described the physical scientists at the institute as "flabbergasted to discover how mathematically rigorous theoretical economists are. Physics is generally considered to be the most mathematical of all the sciences, but modern economics has it beat" (Pool 1989, 701). The point is that the physicists do not actually feel "beaten," since unlike economists, they do not regard mathematical rigor as something to be admired for itself. They have used the Schrödinger equation happily since 1926 without knowing whether it has solutions in general. They can't solve the three-body problem but can simulate the path of the moon to any required degree of approximation.

Economists assure each other that Science involves axiomatic proofs of theorems and then econometric tests of the implied correlations. But the economists are mistaken, as they could see if they looked outside the math department for their model of science. "It is to be admitted," wrote the philosopher of science Paul Feyerabend, "that some sciences going through a period of stagnation now present their results in axiomatic form, or try to reduce them to correlation hypotheses. This does not remove the stagnation, but makes the sciences more similar to what philosophers of science think science is" (1978, 205).

In truth the physicists could care less about mathematical proofs and very little about correlation hypotheses. Go over to the library some day and take down a copy of the *Physical Review* and look at it for a while. I guarantee you won't understand the physics at all and will have only a vague idea what the pages and pages of algebra are about. But you will see if you look for it that physicists *never* use proof of the math department, existence theorem sort and *never* ever use statistical significance. They seek oomph. They simulate, they calculate, they spend their time reading the physical equivalent of agricultural economics or economic history. Pure pencil-and-paper guys are common enough in physics departments, but they do not set its intellectual agenda, and even they are driven by the ethos of the field to offer in each paragraph a claim that this or that piece of mathematics will make it easier to calculate oomph. Our own Buz Brock found to his surprise that it is important for the economics reader . . . to realize that many natural scientists are not impressed by mathematical arguments showing that "anything can happen" in a system loosely disciplined by general axioms. Just showing the existence of logical possibilities is not enough for such skeptics. The parameters of the system needed to get the erratic behavior must conform to parameter values established by empirical studies or the behavior must actually be documented in nature. (1989 [1988], typescript p. 2)

Actually documented in nature: that's what interests scientists. Well, I'll be darned. Fancy that.

Ask any physicist of your acquaintance. She will tell you that existence theorems are of no interest to physicists. The crazy notion that one can establish "existence" *independent of how large in substance the effect is* is not one that physicists believe. The mathematicians have always found repulsive the physicists' lack of rigor (read: lack of interest in matters of mere existence or of axiomatization). Hans Lewy, a member with Richard Courant of the amazing group of physically interested mathematicians gathered around Hilbert at Göttingen in the 1920s, recalled:

> I was very much repelled by what the physicists [such as Heisenberg, Born, Pascual Jordan] were doing. . . . To my mathematical mind they were too sloppy and also their way of talking was so glib I had the impression—which was wrong, of course, as it turned out—that they were fourflushers. . . . They obviously had some physical intuition which I didn't have, but their mathematics was objectionable. (Qtd. in Reid 1976, 113)

Constance Reid notes that

> Courant's primary concern was *existence*. The significance of this concern on the part of mathematicians is sometimes questioned by even quite sophisticated physicists. They are inclined to feel that if a mathematical equation represents a physical situation [the standard of "representation" being quantitative, calibrated simulation, oomph], which quite obviously exists, the equation must of necessity have a solution. (1976, 95)

Well, fancy that: if a solar system or an economy seems to be pretty well following a rule of inverse square attraction or the picking up of profitable opportunities, then what matters is *how big* an effect of Jupiter on Mars is or *how big* an effect of taxation on investment is, not whether "a solution exists."

To the seminar question asked by an economist, "Where are your proofs?" the physicist replies, "You can whip up theorems, but I leave that to the mathematicians" (Pool 1989, 701). At the Sante Fe Institute one afternoon a problem came up in a seminar. The best physicist present solved the problem overnight with a calibrated computer simulation, approximately, while the best economist found overnight an analytic solution, exactly. Who is the more mathematical? And who the more scientific?

Economists arguing over the federal budget next year or the stability of capitalism forever should want to know *how big* a particular effect will be. Will the distribution of income be radically changed by the limiting of interest? Will free trade with Mexico raise American national income much? *Mathematics does not care about such questions of magnitude.* Disproving the Goldbach Conjecture, which is empirically true for every calculated case but is unproven in general, would take only one even number, N, that could not be expressed as the sum of two primes. Mathematics does not care if this N were the only such number: the Conjecture would be false. Period. By contrast, science always cares about magnitudes, not existence. For engineering purposes, the Goldbach Observation works fine up to immensely large numbers, *whether proven as a theorem for every conceivable number or not.*

So economics needs to imitate physics and stop imitating mathematics. Notice: I did not say "stop *using* mathematics." Please, please, listen here. It would be idiotic to complain about *using* mathematics. You might as well complain about using English or using diagrams. But the A-Prime/C-Prime Theorem proves (ha, ha) that we are overinvesting in math department questions of existence and underinvesting in physics department questions of magnitude. No one of sense is "against theory" or "against math." But almost all physicists, and some economists, are against the math department's ideas of how to work.

In Brief, It's Arrogant and Unscientific

Invited for the Neue Zürcher Zeitung *(Aug. 31–Sept. 1, 1991),*
printed in German and then reprinted in its English monthly.

Economists are certainly arrogant enough for the role of modern medicine men. The other experts by comparison seem timid. For a moderate
fee an economist will tell you with all the confidence of a witch doctor
that interest rates will rise 56 basis points next month or that dropping
agricultural subsidies will increase Swiss national income by 14.8 percent.

Observing such confidence, most people attribute it to ideology.
They suppose that the economists are merely writing down their politics
in numerical form. That's not so. Yet even economists with little apparent in the way of political preconceptions are arrogantly self-confident
about their beliefs. A physicist named Richard Palmer attended a conference with economists and told a reporter afterwards: "I used to think
physicists were the most arrogant people in the world. The economists
were, if anything, more arrogant."

What makes economists more arrogant than physicists is that they
are more mathematical than the physicists. More mathematical than the
physicists? How can that be? Surely the physicists, the princes of knowledge since the philologists gave up the throne, know more mathematics
than the economists. Walk the aisles of the university bookstore and
open some of the advanced undergraduate books in physics (or in the
much-despised civil engineering, for that matter). It makes the hair stand
on end. Bessel functions abound. Group theory is routine.

The proposition, however, is not that the economists *use* more
mathematics; it is that they are "more mathematical." In the economics
department the spirit of the mathematics department reigns. The spirit is
different over in the physics department. The late Richard Feynman, a
Nobel laureate in physics, introduced a few simple theorems in matrix

algebra into his first-year class at the California Institute of Technology with considerable embarrassment: "What is mathematics doing in a physics lecture? . . . Mathematicians are mainly interested in how various mathematical facts are demonstrated. . . . They are not so interested in the result of what they prove." Feynman's rhetorical question startles an economist. In advanced economics it would be, rather: "What *besides* mathematics should be in an economics lecture?" In physics the familiar spirit is Archimedes the experimenter. But in economics, as in mathematics, it is theorem-proving Euclid who paces the halls.

Economists think of themselves as the physicists of the social sciences. But they know nothing about how physics operates as a field. The economists, to put it another way, have adopted the intellectual values of the mathematics department—not the values of the departments of physics or electrical engineering or biochemistry they admire from afar. The situation is odd on its face. Philip Anderson, the distinguished physicist who helped bring the Sante Fe Institute together, explained the differences with "the differences in the amount of data available to the two fields" (701). This is silly. Economists are drenched in data, as hard as they want them to be.

In truth, economics in the universities has become a mathematical game. The science has been drained out of economics, replaced by an Intendo game of assumption making. It began in 1947, when Paul Samuelson, then a young professor at the department of economics at MIT, published his Harvard dissertation, modestly entitled *The Foundations of Economic Analysis*. It was a brilliant piece of French rationalism, promising to put economics on an axiomatic basis (well . . . actually his brother-in-law, Ken Arrow, who reads French with ease and had a degree in math, was even better at the ceremonies of axiomatization à la Bourbaki and set the standard, but anyway the combined effect of these two was enormous). Samuelson's book contained no facts about the economy: in the new program the facts were left to the econometricians, another set of mathematical folk, though more in tune with British empiricism than French rationalism.

Economists were dazzled by the promise of rationalism and empiricism harnessed. In that bright dawn it seemed that economics could become what it always had wanted to be, a social physics. Over the next 50 years Samuelson's dissertation was translated into first-year graduate programs across the United States, first in a book by Henderson and Quandt and more recently in another by Varian, killing off local traditions of market economics at the universities of Chicago, California at Los Angeles, Washington, and elsewhere.

It was not merely an American development. In fact in the style of many other antipragmatic movements (such as the Bauhaus in architecture and Mondrian-type abstraction in painting) the Europeans, especially Dutchmen, took a leading role in devising the new game, which was then re-exported to the world through America. The first winner of the Nobel Prize in Economics, the Dutchman Jan Tinbergen, was a pioneer of the econometric side of the program, and on the theoretical side another Dutchman, Tjalling Koopmans, in 1957, advocated separating theory from observation, "for the protection of both. [The program] recommends the postulational method as the principal instrument by which this separation is secured."

The news today: the program has failed miserably, and many economists are becoming aware that it has. Economics has learned practically nothing from the dual triumph of mathematical economics and econometrics, if "learning something" means learning about how actual economies behave. That is not to say that economics has not advanced. It has. We know more than we knew in 1947. But not because of the formal program launched by Paul Anthony Samuelson.

Or, to be completely fair to the program and the many excellent minds it has drained off from serious scientific work, we have learned a negative theorem: we have learned that one cannot solve great social questions standing at a blackboard. Over and over again since 1947 economists have on the contrary believed for a moment that this or that theorem would tell How Big in the world. It is Kant's synthetic a priori. It didn't work. When someone proved on a blackboard that expectations are "rational" and therefore central banks cannot steer the business cycle someone else proved a few months later that with a slightly different set of assumptions central banks *could* steer the business cycle. To speak mathematically, searching the hyperspace of possible assumptions proved to be a waste of time, except for showing that it was a waste of time. This is *not* to say that the idea of rational expectations is to be discarded. It *does* say that the only way it matters is a calibrated model in which questions of How Big can be posed. Existence theorems—those math department devices—are useless for such calibration, as physics has always known.

The same holds for standing at a computer, running econometric models, to maximize goodness of fit. Over and over again economists have learned that if Professor X could show with statistical "significance" that the money supply determined the interest rate, Professor Y could in a few months show the opposite with the same set of data. Using statistical significance has proven to be a waste of time, except for showing the limitations of using statistical significance. Again, the physicists already knew this. You will not find a single use of statistical significance in the *Physical Review*. Go ahead: look.

Well, so what? A group of economics professors have wasted their time of existence theorems since 1947. What of it?

The answer is that economists are crucial experts these days. The questions economists are asked are world-makingly important. No one doubts that the world would be better off if everyone achieved the income of once poverty-stricken Switzerland, say, or learned to innovate in the way of Americans. How to do it is a scientific question. Each dollar spent discovering the causes of modern economic growth or finding the cure to the business cycle or understanding the causes of monopoly or persuading governments to adopt free trade would mean more to humankind than a hundred dollars spent on space telescopes and particle accelerators. That economics has wandered so far from its high-return science is a practical disaster.

The best minds in economics have been diverted into an intellectual game, I say, with as much practical payoff as chess problems. (I think of the early career of my teacher in graduate school, Hendrick Houthakker, wasted on the last gasp of the silliness about whether ordinal or cardinal utility existed.) Instead of producing historical economists who know how banking came to Germany or why British economic growth slowed a century ago, the graduate schools in economics have been producing scientific illiterates. They have produced macroeconomists who have not read a page of John Maynard Keynes and policymakers who do not know how their portion of the economy came to its present state. Arjo Klamer and David Colander in their astounding book *The Making of an Economist* asked American graduate students whether having a thorough knowledge of the economy was important for academic success in economics. How many thought so, by contrast with the 60 percent for mathematics and "theory" conceived as existence theorems instead of calculable models testable in the world? Only 3.4 percent.

Many of the senior figures in economics have private doubts that they were right to follow the Samuelsonian program and are appalled by the current generation of graduate students (the graduate students themselves are appalled, as Klamer and Colander show). Few speak out, because they are still fighting the battle of their youth against the foolish opposition to any sort of mathematics. Most economists and I agree with the great economist Léon Walras, a century ago:

> As for those economists who do not know any mathematics, who do not even know what is meant by mathematics and yet have taken the stand that mathematics cannot possibly serve to elucidate economic principles, let them go their way repeating that "human liberty will *never* allow itself to be cast into equations" or that "mathematics ignores frictions which are *everything* in social science."

But economists know that a qualitative argument for something does not fix its quantity. We need some rain but not floods, sunshine but not the Sahara. A recent study by the American Economic Association has found that graduate schools are not teaching economics (Bob Lucas was on the committee and blocked any change). Most thoughtful economists think that the games with existence theorems and statistical significance have gone too far, absurdly too far. It's time to bring economic observation, economic history, economic literature, and the question "How Big Is Big?" back into the departments of economics.

Economists would be less arrogant and less dangerous as experts if they had to face up to the facts of the world. Perhaps they would become more modest, as modest even as the physicists of renown.

Quarreling with Ken Arrow about Existence Theorems

Eastern Economic Journal *(winter 1998).*

I've praised Kenneth Arrow here from time to time. But in the January 1998 meetings of the American Economic Association in Chicago, at which Ken for theory and Ed Leamer for econometrics and Barbara Bergmann in the chair, discussed my new book *The Vices of Economists; The Virtues of the Bourgeoisie* (University of Michigan and University of Amsterdam Presses, 1996), I did not.

Earlier columns here have given you the gist (which is a *poor* excuse for not buying the book, dears; I need the money and you need the amusement of seeing your colleagues go red when you use arguments out of it). It is: Economics is in serious trouble because of the three "vices" of statistical significance, blackboard economics, and social engineering. A bourgeois and antiaristocratic virtue, the virtues of bench-and-field scientists like Rosalind Franklin (Sayre 1975) and Edward Wilson (1996) or theorists with a serious interest in the world like Richard Feynman (1985), can bring economics back to its scientific senses.

At the Chicago meetings I focused on the first two vices—statistical significance and blackboard economics. Since Ed Leamer has been a leader against mindless use of statistical significance (1978, 1983) and Ken declared decades ago that its common use is indefensible (1959) and Barbara has long and consistently advocated calibrated simulation as the scientific alternative (1990), I did not get any disagreement on point 1: Statistical significance is bankrupt; all the "findings" of the Age of Statistical Significance are erroneous and need to be redone; economists have thrown away gigabytes of scientific time better spent on finding out how big is big—observing and estimating and arguing rather than pseudo-testing by Student's-*t*. That's news: leaders of the economics profession think that the main empirical rhetoric in economics is nonsense.

Point 2, the futility of blackboard proofs of existence, evoked a lot more quarreling, predictably between Ken and me. Kenneth Arrow, with his sister's husband's brother Paul Samuelson, was the pioneer of blackboard economics and by 1950 had set the standard for chalk talk in the field. I was an eager student in the 1960s of such mysteries but eventually decided that they were not science. At Chicago that January in a big Hyatt ballroom filled with economists we quarreled. "Quarreling" is not necessarily a bad thing. C. S. Lewis pointed out once that "quarreling— as against mere angry abuse—means trying to show that the other man [or woman, if you please] is in the wrong. *And there would be no sense in trying to do that unless you and he had some sort of agreement as to what Right and Wrong are*" (1952 [1996], 18; italics added). Ken and I agree on the definition of scientific right and wrong. We agree that economics is an empirical science, not mainly philosophy. We agree that people like Rosalind Franklin and Edward Wilson and Richard Feynman are in this empirical sense scientists. They want to know about the world. As smart and admirable as the other kind of people may be—people like David Hilbert or Bertrand Russell or T. S. Eliot or for that matter C. S. Lewis when talking about theology rather than his scientific specialty of medieval literature—they are not worldly scientists.

So here's my side of the quarrel, trying earnestly to show that the defenders of the blackboard with its axiom and existence proof are in the wrong *by their own standards of what constitutes empirical science.*

We all agree that there are two things we need to do as scientists if we are going to find out the world. Thinking and watching. Theorizing and observing. Imagining and feeling. Speaking and listening. Models and history. Metaphors and stories. Projecting our ideas out onto the world and accepting with humility the facts in the world.

You can view these two if you want as yang and yin, the male and female principle. It is the case that men seem on average to be more comfortable with theoretical models, women with empirical observing. There's plenty of overlap, obviously, but an interestingly large difference in first moments. It's not necessarily a matter of comparative advantage. Contrary to the usual routine in (blackboard) economics, tastes after all do differ. The great biologist Barbara McClintock was no slouch at theoretical genetics such as it was in the 1940s but wanted also to acquire by observation, as she put it, "a feeling for the organism" (qtd. in Keller 1985). In his classic of self-serving autobiography, *The Double Helix,*

James Watson claimed about "Rosie" Franklin that "model-building did not appeal to her" (qtd. in Sayre 1975, 133). Well, yes and no. Rosalind Franklin had done brilliant model-building work on the chemistry of coal before she studied DNA. But, as Anne Sayre puts it in her reply to Watson: "Models are not built out of thin air. . . . If nothing is known about a substance, a model cannot be built at all" (134).

What is plain is that we need both, preferably in the same person, a sort of scientific androgyny. Economists are fond of defending the split of thinking and watching by appeal to specialization. Sure. I get it. I can even draw the diagram on the blackboard. But if you don't then *trade,* the economics is not being correctly appealed to, is it? Unless the thinking and the watching are brought together in a scientific argument, such as Wilson's sociobiology (to pick a controversial example) or Stephen Gould's and Richard Lewontin's punctuated equilibria or the Alvarezes meteor account of mass extinctions or Simon Kuznets's account of modern economic growth, nothing scientific happens. You get what professional historians sneer at as "antiquarian" writing, mere piling up of facts; or what professional physicists sneer at as "math-mongering," mere piling up of proofs. This is not controversial. Two centuries ago Immanuel Kant said that facts without concepts are blind and concepts without facts not much use either.

But you've got to do the real thing. You have to really be thinking—about the world. And you have to be really watching—the world. The trouble is that the two master techniques of modern economics, statistical significance and existence theorems, are not the real thing. They look like the real thing, really thinking about the world and really watching the world, but aren't. They've crowded out the real science.

The existence theorems which flood the journals—and by this I mean *any "demonstration" of the "existence" of an effect that does not ask How Big*—are not real science. The economists have adopted the intellectual values of the math department—not the values of the departments of physics or electrical engineering or biochemistry or for that matter history. Gerard Debreu, in his presidential address to the American Economic Association, notes that the mathematical economist "belongs to the group of applied mathematicians, whose values he espouses" (1991, 4). He speaks of "the values imprinted on an economist by his study of mathematics" (5). Debreu realizes that physicists do not share these values: unlike economics, "physics did not surrender to the embrace of mathematics and to its inherent compulsion toward mathematical rigor," but on the contrary occasionally was led "to violate knowingly the canons of mathematical deduction" (2). You're not kidding. Physicists use with abandon self-contradictory mathematics when it works as calibrated simulation, the first few terms of divergent infinite series, for example. But economists, says Debreu, do not have enough experimental data and therefore must rely on deductive methods. Considering, he claims, that economics is "denied a sufficiently secure experimental base . . . economic theory has had to adhere to the rules of logical discourse and must renounce the facility of internal inconsistency" (2). That is, we have to stay on the blackboard and be rigorous there by the standards of the math department dealing only with existence instead of magnitude, because we poor economists have so little information about the world. Would that we were physicists and had all those data! But sadly it is not to be, and we are condemned to the blackboard.

It needs to be said how mistaken this argument is. For one thing economists are drenched in data, as hard as may be, and recently even experimental data. Unless astrophysics and geology are to be accounted nonsciences because they do not experiment much, observational data are data, too, what we mainly can hope to have in paleontology or history or economics. The word *data* anyway shows the real problem: it means in Latin "things given," which suits the scholasticism of blackboard theory but not modern science. The better, less mathematical, and more scientific word would be *capta*, "things seized" in long, cold nights at the telescope or long, dry days in the archive. The data are not "given" to physics: they are seized, with great difficulty. An astrophysicist studying quasars stars has thin and puzzling data, but she examines them closely and lusts to have more. A theoretical economist, by contrast, fabricates some "stylized facts" out of his head and then devotes the rest of his career to axiom and proof.

And for another thing the claim that consistency mongering can lever us up into a scientific world is obviously wrong. Debreu has not thought much about *why* you would want to elevate consistency to the only intellectual value. He brings out the old chestnut that "a deductive structure that tolerates a contradiction does so under the penalty of being useless, since any statement can be derived flawlessly and immediately from that contradiction" (1991, 2). But if this is true, if a deductive structure that tolerates a contradiction is in practice useless, then calculus for the first two centuries of its existence was useless. And much of economics before G. Debreu and K. Arrow and their less gifted students came over from the math department to slay Inconsistency was, according to his criterion, similarly useless. The notion that "if not consistency, then chaos" is not admitted even by the best logicians. In the work of logicians such as Anderson and Belnap, reports James McCawley, "a contradiction causes only *some* hell to break loose" (1981, xi). Consistency is not to be spurned, but it is not the master virtue, except in the math department.

My remarks about his friend Debreu did not please Ken in Chicago. He tried to claim that I was thereby "against theory," a claim that makes it sound easy to deflect my case. My case is a narrow one—though not on that account unimportant, alas—against existence theorems, against qualitative theorems about possible effects that give no promise, ever, of calibrating to the world. I'm not of course against theory as a set of reflections on how we should measure the actual world, how it hangs together, how one part might be a function of another. On the contrary, I'm in favor of it, the more mathematical the better. Far from being against math, I like it in any theory, as Robert Fogel and other economic scientists do, because it gives you ways of simulating How Big: once you have a parameter symbolized you can think coherently about measuring it. A good example of what I mean is Solow's old paper in 1957 about technological change: no existence theorems; no Samuelsonian qualitative theorems; just a suggestion, theoretically motivated, for measuring A in $Q = AF(K,L)$. Another example is Arrow's own paper about learning by doing, which said, $A = f$(cumulated sum of past Q).

And, anyway, the case is not about the *existence* of existence theorem theory. The issue is quantitative, a matter of magnitude, the *amount* of it. I'm willing to let a rump of admittedly unemployable math department speculators devise as many qualitative theorems as they wish. I'm trying to be agreeable and don't want to fire anyone who is enjoying himself. I just want the bulk of the field to be doing actual science, real applied math, serious calibrated simulation. At present, despite appearances (namely, talk about "policy implications" of theory-without-magnitudes), it isn't.

So it just won't do, these qualitative defenses of endless A-prime, C-prime theorizing, one damned existence theorem after another. The crux of the matter between me and Ken is scientific, that is, quantitative. Even if you thought, as I do, that some very few economists should be assigned to exploring the nonquantitative connections between assumptions A and conclusions C, the percentage of academic economists who now spend their days on such stuff—in the "best" departments on the order of half of the person hours (the rest of their time is spent on statistical significance)—is bizarre. Ken tried to argue that mathematical economists are a beleaguered minority, which I hope is correct. Want a job? Flee formal theory. For the future of our science I hope he is right. But the trouble is that, meanwhile, the *A*-primers have persuaded everyone to do their same job, spending all day on qualitative logic when what matters for science is quantitative logic.

That was our quarrel: the quantitative question of how much time economic scientists should spend on quantitative questions of How Big. Ken and I differ sharply on this. Ken wants *more A*-prime, *C*-prime theorizing in the absence of quantitative discipline (Student's-*t* is *not* a "discipline" even on his own account), the usual exploration of assumptions, lowbrow or highbrow, diagrams or fixed-point theorems, words or math, more jobs for "theorists." I want less. How much less? About a tenth of what we have.

And here's the odd part: Ken agrees with my definition of science. As I said, there would be no sense in quarreling unless he and I had some sort of agreement as to what Right and Wrong are. Why then doesn't he agree with my quantitative judgment, that we're spending too little time on quantitative work by a factor of 10? You'll have to ask him and the other economists who defend the unscientific status quo. He'll be polite and masterful as always. But as in the ballroom in Chicago, I think, he won't really know.

Rule 13
Take Rules 11 and 12 Entirely Seriously

Why Don't Economists Believe Empirical Findings?

A report on the outcome for economic science, Eastern Economic Journal *(summer 1994)*.

The Centre for Policy Research is a lively operation, founded in London in 1983 but involving economists from all over the world and especially Europe. It is a sort of European National Bureau of Economic Research, tending to Brookings Institution (which distributes its papers in the United States), describing itself as "pluralist and non-partisan, bringing economic research to bear on the analysis of medium- and long-run policy questions." Among its many virtues is that it takes international comparisons seriously, takes economic history seriously, and takes the facts seriously. So the center does serious science. It's not mainly about *A*-prime, *C*-prime existence theorems.

The center sponsors a lot of conferences of economists trying to work things out. During mid-March to early August 1994 alone it sponsored or cosponsored 21, 6 of them in that great center for talk, Brussels, two in London, and the rest scattered from Cambridge (Mass.) to Kiev. Out of the conferences come discussion papers and a fine *Bulletin* summarizing the conferences and the papers in English that any economist can grasp (write to the center at 25–28 Old Burlington Street, London, W1X 1LB, UK). So the center explains its scientific result clearly.

The *Bulletin* therefore is a good place to do a little experiment in how economists persuade. I read the winter 1993–94 issue with some care from cover to cover, 44 double-columned printed pages, asking myself how I as an economist reacted to the hundreds of arguments and findings reported there. I don't think my reactions are atypical. I've read a lot of applied economics in the past 30 years and probably read it no better or worse than the average economist. Being an economic historian, my interests in economics are perhaps broader than some. I was trained in econometrics well for someone of my generation, which means I'm an econometric idiot who doesn't know it. My first job as an economist was as a transportation economist, which means I know that engineers know more than economists do. Admittedly, my economic priors are those of a Chicago School economist (subspecies *Femina coasiana fogelfania*). But everyone has priors, and in my experience it's wrong to believe that those of Chicago are especially tight. People say it, I know, since Mel Reder first articulated the charge, but they're wrong about everyone except George Stigler and are often speaking from a tighter if politically middle-of-the-road dogmatism of their own. In short, as a sample of $N = 1$, I'm not hopelessly biased.

The *Bulletin* reports on good stuff, all of it at least trying to be relevant to the actual economic world. I marked with a plus sign the findings that were at first blush scientifically believable and surprising and put a zero beside those that were believable but unsurprising. In other words, when I felt myself learning something new about the world economy or about the logic of economics (note: existence theorems have nothing to do with this, though math sometimes does), I marked it with a plus. In 44 tightly packed pages there were 32 pluses. When Angus Maddison said that the high growth rates of the postwar period probably have a lot to do with the chaos before and during the war, it got a plus, partly because I know Angus and his seriousness about economic science. When Robin Matthews said that measuring hours of work outside of the manufacturing industry is hard, I learned something, partly for the same "ethical" (that is, characterological) reason as for Angus. When Richard Baldwin said that in the United States labor is mobile and in Europe capital is, I could see something I hadn't noticed before. When Gianni Toniolo and Konosuke Odaka said that beginning levels of economic growth were higher in Sweden and in Japan in the eighteenth century than has been realized, I sat up and listened. When Mathias Dewatripont said that a corporate culture was like infinite-lived game players, I saw something new (repeat: existence theorems of the Math Department sort have nothing whatever to do with the persuasiveness of this mathematical and metaphorical point; the "rigor" of the theorems is entirely meaningless as science). The pluses were what is called in physical science the "Aha!" effect. I could see my mind changing a little, learning more about the economic world. Mainly, they came from what statisticians call "interocular trauma," a result that hits you right between the eyes.

But what surprised me is how uncommon the experience was and how often I doubted what my fellow economic scientists were earnestly telling me. The result of reading 44 pages summarizing hundreds of scientific results from the front line of applied economics was mainly that I believed surprisingly little of it. The minuses and zeroes far outnumbered the pluses. Sometimes a minus seemed intellectually crude, ignorant about the history of the discipline, such as the assertion that "the Solow model" (of economic growth) was the same thing as "growth accounting," which it is not. Or: "the academic literatures on 'new growth' and economic geography have produced a variety of new theoretical and empirical insights" (on the contrary, they have reinvented the wheels of Smith and Marshall and the economic historians). You don't believe a writer who doesn't know what she is talking about.

Sometimes a minus contradicted itself, leading to indifference. Margaret Thatcher's reforms are said in successive sentences to have worked and to have not worked in raising British performance. Or on one page John Kendrick said that OECD countries converged after World War II, and on the next page Bart van Ark said they did not. A brief summary, of course, can hardly do justice to a putative demonstration that the share of tradables in Swedish national income has fallen, but on it's face it's hard to believe, and I for one don't. No one really believes a scientific assertion in economics based on statistical significance, and the *Bulletin* contains quite a few (fewer than I had anticipated, though: I see that my prediction that calibrated simulation would become the dominate rhetoric in economics is coming true). I therefore am not being weird when I disbelieve the statistically significant finding that knowledge services (for example, computer consultations) don't affect manufacturing productivity. Nor does anyone in economics believe most of the arguments based on blackboard proofs of existence, which even in such applied circles are embarrassingly common, such as Paul Krugman's blackboard proof that growth in places like Mexico City is a matter of complexity theory and nonlinear dynamics. Richard Baldwin and Jürgen von Hagen remarked of this one that "empirical . . . applications of complexity will pose major challenges." That puts it mildly.

I think you would have the same reaction. In fact, I think you have it daily when you read the journals or listen to a colleague's talk or browse through the conference volumes produced by the Centre or the Bureau or the Institution. Scientific results pour over you daily, but only a small percentage of them stick. Economists don't believe one another.

Now in a way this is not shocking. Most science has to be wrong or irrelevant, or else science would advance at lightening speed. It doesn't. The crystallographer and philosopher of science Michael Polanyi pointed out long ago that science supersedes itself, and therefore most of what even the best scientists believe will eventually prove to be mistaken. As John Maddox, the editor of *Nature,* put it recently, "Journal editors, if they are honest with themselves, will acknowledge that much, perhaps most, of what they publish will turn out to be incorrect."

But I think it's worse in economics than in what we English speakers call "science." And I know it's worse than in historical science. Historians don't believe everything they read in the library. But they expect, rightly, to be able to rely on sheer factual assertions by their colleagues and to have some confidence in their interpretations, if signs of haste or of party passion are absent. (You can work out the signaling equilibrium here and make a pretty accurate prediction about what the profession of history is like.)

I would claim that in economics we have nothing like this degree of scientific agreement. To repeat, I don't believe it's merely a matter of my personal priors crashing up against the facts. You could put a minus sign in front of my priors and come to similar results. Most of the *Bulletin,* and most allegedly empirical research in economics, is unbelievable or uninteresting or both. It doesn't get down to the phenomena. It's satisfied to be publishable or clever, by the sad standards of statistical significance or A-prime, C-prime proofs of existence. It's unbelievable, unless (because deans don't do their jobs) you have to believe temporarily to get tenure.

Beyond the catastrophic technical failures to justify Student's-t or "there exists for every epsilon greater than zero" as methods of economic science, I reckon we are seeing here an ethical failure. Economists when they write are tendentious. Good word, that: it means what we statistical sophisticates understand by "strong priors." Because they know always already (a useful phrase from German philosophy, that), they are not curious about the world. Contrast the books in history or biology or astronomy. The results come thick and fast and surprising. I read a book a while ago by E. C. Pielou called *After the Ice Age: The Return of Life to Glaciated North America,* and it was a page-turner, though it concerned three-spined sticklebacks and the East Coast refugia. Like economics, evolutionary biology and geology use stories constrained by simple principles of maximization. Why don't economists therefore write books as gripping as Adrian Desmond's *The Hot-Blooded Dinosaurs?* I have a British acquaintance, Michael Summerfield, who is a geomorphologist (we hiked up a mountain in Italy together, and I tell you that a geomorphologist is the ideal guide for such an expedition). He wrote a textbook, *Global Geomorphology* (1991), 537 big pages in double columns filled with fact and argument about the landscape, without a dull paragraph. Why? Because it's all about the world, and it's all documented and believable. It's motivated by curiosity (which is why a lot of economic history or legal economics is better economic science than most economics).

Other fields have the same problem. I suspect that physics, for all its prestige, has something like the same oversupply of dull or clever unbelievabilities. Anthropologists, who on the whole fear and loath economics and therefore never bother to learn any, seem at first more curious. But read anthropology that takes as the last word on What Happened under Capitalism the journalistic book by Karl Polanyi in 1944 (Karl was Michael's less smart brother), and you'll find that they too are reading the world as they want it to read, tendentiously and therefore unbelievably.

Economists in other words are not curious enough to get their own data, talk to the economic actors, get right down into what is certainly the most interesting set of events in social life, the economy. They already know. How? This diagram on a blackboard. This clause in the platform of the Democratic Party. What economist do you know who has changed her mind? Bob Fogel has, four times. I have three times. Both are well above the median and modal number of times for academics, which is zero. But it's not a record that either of us can be proud of, considering how hard it is to know anything about the world for sure.

I think we should be worried that so much of economics is unbelievable tendentiousness. I think—don't you?—that economics ought to start getting serious about learning the economy. If even the Centre for Policy Studies and the NBER are going in circles, we've got a scientific problem.

Ask What the Boys in the Sandbox Will Have

A later summary attempt, in the (London) Times Higher Education Supplement *(1996). It is the introduction to* The Vices of Economists *(1996). The mild feminism in the piece enraged some male readers, such as Douglass North.*

Economics as a field of study has a problem nowadays. The problem is that its methods are wrong and produce wrong results. The methods claim to implement Francis Bacon's new science of 1620, in which "the mind itself is from the very outset not left to take its own course, but guided at every step, and the business be done as if by machinery." It hasn't worked.

The three methods that dominate modern, mainstream, "neoclassical" economics were invented by three men of the 1940s, the Americans Lawrence Klein and Paul Samuelson and the Dutchman Jan Tinbergen. They are,

- The Kleinian notion that "statistical significance," using the phrase in its technical sense, is the same as scientific significance.
- The Samuelsonian notion that blackboard "proofs of existence" are scientific.
- And, most important for practical affairs, and justifying the other two, the Tinbergean notion that these first and second pieces of pseudoscience—statistical significance and blackboard proofs—can be applied to the making of economic policy, in a sort of social engineering.

Klein, Samuelson, and Tinbergen, these three. But the greatest is Tinbergen. Statistical significance, blackboard economics, and social engineering, these three. But the greatest is social engineering.

I do not sneer. The three men were geniuses, honored with the Nobel Memorial Prize in Economic Science in the twelfth, the second, and the very first years in which it was awarded. They are connected in the history of economics during the 1940s. Klein was then Samuelson's Ph. D. student. Tinbergen inspired the approach that Klein took to statistical fitting of macroeconomic models, a program, Klein relates, that Samuelson himself encouraged.

It's wonderful stuff. I was dazzled when I first came upon it in graduate school in the 1960s. But in the hands of some of their less sophisticated enthusiasts, such as I was for so long, the brilliant ideas of the 1940s have ended as boys' games in a sandbox. The boys (women are not so interested in the game) are the intellectual sons or grandsons or even now great-grandsons of Klein, Samuelson, and Tinbergen. By now the sandcastles are very tall, and many careers have been spent building them, though strictly within the sandbox. The games are a sad parody of the science of Smith, Mill, Keynes, or even of Klein, Samuelson, and Tinbergen.

No economist who understands statistical theory believes that a narrow "statistical" significance is the same thing as quantitative, scientific significance. Likewise, no economist acquainted with other sciences believes that searching through all conceivable axioms is science. And no economist who has paid attention to the revolution in thinking about expectations—summarizable in the American Question: "If you're so smart, why aren't you rich?"—believes it is possible to predict profitably in aid of social engineering. Yet the three self-contradictory attempts to mechanize economics have come to dominate the output of the field. Half the high-science articles in economics mistake statistical for actual significance, and the other half ring the changes on the infinitude of axioms undisciplined by fact. The low-science articles consist of using these two sandbox games to recommend steering the economy this way or that. It's a scandal.

And sad. The sadness is that the economists, mainly men, are confident that their mechanical methods are correct and produce correct results. The men stride about offering advice to governments and criticisms of each other's work as though they were doing real science. They are so happy and so proud of their masculine achievements. Their business suits are impressive, their reports fluent, their numbers weighty. Lord, Lord, one would like them to be right! They are intelligent and hardworking. They have followed the rules for machine minding produced by the best men among them. They are of goodwill and have good minds. They do not deserve to end up with a science lacking scientific findings. No one with an ounce of human pity would be happy that such a good group of men are so wrong.

The scene is like an aunt watching her three-year-old nephew and his friends playing in a sandbox. They are so earnest in their play, so full of life and confidence, so sure that what they are playing is reality. The aunt would have to be a monster to be happy they are wrong. She indulges them and tells them all is well. Yes, David, you are building a great fort in the sand. My, how wonderful. Yes, Gerard my dearest, yes.

It is the essential sadness of boys' games. Unlike the games of girls, which so often in their practice have a human point of making solidarity, the boys' games in the sandbox are autistic and pointless. The sad, unspeakably sad, fact about modern economics is that much of what it claims to have accomplished since 1945 is a boys' game in a sandbox.

A surprising feature of this sad fact is that it is easy to show from within economics. What's wrong with the Three Methods is not hard to understand. The criticisms are not original with me. And they are not controversial among economists. Well, that last is not quite right. It *is* controversial to conclude as one must that nothing can be salvaged from the three wrong methods. Most of economics since World War II has to be done over again. Literally, most of the allegedly "scientific" findings of economics have to be redone with another method before anyone should believe them. That's *very* controversial, and me saying it in so many words will drive up the blood pressure of most economists. You can see why a man would get agitated by some woman claiming that his life's work has been pointless.

But if you sit down with an economist in his study and talk quietly about the three mistaken methods he'll come to agree to each one, if you speak softly and reasonably. (He'll agree, I should say, unless he realizes what the consequence is going to be and wants to save his job; but I can't imagine anyone being so craven and unscientific.)

I sincerely do not want to infuriate my colleagues in economics, mainly because I want them to listen, really listen, for their own good, to what Aunt Deirdre is saying. But I want to be clear to everyone, including noneconomists. So I'll say it again in stark and, I am afraid, infuriating form. No economist can answer the three criticisms. That is not because I am especially clever or the criticisms especially subtle. The economists already know them and know they are correct. They only have to look candidly at what they are doing to see it for what it is, a sandbox game.

There's a woman's point here. What grates on women is male pomposity. I was talking in Holland with some other women economists, and we were trying to think how we could bring economics back to the world. Someone came up with the idea of womanly sarcasm. It always terrifies the men, this laughter of women. If you could get a critical mass of women in the seminars—three times the current number, say—we could in short order shame the men into a less pompous attitude toward their intellectual games. The man presenting the latest misuse of statistical significance or the latest set of axioms or the latest "policy implication" from a blackboard would get the embarrassing praise an aunt showers on her three-year-old nephew: "Oh, Paul, what a *wonderful* sandcastle you have. It's *so* much better than anyone else's!" I am not going to use such womanly sarcasm on economics. But, Lord, it would be easy.

The sadness is deepened by a lost opportunity for actual science. Economics really is the queen of the social sciences. It is an amazing and wonderful set of intellectual tools, the study of prudence. Any economist can give hundreds of examples of its fruitfulness. I myself once wrote a book called *The Applied Theory of Price* that does so, and I and other economic historians have shown how prudence works as a way of telling history. You can see how wonderful economics is by the worshipful way that other scientists who study politics or sociology or law approach it. Economics has had a great influence in these other fields during the very period that it went into the sandbox. Law schools now hire economists; departments of politics, especially in the United States, have transformed themselves into imitations of economics departments; sociologists are properly impressed by rational choice models; philosophers use them to solve age-old questions of justice. John Rawls, Robert Bates, Richard Posner, Robert Putnam, Robert Nozick, Jon Elster are not fools. Economics *is* impressive. It really is.

In other words, I'm not trying to tear down the field. I do not want anyone to conclude, "Well, thank God I don't need to learn any economics, if it's such a great mess!" A student of society who took that view would be making a mistake. Prudence is too important a motive for human behavior for the science of prudence to be simply ignored, as most intellectuals have ignored it since the late nineteenth century. And capitalism is too successful an economic system to leave its analysis in the hands of noneconomists. I love economics and sincerely admire its intellectual traditions. I do not want merely to end the conversation.

On the contrary, I am trying like a concerned aunt to correct a nephew with great potential who has fallen recently into bad habits. She indulges his fantasies in the sandbox at age 3, but at age 13 or 30 he's got to get over them if he's going to have a worthwhile life. If she loves him for his own sake, she wants passionately for him to grow up. If I thought that economics was a silly subject or that markets and capitalism were evil or that economists were stupid, even as an aunt I might not bother.

So I don't want you noneconomists to be happy that this strange and arrogant field called economics is not perfect. "Not perfect" is an understatement if the three methods are as wrong as I say they are, which I'm afraid they are. Most of the allegedly scientific "output" of economics, most of what appears in the scientific journals these days, is not just trivial—after all, most normal science is trivial, or else science would advance by Newtonian or Einsteinian leaps every day. It is wrong. The findings, assurances, recommendations: wrong.

That's surprising: a scientific field can be shown to be wrong from arguments everyone in the field would agree to. And yet the solution is obvious. An economics that got out of the sandbox would look seriously at magnitudes, would theorize sparingly, and would recommend policies cautiously. It would resemble geology or history or other real sciences. Or an economics with three times more women than it now has.

Cassandra's Open Letter to Her Economist Colleagues

Cassandra, you know, was the most beautiful of the daughters of Priam, king of Troy. The god Apollo fell for her and made her a prophetess. In exchange he wanted sexual favors, which she refused to give (we needed laws about sexual harassment in 1250 B.C. as much as we do now). So he cursed her, in a most peculiar way. He had already given her the gift of prophecy, to know the future of the interest rate, say, or of the S&P 500, or to know what was going to happen if the Trojans brought that big wooden horse into the city. The curse? That although she would continue to be correct in her prophesies no one would believe her.

Cassandra [to Trojan guys proposing to bring the horse in]: You dopes! The horse is filled with Greek soldiers. If you bring it in Troy is lost!

Trojan Guy: Uh, yeah. I see what you mean, Cassie. Good Point. Enemy soldiers. Inside. Our city lost. Thanks very much for your prophecy. Really. Great contribution. [Turning away.] Well, come on, guys, let's bring this sucker in!

I have to admit, guys, that I feel like Cassandra. I tell you plainly that existence theorems and statistical significance are useless for a quantitative science like economics. I give you reasoning and evidence that none of you can answer, even the best of you—I mean Nobel laureates; I mean Ken Arrow, Bob Solow, Gerard Debreu, Doug North; name your laureate. When you try to answer my (blindingly obvious and therefore rigorously true) points you just make fools of yourselves, showing that you haven't thought through the place of existence theorems or of statistical significance in a real science. I invite you to look at a copy of the *Physi-*

cal Review (version C, say, the one about nuclear physics, the issue of November 1990, just as an example) and confirm that its 2,263 pages contain not a single use of existence theorems or of statistical significance, though every page has mind-stunningly difficult mathematics, and data or simulations actually or hypothetically measuring the oomph of the effect the math has isolated. I explain patiently to you that real sciences like physics care only about How Big (actually or hypothetically) and not at all about "existence," whether in the mathematical or the (allegedly) statistical sense. I ask you to consider any other science you care to— geology, say, or evolutionary biology or social history—and notice that all of them spend all their effort on questions of How Big, which never can be settled by an existence theorem or by an unadorned test of statistical significance.

I take Gerard Debreu's feeble defense of existence theorems to pieces at length (1994, esp. chap. 10 and 11); I debate publicly with Ken Arrow and he loses (1998a); I utterly demolish significance-without-loss-functions, citing all the best authorities in theoretical statistics (1985; 1998b, [1985]); I put the two points together in a semi-popular form that anyone can understand (1995a, 1995b, 1997). Steve Ziliak and I show you empirically that you in fact use statistical significance, for no scientific gain, in most of your empirical papers (1996). I guess it's obvious that you use existence theorems in most of your theoretical papers for no scientific gain, although I note a promising trend in the papers during the 1990s: having proven existence, pointlessly, the papers often then show that the effect has oomph, matters quantitatively, by simulation. But I've gotten merely strange looks when I suggest to the theorist that she dispense with the useless, math department existence theorems and allocate her time to actual scientific work on the simulatable results.

I get plainer and plainer about these two points, and say them to you every chance I get, because after all if I'm right then most of what passes for science in economics is simply a waste of time—which is an urgently important fact about our science, if true. "Guys," I say, "You bring either of those two horses into the city of economics and the city will be ruined. Leave them alone. Get back to using mathematics and statistics for real measurements."

The curse? No one believes me. When I chose my new name a few years ago I guess it would have been prescient to choose Cassandra. "Yeah, I see what you mean. Statistical significance and existence theorems are useless for science. Uh-huh. Yup. Wow, you sure are a good writer! Iowa, eh? Hey, how about them Hawks! (Turns back to 'work.')

OK, guys, bring in the two wooden horses!" Poor Cassandra. No one believes her. Well, not quite no one. I get letters of support from a few graduate students and professors, for which thanks. They sound furtive, like people in a police state whispering their politics. Arthur Goldberger has spoken out, devoting a page in his book on econometrics to McCloskey's Criticism (1991, 240–41). Thank you, Arthur; I wish your econometrician colleagues would teach the point. (It would be bitchy of me to note that Arthur's page is one out of hundreds, the other hundreds being devoted to showing how to misuse statistical significance; so I won't compare Arthur's lucid act to including a long page on safe sex in the *Kama Sutra*.) I hear news of people saying, "Hmm. She's right." Thank you, thank you, on behalf of our amazingly misled science, which is not going to make progress in understanding the world until it gets over the strange conviction that blackboard existence theorems and tables of Student's-*t* can in themselves test our scientific hypotheses.

I have mixed feeling about the experience. Part of me says, "Grow up, Deirdre. Of course Normal Science resists listening to critics: what do you expect?" After all, Deirdre knows that science is a matter of rhetoric. Science is not a matter of just laying down your cards of reasoning and evidence and then winning the rubber, as people who haven't followed science studies since Thomas Kuhn think. Science is persuasion, a matter of wordcraft. The rhetorical theory of science says that every scientific advance, even in method, is a matter of persuasion. Science is rhetoric, persuasion, all the way down. It must be so if it is going to be a science in a free society. (Another, pure-prudence theory of science, popular among economists, would say that scientists are Max U-ers, and will therefore of course do any silly but profitable thing as long as journal editors let them. Don't I believe in economics? [Answer: no, not as an ethical guide.]) So if Larry Summers and Jim Buchanan and Franklin Fisher and Roger Back-house and Ed Leamer and Wassily Leontief and Tom Mayer and Mark Blaug and I can't persuade, well, that's life, Toots.

And yet, even though I know that science is rhetorical and though I have been saying it even longer than I have been saying that existence theorems are pointless and that statistical significance without a loss function is silly, you can see I am indignant. Why? People get indignant when they feel some ethical norm is being violated. Persuasion in science is at bottom an ethical matter. One should be ethical in science, right? That doesn't mean, "Shut up and go along with the way we do things regardless of how indefensible it is," although I realize that my violation of this Shut-Up norm of normal science is what makes people angry at me. It's why I've stopped attending most seminars in economics; I make people so angry by suggesting that we not use the nonsense procedures in modern economics and that we instead use the theory and econometrics for simulations of How Big that it's only polite to absent myself. I don't want to hurt my colleagues, whom I love, and it hurts them to hear my two criticisms, which they don't understand.

Ethics in science means—doesn't it?—something like the opposite of the Shut-Up norm, Max-U, do-anything-the editor-will-allow, go-along-to-get-along. It means looking seriously at serious criticism, and if you can't rebut it, accepting it and changing your practice to suit. In the end the reaction to the Lucas Critique, for example, was to agree with it and change practice. (But I have in mind the example of the Coase Critique, too, which at one level is the same as my existence-theorem criticism. The Coase Critique has not been understood by most economists [McCloskey 1998c]. So they haven't agreed with it and have not changed their practice of blackboard economics.)

I think the reaction of most (I mean 95 percent) economists to my two very simple points has been in this sense "unethical." It's been the Shut-Up reaction. That means you, I'm afraid, dear. At any rate the odds are good, adopting a 5 percent level of significance.

Try to forget that I am a mere economic historian or a mathematical novice or a statistical idiot or a gender crosser or an Iowan or a Chicago-School economist or an irritating woman in seminars or whatever else about me you think disqualifies me from observing that the two emperors of modern economics, Existence and Significance, are naked. Try to act like an adult in science and respond to the actual case being made instead of seeking refuge in resentment about its tone or venue or whatever other piece of "mere" rhetoric you don't like.

I make a lot of jokes but actually I'm a pretty serious person, as you can see by having a look at my scientific work in economic history, or for that matter in economic rhetoric. So, a serious person makes two devastating, internal criticisms of the way modern economics has run itself since World War II, yet no one listens. (The criticisms are "internal" because they are not criticisms of the sort, "Gosh, you economists depend on Max U when everyone knows that people have other motives" or "I wish you would pay more attention to class and gender" or "I hate math: why do you do so much of it?" Mine are criticisms that bracket off the substantive criticisms, good or bad, that come from outside the mainstream of economics. My two criticisms by contrast come from within the very scientific program they criticize, namely the noble ambition of

Samuelson, Arrow, Klein, Tinbergen, and others of the 1940s to make economics into a real science like physics or history. That's why the criticisms are "internal": Cassandra came from within Troy and was making an argument that Trojans would have agreed with if not under Apollo's spell.)

What should one—I mean you, dear reader—do when hearing my criticisms? It seems to me that one should, ethically, either:

1. Come up with counterarguments that are at least as serious in their practical and philosophical reasoning as the Cassandra Critiques. This requires understanding them. It won't do to "reply" by saying things like "But we must do theory" (of course we must, you silly man, but existence theorems are not theories in any science) or "You are against statistics" (that's ridiculous; I'm against misuses of statistics that every theoretical statistician since Neyman and Pearson has been against, too).

Or one should:

2. Agree with Cassandra and stop offering existence theorems and statistical significance as "science."

What is not open to a serious scientist is to:

3. Skulk around looking for opportunities to put arrows into Cassandra's back.

Unhappily, that third, unethical option is what most of my colleagues, near and far, have done. They won't face my arguments; they won't listen; they don't understand. They are so angry.

My thesis supervisor, Alexander Gerschenkron, wrote a devastating review of a translation from Russian of a book in economics, attacking in detail the translator's apparently feeble command of the Russian language. Later at a conference the translator had the temerity to approach Gerschenkron and say amiably, "I want you to know, Professor Gerschenkron, that I'm not angry about your review." Gerschenkron turned on him: "Angry? Angry? Why should you be angry? Ashamed, yes. Angry, no."

If you haven't got serious answers to my two internal criticisms of modern economics you shouldn't be angry. You should be ashamed. (The same holds for the external criticisms, by the way. If you haven't got an answer to the Marxist's criticism that class interest governs the economy or the Austrian's that entrepreneurial creativity does or the feminist economist's that gender does, you should be ashamed. What kind of scientist are you? These are serious, intelligent people; what's wrong with you that you haven't got the wits or will to reply? But you should be *really* ashamed if you can't even make your *own* program cohere.)

It's time to get serious about scientific rhetoric, about how economists ought to persuade. If you disagree with my two criticisms I think you have a responsibility as a serious scientist to answer them.

Let me restate them (my fingers are wearing out doing so over the years, but I've observed that people need them to be stated over and over and over again before their truth and importance sinks in; and there's no reason that everyone should be conversant with my works; so here's the short version):

1. A theorem that asserts the existence of an effect is useless for science. What makes the mathematical assertion of the effect useful for science is accompanying reasoning (mathematical, for example, or observational or experimental) that can lead to a way of judging How Big the effect is.

For example, general equilibrium theory is in this sense useless. And (just in case you thought I would stop with an old-fashioned example that by now pretty much everyone in economics agrees is useless) so is most of game theory. An example of useful and mathematical theory is Solow's way of splitting increases in output per labor input into increases in capital per man and change in a neutral factor, A, called "technical change," stuck in front of the production function. Another is supply and demand curves, with functional forms and guesses as to the parameters. So for that matter are general equilibrium simulation models. All these ask How Big. Useful theory shows the way to answering How Big.

2. No test of significance that does not examine the loss function is useful as science. What make tests of significance useful are situations in which the sampling error is the scientific issue (which it commonly is not, by the way) and in which the costs of accepting or rejecting the hypothesis are explicit and sensible.

Thus unit root tests that rely on statistical significance are not science. Neither are tests of the efficiency of financial markets that rely on statistical instead of financial significance. Though to a child they look like science, with all that really hard math, no science is being done in these and 96 percent of the best empirical economics (McCloskey and Ziliak 1996; the 96 percent is the figure for the 1980s in the *American Economic Review*; we are retesting on the 1990s). Scientifically meaningful statistical procedures are answers to the question How Big.

Anyone who has a serious answer to either of my points is invited to submit them to the *Eastern Economic Journal*. Or to any other journal. Make your scientific fortune. Ingratiate yourself with the powers that be. Get a job at Princeton. Show that the way economics is presently being done is scientifically defensible. If you can.

But please, no skulking. No cowardice. No Shut-Up ethics. No saying in seminars, "You can't raise that point because it's too fundamental." Send me a copy of your answer, and be ready for me to point out that you are still not bothering to look into how actual sciences operate. And if you're going to shoot arrows at me have the courage to shoot them with me facing you, my own little bow in hand.

Hmm. Diana, the huntress: that would have been a good name, too.

A Brief List of Devastating Internal Criticisms of Modern Economics
That Have Not Been Answered

Arrow, Kenneth. 1959. "Decision Theory and the Choice of a Level of Significance for the t-Test." In *Contributions to Probability and Statistics: Essays in Honor of Harold Hotelling,* edited by I. Olkin and others. Stanford: Stanford University Press.

Backhouse, Roger E. 1997. *Truth and Progress in Economic Knowledge.* Cheltenham: Elgar.

Blaug, Mark. 1992. *The Methodology of Economics.* 2d ed. Cambridge: Cambridge University Press.

Buchanan, James. 1964 (1979). "What Should Economists Do?" *Southern Economic Journal* 30 (January), 213–22. Reprinted in *What Should Economists Do?* by J. Buchanan. Indianapolis: Liberty Press.

Dalen, Harry P. van, and Arjo Klamer. 1997. "Blood is Thicker than Water." Research Centre for Economic Policy, Erasmus University of Rotterdam, Research Memorandum 9704.

Dalen, Harry van, and Arjo Klamer. 1996. *Telgen van Tinbergen: Het Verhaal van de Nederlandse Economen.* Amsterdam: Balans.

Fisher, Franklin. 1989. "Games Economists Play: A Non-Cooperative View." *RAND Journal of Economics* 20 (spring): 113–24.

Gibbard, Allan, and Hal R. Varian. 1979. "Economic Models." *Journal of Philosophy* 75: 664–77.

Goldberger, Arthur. 1991. *A Course in Econometrics.* Cambridge: Harvard University Press, 240–41.

Heilbroner, Robert, and William Milberg. 1995. *The Crisis of Vision in Modern Economic Thought.* Cambridge: Cambridge University Press.

Keuzenkamp, Terence W., and Jan R. Magnus. 1995. "On Tests and Significance in Econometrics." *Journal of Econometrics:* 5–24.

Klamer, Arjo, and David Colander. 1990. *The Making of an Economist.* Boulder: Westview.

Leamer, Edward. 1983. "Let's Take the Con Out of Econometrics." *American Economic Review* 73 (March): 31–43.

Leamer, Edward. 1978. *Specification Searches.* New York: Wiley.

Leontief, Wassily. 1982. "Letter: Academic Economics." *Science* 217: 104, 107.

Mayer, Thomas. 1993. *Truth versus Precision in Economics.* Cheltenham: Elgar.

McCloskey, Deirdre. 1985. "The Loss Function Has Been Mislaid: The Rhetoric of Significance Tests." *American Economic Review* 75 (May): 201–5.

———. 1991. "Economic Science: A Search through the Hyperspace of Assumptions?" *Methodus* 3 (June): 6–16.

———. 1992. "The Bankruptcy of Statistical Significance." *Eastern Economic Journal* 18 (summer): 359–61.

———. 1994. *Knowledge and Persuasion in Economics.* Cambridge: Cambridge University Press, Chs. 10 and 11.

———. 1995a. "The Insignificance of Statistical Significance." *Scientific American* (April): 32–33.

———. 1995b. "Computation Outstrips Analysis." *Scientific American* (July): 26.

———. 1997. *The Vices of Economists; The Virtues of the Bourgeoisie.* Amsterdam: University of Amsterdam Press and Ann Arbor: University of Michigan Press.

———. 1998a. "Quarreling with Ken." *Eastern Economic Journal* 24 (winter): 111–15.

———. (1985) 1998b. *The Rhetoric of Economics.* 2d rev. ed. Madison: University of Wisconsin Press.

———. 1998c. "The So-Called Coase Theorem." *Eastern Economic Journal* 24 (summer): 367–71.

McCloskey, Deirdre, and Stephen Ziliak. 1996. "The Standard Error of Regression." *Journal of Economic Literature* 34 (March): 97–114.

Mehta, Judith. 1993. "Meaning in the Context of Bargaining Games—Narratives in Opposition." In *Economics and Language,* edited by Willie Henderson, Tony Dudley-Evans, and Roger Backhouse. London: Routledge.

Mini, Piero V. 1974. *Philosophy and Economics.* Gainesville: University of Florida Press.

Mirowski, Philip, and Steven Sklivas. 1991. "Why Econometricians Don't Replicate (Although They Do Reproduce)." *Review of Political Economy* 3: 146–63.

Mirowski, Philip. 1989. *More Heat Than Light: Economics as Social Physics, Physics as Nature's Economics.* Cambridge: Cambridge University Press.

Morishima, Mischio. 1984. "Good and Bad Uses of Mathematics." In *Economics in Disarray,* edited by P. Wiles and G. Routh. Oxford: Blackwell, 51–74.

Mueller, Dennis. 1984. "Further Reflections on the Invisible-Hand Theorem." In *Economics in Disarray,* edited by Peter Wiles and Guy Routh. Oxford: Blackwell.

Pool, Robert. 1989. "Strange Bedfellows." *Science* 245 (August 18): 700–703.

Summers, Lawrence. 1991. "The Scientific Illusion in Empirical Economics." *Scandinavian Journal of Economics* 93 (2): 27–39.

Weintraub, E. Roy. 1991. *Stabilizing Dynamics: Constructing Economic Knowledge.* Cambridge: Cambridge University Press.

Woo, Henry K. H. 1986. *What's Wrong with Formalization in Economics?* Hong Kong: Victoria Press.

Rule 14
Simulate, Simulate; Calibrate, Calibrate

Calibrated Simulation
Is Storytelling

Scientific American (Feb. 1995). With the piece the magazine used a late Victorian painting of reading Homer, which I liked.

Determining what drives economic growth or decline depends as much on storytelling as on data. Since 1980 a new crop of theorists, including Paul Romer of the University of California at Berkeley and Robert Lucas of the University of Chicago, has been pushing "endogenous" growth. They argue that development results entirely from *economic* factors: once upon a time the United States was poor; then its population grew and became urbanized, allowing business to exploit economies of scale; as a result, the country became rich. There are mathematical models to "prove" it. Economists understand all the variables in this story—and so it's called endogenous (inside the economics).

Economic historians such as Joel Mokyr of Northwestern University and Nathan Rosenberg of Stanford University, meanwhile, favor "exogenous" explanations based on outside factors, in particular technological change and the set of economic *and* noneconomic variables that might affect it—freedom of speech, for instance. Once upon a time we were all poor; then a wave of gadgets swept over England; as a result, we are all rich, or well on our way to it, if we will let people alone. This story does a better job of explaining, for instance, why China's per capita income now grows by 10 percent a year: the Chinese, like the Koreans and Japanese before them, adopt the best methods invented thus far and quickly catch up with more advanced nations, regardless of endogenous factors in their economy. And they are beginning to leave people alone.

The historians' exogenous version has its own problems, but one of the major reasons the endogenist economic theorists argue against it seems to be that it offends their narrative sense. They do not like to have to step outside of economics to talk about the nature and causes of the wealth of nations.

Are the economist endogenists being unscientifict this way in wanting to tell one kind of story rather than another? Is economics as a whole simply *not* a science because its practitioners rely on narrative? No. The Nobel Prize–winning physicist Steven Weinberg wrote a paper in 1983 call "Beautiful Theories" to make the point that aesthetic principles are at the heart of good physics. The astrophysicist Subrahmanyan Chandrasekhar wrote an entire beautiful book on the matter, *Truth and Beauty: Aesthetics and Motivations in Science* (1987). The same issues of narrative aesthetics appear in paleontology. Classical Darwinian evolution proceeds like a film in dignified slow motion: punctuated equilibrium interleaves still photographs with burst of silent movies run at fast speed.

The notion that "science" could be divorced from storytelling arose largely during the past century and a half. Before then the English word *science*—like its French, Tamil, Turkish, and Japanese counterparts— meant "systematic inquiry." The German word for the humanities is *Geisteswissenschaft,* or "systematic inquiry into the human spirit," as opposed to *Naturwissenschaft,* which singles out the external world. When Freud's translators rendered *Geisteswissenschaft* as "mental science," they left many readers wondering why a science in the English sense had so much to do with Oedipus and other literary tales.

Most sciences do both storytelling and model building. At one end of the spectrum sits Newtonian physics—the *Principia* (1687) is essentially geometric rather than narrative. Charles Darwin's biology in *The Origin of Species* (1859), in contrast, is entirely historical and devoid of mathematical models. Nevertheless, most scientists, and economists among them, hate to admit to something so childish-sounding as "telling stories." They want to emulate Newton's elegance rather than Darwin's complexity. (Still, one suspects that the relative prestige of the two methods has more to do with vintage than anything else. If a proto-Darwin had published in 1687 and a neo-Newton in 1859, it seems likely the prestige of storytelling versus timeless modeling would be reversed.)

Even when economists rely on timeless models the decisions about what to include or what conclusions to draw can turn on some principle of storytelling. Particularly important is the sense of beginnings and endings. To an eclectic a Keynesian, the story "oil prices went up in 1973, causing inflation" is full of meaning. For a monetarist, it ends too soon: a rise in oil prices without some corresponding fall elsewhere is not an equilibrium. Meanwhile, Keynesians accuse the monetarist plot line of an ill-motivated beginning: focusing on money as though it were causeless, ignoring where it comes from and why.

So when forecasters debate the impact of the Federal Reserve's latest fiddle with discount rates they are not just contesting the coefficients for their equations. They are debating which narrative style best describes the economy. And in economics, as in other sciences, you can't get away from the aesthetics of human stories.

Calibrated Simulation Is Outstripping Analytic Solutions

Another Scientific American *column (July 1995).*

The law of demand—that people will buy less of something if its price goes up, more if its price declines—is about as secure a proposition as economics offers. An important example is computation. At any given time since 1965 or so the cost of adding or multiplying two numbers has been half of what it was 18 months earlier (that's another law: Moore's). At Los Alamos in 1943 a "calculator" was a woman who did calculations for a team organized by Richard Feynman. Today systems of hundreds of equations are an easy job for an average PC. Someone calculated that if the price of Ferrari automobiles had fallen at the rate that calculation has in the past 30 years they would sell now for 12 cents a copy.

The change in degree has become a change in kind. Instead of reasoning about the economy on the basis of a few highly simplified, mathematically tractable assumptions, researchers can build realistic models of economic behavior and see how they run. The notion has been taking hold throughout the sciences. In their book *Darwinism Evolving: Systems Dynamics and the Genealogy of Natural Selection* David J. Depew and Bruce H. Weber trace similar stages in evolutionary theory. From Charles Darwin's publication in 1859 until about 1900 was the prequantitative beginning, from 1900 to 1975 or so the "Boltzmannian" statistical stage, with formal mathematical models in ascendance, as they are now in economics. And then in evolutionary theory, with the fall of computation costs, came the age of the computer.

The statistical stage is the one that most observers of science are familiar with. Ludwig Boltzmann introduced statistical methods into physics to deal with the aggregate behavior of a gas. In 1877 no one could even imagine following the individual histories of thousands of gas molecules colliding with one another, and so Boltzmann opted for following average behavior, which is what statistical theory is good at.

Economics is just finishing its Boltzmannian, statistical stage. The statistical techniques used by economists were invented in agronomy and perfected by agricultural economists in the 1930s. During the 1940s and 1950s such techniques, which let economists deduce properties of individual actors from gross measures such as price levels, spread to the rest of economics. In discussions of monetary policy, for example, the prequantitative stage contends with philosophical issues such as "Should the government interfere in financial markets?" or "Does it seems reasonable that raising interest rates will throttle demand and reduce growth?" Boltzmann-style analysis looks instead at whether the numbers show connections between the discount rate and gross national product. The Boltzmann era ended and the great age of calibrated simulation began in the 1990s, when economists had enough computing power to test directly their ideas about how molecules of economic behavior will interact in a mass. Assuming researchers agree on underlying economic behavior (such as that law of demand), the answers are unobscured by all the confounding factors that beset real data. They are quantitative thought experiments.

The story of evolutionary progress highlights the two competing intellectual traditions long coexisting, with differing attitudes toward computation. In the Greek tradition the theoreticians prove things on abstract principles. The proof of the Pythagorean theorem does not depend on the particular sizes of the right triangles in question. The Babylonian tradition, in contrast, discovers by brute force that a million different right triangles all seem to exhibit approximately the same relation among the squares of their sides.

In modern economics the Greek tradition reached its peak in the work of the Nobel laureates Paul Samuelson and Kenneth Arrow, who during the 1940s and 1950s applied mathematical reasoning to a minimum of data. The Babylonian tradition in economics is more checkered. In Isaac Newton's time it allowed calculation of hypothetical costs to show that the Somerset Levels wetlands should be drained at public expense. Wesley Clair Mitchell advocated calculation of business cycles, which Tjalling Koopmans (the unacknowledged heavy in the triumph of Greekism in economics) attacked as "measurement without theory." In 1973 Wassily Leontief won a Nobel for input-output analysis, a much more Babylonian approach to economic thinking than Samuelson's or Arrow's timeless proofs.

My point? The law of demand means that Mitchell and Leontief will eventually win. The decreasing cost of computation puts Greek mathematics on death row. Elegant analytic solutions still cost as much time and effort as they ever did, but number crunching becomes cheaper and cheaper, and more and more of it is demanded. That's the way the marketplace of ideas works, and it works even in the science of marketplaces. Calibrated simulation is the future of science.

Simulating Barbara

A shortened version appeared in 1998 in the new journal Feminist Economics *for a special issue honoring Barbara Bergmann.*

I first met Barbara Bergmann years ago, and we got along fine. This may seem odd, since our politics are not the same. I'm a postmodern free-market feminist, and in those days I was just a free-marketeer, without the postmodern or the feminist parts. Barbara is not a 100 percent "statist," as we label the enemy in libertarian circles, but she's nothing like as worried as I am that the next intervention by the federal government will end up somewhere between the Soviet gulag and United States Postal Service.

I think we've gotten along fine in our few encounters because we have the same intellectual style and purpose. This itself might seem odd, because our backgrounds are not the same. I was a Harvard professor's son; Barbara was not. But Barbara's purpose, like mine, is to find How Big Is Big; and in finding it our style is a little confrontational.

"Confrontational" in a good sense. For example, unlike some people with a confrontational style, Barbara is consistent and doesn't get sore when other people are confrontational back at her. She showed this in her calm reaction to Donald McCloskey's bizarrely large role in the Great Market Debate on the listserve FemEcon in the spring of 1994. When other people, especially women, were becoming *very* angry at Donald's domination of the airwaves (a later statistical study showed that Donald's interventions were *eight standard deviations* above the mean in frequency and length; *oy,* guys), Barbara defended him—not his views on the cuddly sweet nature of The Market, Lord knows, but his confrontational style. (Donald took up every challenge, and I can report from inside his head that he had a masculine reason for doing so: "She thinks *she's* so tough, well, let's see if she can answer *this.*" It's stupid, an atmosphere of testosterone like that inside Kenneth Starr's office when prosecuting Clinton, but there you are.)

Like me, Barbara believes that confrontation gets us right to the point and keeps us there. Barbara said on FemEcon that when she was a graduate student she was the most outspoken member of the class, challenging the professors, asking questions, getting to the point and staying there. At Harvard in the late 1950s such behavior was not, she noted, popular in a young woman. It was more acceptable, even encouraged, at Harvard in the middle 1960s in a young man.

When Barbara saw me for the first time as Deirdre, in Mexico City in July 1997, we wandered through the streets together trying to find the hall for the International Association for Feminist Economics reception, and she immediately, with no social chitchat, started quizzing me on my views about some economic issue—I think it was the minimum wage but confess that I was so overwhelmed by her eagerness to Get to Work that I can't remember. Her attitude was, Here I have a living, breathing member of the Chicago School. What a *great* opportunity to sharpen my own arguments! Let's see if she has anything to say on the issue. (I didn't, but that didn't stop Bergmann.)

The idea is that through confrontation we improve each other's ideas. We Consistent Confrontationists don't get angry at the other person's Getting to Work, because we regard the friction of confrontation as a great *favor* that our opponent is doing for us. We don't get "offended," a favorite word of the nonconfrontationists. They are always getting offended and going off in a huff. Not Barbara. She stays and confronts and learns something. It's not a feminist style, in one version of that essentially contested concept, though it easily could become so. It's even a little macho, which I don't think troubles Barbara one bit. After all, she advocates us getting into men's jobs just as fast as we can and proving what the Canadian feminist Charlotte Whitton (1896–1975) said somewhere: "Whatever women do they must do twice as well as men to be thought half as good. Luckily this is not difficult."

So too for academic confrontation. With a feminist flavoring, luckily, it is not difficult. What is crucial, writes the philosopher Amelie Oksenberg Rorty, is "our ability to engage in continuous conversation, testing one another, discovering our hidden presuppositions, changing our minds because we have listened to the voices of our fellows. Lunatics also change their minds, but their minds change with the tides of the moon and not because they have listened, really listened, to their friends' questions and objections" (1983, 562). The confrontation is good if it involves listening, really listening. Barbara asks, "What is truth?" and stays for the answer.

There's something else going on here, which is perhaps worth making explicit. I have a friend who is from California, a wonderful woman. But she is made uncomfortable by my interruptions. In her Californian conversational culture, which she understands as Simply Good Manners, everyone waits for the speaker to finish. Really finish. Then there is a brief pause to make sure that she has *really* finished. Then the other Californian starts up and says something, preferably supportive.

I don't. Neither does Barbara, in spirit at any rate (Barbara does pause sometimes to reflect, which is an unusual use of conversational time; the only other economist I know who does it much is Al Harberger of UCLA and Chicago). The frequent interruptions and overlapping Barbara and I engage in are not because we are terminally impolite or because the California style is the only conceivable way that people can talk to each other politely. It's because we were brought up as urban Easterners. (In all such characterizations of difference one must avoid the Charybdis of essentialism while skirting the Scylla of silence about something that should be noted. One must ask every time whether it really *should* be noted. This one I think should be, because it can help people understand each other, tolerantly, and listen.)

Being interrupting, confrontational, enthusiastic, loud, emphatic, unsupportive, sarcastic, even a little bit nasty is an Eastern, urban style. It's not bad in itself. Like all language, its goodness or badness depends on its pragmatic effects, ethically or unethically performed in a context in which people understand the performance. When we Easterners interrupt we are often trying in the excess of our hot Easternity to *support* the point the other person is making. When we confront we are surprisingly often trying to get at the truth. When we are sarcastic we are often trying to unveil hypocrisy and pretension and pomposity.

Of course, *sometimes* we Eastern urbanites are just trying to win, like guys in a pickup basketball game, though neither Barbara nor I do this by habit or intent. (Even Donald didn't.) It's easy to cheat on the conventions of an Eastern, urban style of conversation, to secretly have only winning in mind, not truth telling or friend supporting or hypocrisy unveiling. But that's so of the opposite, Californian style, too. It also can be used for aggression, as I have found, for example, in controversies about statistical significance. With a flamboyantly Eastern, urban style I confront this silly procedure, which has ruined empirical work in economics (Barbara has long known that calibrated simulation is the way out and has said so), and get stonewalled by non-Easterners. They've learned that they can protect any stupidity in their argument by . . . not answering. One of those long Western pauses. And then they can justify

getting sore if you act Eastern. They can divert attention from your devastating criticism of their position to your cultural style and ethnic background. If you can't say anything nice . . . (to which the Eastern Con-
frontationist says: come over and sit by me).

To interpret confrontation and the speech habits that go with it as
Badness is to miss that it is cultural, a matter of difference, not just Bad.
(There are some cultural differences that *are* Just Bad: throwing Hindu
widows onto funeral pyres, for example, or burning English witches, or
the doctrine of coverture; my point is that "impolite" speech customs are
sometimes not impolite in the right context.) The point gets to the heart
of feminism in economics and elsewhere. In her collection of academic
essays on linguistics Deborah Tannen has a paper about interruptions in
conversation. She concludes:

> As a woman who has personally experienced the difficulty many
> women report in getting heard in some interactions with men, I am
> tempted to embrace the studies that find men interrupt women: it
> would allow me to explain my experience in a way that blames oth-
> ers. As a high involvement style speaker [her technical label for what
> I am calling "Eastern urban" style], however, I am offended by the
> labeling of a feature of my conversational style as loathsome, based
> on the standard of those who do not share or understand it. As a
> Jewish woman raised in New York who is not only offended but
> frightened by the negative stereotyping of New Yorkers and women
> and Jews, I recoil. (1994, 74)

So do I, and I imagine Barbara Bergmann would, too.

As Tannen says, the style is specifically, if not exclusively, Jewish. I
had an Italian father-in-law from Vermont who was that way. I myself
picked it up in an Irish/Norwegian/English home in eastern Massachusetts. But I have argued with an awful lot of New York Jewish intellectuals in my career, and I can see something interesting about the difference
from other ethnic groups in the Talmudic style. Robert Fogel, for example, was a college classmate of Barbara's, Cornell class of 1948. I think
they knew each other. Bob was at the time an enthusiastic Communist
and later became a paid organizer for the Party (paid by the FBI, we now
know). What Bob carried at first over into his later, Chicago School life
was the flamboyantly Eastern and urban and Jewish style of argument in
the Party in those days. Fogel's work has become slowly, steadily duller
as he has grown away from his roots and opted for what he conceives of

as Science instead of argument. In his great and exciting book of 1964, *Railroads and American Economic Growth,* Fogel's rhetoric is unusually lawyerly, argumentative, aware of itself as rhetoric. The prose is confrontational: no indirection here; just bang, bang, bang. The book inaugurated a new style of economic history, a confrontational, forensic style that has become important in cliometrics. (It was important to Donald, at any rate, who imitated it in his historical work.) Fogel brought to American economic history, which up until then had been a distinctly right-wing and goyish field, the traditions of flamboyantly Talmudic disputation characteristic of New York Jewish intellectuals, especially left-wing intellectuals. The combination of a somewhat heated tone and the methodical treatment of every imaginable point—known anciently as *indignatio, diasyrmus, digestion,* and *diallage*—was invented by Marx himself (Marx the son of a lawyer and grandson of a rabbi) and attached by him to self-conscious scientism. In the 1940s you see it in the cases prepared by labor union intellectuals about such mundanities as the construction of cost-of-living indices—pieces of science, but tough, disputatious, lawyerly science. So in Fogel, and in Bergmann.

I had not read much of Barbara's work until recently. In academic life we get along on reputations and rumors, especially in economics (historians are more insistent that if you are going to have an opinion about someone you ought to know the work of the person you are talking about, by doing the reading; it's a much better policy for hiring and promotion). I was satisfied with an amiable assumption that Barbara was, I guess, a good economist. This is at least a better default assumption than the one most economists seem to favor, that anyone they haven't read (a sociologist, say, or a philosopher or someone in another school of economics) is probably an idiot.

When I recently started reading her, nonarrogantly, I was astonished at how similar our views are. Well, not about policy and politics. What we agree on is how to go about being an economist. That is, we agree, again, on how to talk as an economic scientist. We agree on the proper rhetoric for our field.

In particular Barbara has been an early and insistent advocate, as I noted, of calibrated simulation. So have I. Understand right at the outset that calibrated simulation is a radical alternative to the way we do economics now. The way we do it now, and have since Barbara and I were graduate students, is mainly either to prove things on the blackboard or to measure the statistical significance of fitted hyperplanes. We therefore have gotten nowhere in economic science since 1955. You can prove anything if you are free to play with the assumptions, so proof (what philosophers call "validity") is no guide to social truth. On a blackboard you can prove that the minimum wage is, under some assumptions, wonderful or, under other assumptions, terrible. Take your pick (people do). And the statistical significance of a finding is irrelevant to its scientific significance. They overlap only by accident.

By contrast, calibrated simulation is what physicists and engineers and evolutionary biologists and (in effect) historians do. The recent popularity of simulation in economics has sometimes carried over the math department value of just assuming hypotheses without the discipline of fact from observation or experiment. Uncalibrated. Uh-oh. This is what killed earlier attempts to make simulation the core of economic rhetoric (thus the fashion for it in the 1950s and 1960s at Carnegie-Mellon). In engineering and physics the simulations are always calibrated, that is, made to lie down on the properties of things. A scientific simulation will follow Newton: "Hypotheses should be subservient only in explaining the properties of things, but not assumed in determining them; unless so far as they may furnish experiments" (1672, qtd. in Chandrasekhar 1987, 43). Like Robert Fogel, *hypotheses non fingo*.

In other words, the real scientists ask How Big. Barbara has advocated all through her scientific career getting to the scientific point of How Big Is Big and staying there. I wasn't as early as Barbara in advocating calibrated simulation, and I didn't have the clarity of mind until recently to be as insistent. But I always did it. My Ph.D. dissertation in 1970, for example, asked How Big was the superiority of American over British techniques in iron and steel around 1910 (answer: nil). I did it by imagining the choices of technique the two countries faced and simulating retrospectively their profits and productivities. A lot of theory and statistics was involved, at least by the modest standards of 1970, "theory" in the sense of economic ideas expressed mathematically, but no existence proof or statistical significance. The theory was used to get ideas about functional forms (in calculations of total factor productivity, for example). The statistics (I mean the numbers) were then used to put numerical values on the math, to calibrate the simulation, that essential step that the math department habits of economists so often lead them to miss. I later did the same thing with a portfolio balance model of landholding among medieval peasants, making Markowitz lie down on the properties of yields and famines around A.D. 1300. Economic historians do calibrated simulations all the time—of how changes in life expectancy might affect bequests and retirement, of how much of Southern prosperity depended on a rising demand curve for cotton, of how much of the male-female wage gap is attributable to skill.

It did not impress me then or now that such-and-such Exists. I was muddled then and didn't know exactly why I was not impressed. By the low standards of my graduate student vintage I had adequate math. I was not at all hostile to the unscientific cartel gathering force then. We all read Tjalling Koopmans's *Three Essays on the State of Economic Science* (1957), which outlined a market-sharing agreement between proof-peddlers and significance-sellers, and we thought it was swell. He was selling axiomatization and proof. Unfortunately, axiomatization and proof doesn't result in any scientific findings, merely in endless games with alternative axioms and alternative conclusions and alternative statistical specifications. No serious science depends on axiomatization and existence proof, yet to an economist unacquainted with serious science it seemed in 1957 *so* neat.

Koopmans' program has been widely accepted. In 1984, for example, Frank Hahn thought he was answering the objection that anything can happen in general theorizing by saying: "It is true that often many things can be the case in a general theory but not that anything can be. Everyone who knows the textbooks can confirm that" (6). What he means is that the textbooks line up the sequence of assumptions $A, A', A'', \ldots$ with the conclusions $C, C', C'', \ldots$ True enough. That's nice. But of course it is not an answer to the objection that in economic theorizing, contrary to its declared love of rigor, in fact anything goes: choose A, A', A'', as you will, like taste in lovers, and get the C, C', C'' you want. To his credit, Frank has now changed his mind.

Likewise, I was muddlingly unimpressed with findings that so-and-so is Statistically Significantly Different from Zero. By the standards of the time I was well trained in econometrics. It was just that econometric testing didn't seem to get anywhere (econometric *estimation*, the finding of coefficients, is quite another matter and has accomplished something, as in the estimation of beta coefficients in finance; it's *testing* in the way economists think they can interpret the word that is the silly part). I remember witnessing from one side and then the other, moving in the 1960s from Harvard to Chicago, the Keynesians and the monetarists hurling significance tests at each other and not persuading anyone but themselves. T. F. Cooley and S. F. LeRoy showed empirically in 1981 that, of course, prior convictions about monetarism as against Keynesianism had decisive effects on the econometric tests. I finally figured out why the statistical test of significance didn't persuade anyone: it doesn't do what economists almost universally think it does—tell you How Big Is Big.

In 1933 Neyman and Pearson wrote of Type I and Type II errors: "Is it more serious to convict an innocent man or to acquit a guilty? That will depend on the consequences of the error. . . . The use of these statistical tools in any given case, in determining just how the balance should be struck, *must be left to the investigator*" (Neyman and Pearson 1933, 296; italics added). Abraham Wald went further: "The question as to how the form of the weight [that is, loss] function . . . should be determined, *is not a mathematical or statistical one.* The statistician who wants to test certain hypotheses must first determine the relative importance of all possible errors, *which will depend on the special purposes of his investigation*" (1939, 302; italics added). Morris DeGroot, a statistician with sophistication in economics, was emphatic on the point: "In a given problem, the tail area corresponding to the observed value of U might be very small; and yet the actual value . . . might be so close to [the null] that, for practical purposes, the experimenter would not regard [it] as being [substantively] different from [the null]" (1989, 496).

Among recent econometrics books Arthur Goldberger's is unique in being clear on the point that statistical and economic significance are different, at least on two pages of *A Course in Econometrics* (1991, 240–41). But most do not (and two pages of warning buried in hundreds of pages of sin is a little like including a brief pamphlet on safe sex in the middle of the *Kama Sutra*). Clive Granger, reviewing in the March 1994 issue of the *Journal of Economic Literature* four leading econometrics books, among them Goldberger's, notes that "when the link is made [in Goldberger's pp. 240–41 between the economics and the technical statistics] some important insights arise, as for example the section discussing 'statistical and economic significance,' *a topic not mentioned in the other books*" (1994, 115; italics added). Not mentioned. That is, most econometrics books even now, unlike DeGroot and Goldberger and before them the modern masters of statistics, do not even mention the difference between economic and statistical significance.

In 1965 I was just in my muddled way more interested in actual scientific findings, which I vaguely realized always turn on How Big. Barbara and I are quantitative ladies. We want to know How Big. *You never learn this from existence proofs or statistical significance.* Physicists use calibrated computer simulation, testing its robustness to a range of alternative specifications and empirically observed parameters, using the first few terms of divergent infinite series and other stuff that would make a mathematician faint. Who is the scientist? Who asks How Big Is Big? Not the economists, unfortunately.

There's nothing mysterious about "calibrated simulation." It has been one strand in economic thinking back to the English political arithmeticians of the seventeenth century. It's just sophisticated, theory-using, mathematized accounting. Thomas Schelling is fond of pointing out that what economists really, truly know, and noneconomists do not, are largely matters of accounting. Learning to think like an economist, Schelling argues, consists in good part of learning to speak such bits of accounting logic. Add whatever behavioral equations you think you have evidence for (better not use statistical significance!), and you can find out, sometimes, How Big Is Big.

A good example is Barbara's book *Saving Our Children from Poverty* (1996; economists like Bergmann or Leontief or Adelman or Goldin who favor calibrated simulation tend to write books, which the proof-peddlers and significance-sellers find too taxing to write or to read; when economists get back to books as their characteristic intellectual product you will know they have gotten back to serious scientific work, since serious calibrated simulation often requires a lot of room; though it is gradually becoming more common in the *American Economic Review* [Ballard 1988; Campbell 1993] and is now a regular addendum to "theoretical" papers offering in their first half scientifically meaningless proofs of existence). Barbara's book is an impressive scientific case that adopting a French-style payment for childcare would save millions of American children from pathology-producing poverty. It depends on economic theory to note that ADC has a disincentive effect on job holding (107 and throughout) or that food stamps have a shadow price less than their face value (99) and on statistical theory to make use of numbers gathered from sampling (throughout). But I can't find any place where Barbara uses the bankrupt rhetorical forms "theory says that C" or "the coefficient on Z is statistically significant at the .05 level." She does economics in the physics department way, not the math department way. She asks How Big. And she is explicit about the loss function, as in "How much poverty among children are we willing to tolerate in order to discourage improvident childbearing or to penalize impecunious single parents who avoid paid work?" (138).

After reading her book, I end up back at a theme in the Good Old Chicago School: If you want to help people of X description, you better just give the X the money. It's Barbara's scientific conclusion, too. The

French target the children and try to resist the temptation to punish the adults with the same instrument used to help the children. Yes. If Milton Friedman and I thought American governments would not grossly misallocate most of such money and end up giving most of it to middle-class holders of government jobs and middle-class taxpayers, we would sign on. Milton and I don't agree with Barbara's conclusion. But we have no doubt that she's on the right track in the form of argument she uses.

Calibrated simulation is not usually explicitly defended (Ed Prescott defends it; Ken Judd does it; economic historians have been doing it by the ton since the 1960s), and certainly not with the fervor mixed with confusion that existence theorems and statistical significance have been. An early defender was Guy Orcutt. In 1980 Barbara co-authored a book on simulation with Orcutt, who was a professor of econometrics at Wisconsin and a Distinguished Fellow of the American Economic Association. A decade or two before the fall of computation costs made it feasible Orcutt was trying to model the whole economy as little computer people running around. It's the way one models any difficult system, such as the weather or evolutionary processes or a building subject to wind and earthquakes, and doesn't require analytic solutions of demonstrably imperfect generality. As Barbara put it in 1990, "Highly mathematical accounts of the derivation of individuals' behavior are not infrequently followed by vague verbal descriptions of what goes on when the individuals come together and interact" (100). The "rigor" of the analytic results is of course phony, as even Frank Hahn finally realized. $A => C$. So?

Orcutt visited Harvard when I was a graduate student, and I took two courses from him in 1965 and 1966. Orcutt's pioneering of computer-aided simulation is forgotten, though his asymptotic theorems about significance testing are not, which is a bad sign. He was a scientist rather than merely a mathematician. I had already learned the calibrated simulation of the engineers from John Meyer and his team of transport economists from Harvard and transport engineers from MIT, with whom I worked as a research assistant (Meyer taught my first econometrics course, too). As an undergraduate, I had talked nightly with Gary Fromm in 1963 and 1964 when he was working on the first Brookings model with Jim Duesenberry and Otto Eckstein. I took Econ 1 as a sophomore in college from Eckstein. I took a monetary theory course from Duesenberry as a second-year graduate student. And at Chicago during the late 1960s and early 1970s, before *nouvelle Chicago* and the rise there of axiom-and-proof, the questions was *always* How Big? Margaret Reid attended the

Economic History Workshop every week. Get serious about your numbers. I remember Zvi Griliches in the Quad Club at Chicago commenting sardonically on someone's simulation without calibration: "Vel, your model computes. So?" Come to think of it, my intellectual life in economics has been shaped largely by inveterate simulators and persistent calibrators, not theorem provers or significance testers. How Big? *Nu?*

Barbara was for a long time at the University of Maryland, which was and still is a hotbed of people who think How Big is the big question (one of them, Julian Simon, died in 1999, a great loss for the How Biggers, but my old teacher of mathematical economics, Clopper Almon, is still there and still asking How Big; the death there, also in 1999, of Mancur Olson was a grievous loss for breadth and humanity in economics). I almost went to Maryland when I left Chicago in 1980 in a huff (I was offended by not getting promoted to full professor as soon as I imagined I deserved), and if I had gone there rather than to hilly Iowa I think I would have continued to pursue a career of calibrated simulation instead of starting one on the rhetoric of economics. Though come to think of it an interest in rhetoric is antiphilosophical, anti–math department, and in favor of the values of practical discourse, in the same way that calibrated simulation is.

The point is that careers like Barbara's of calibrated simulation and then feminist economics and careers like mine of calibrated simulation in transport economics and economic history and then inquiry into the rhetoric of economics end up with the same remark about the present state of economics: Good Lord, guys, let's get out of the sandbox and start doing some real science! The proof-finding and significance-trolling of economics since about 1948 is a boys' game in a sandbox.

The boys' game is what the physicist Richard Feynman used to call "cargo-cult science" (1985, 340). In New Guinea after the war (Barbara will know I mean The Big One) the natives built "airports" with coconut shells for "landing lights" and cardboard for "planes," because they wanted a second coming of the real cargo planes. Photographs of the cult airports show them to be amazingly accurate. But the natives weren't doing real cargo work. It looked a little bit like the real thing, as the contents of the *American Economic Review* looks a little bit like the *Physical Review*, but on closer inspection nothing real was happening. Barbara once apologized ironically for her vulgar attachment to asking How Big: "Such simulations seem sleazy to those economists for whom respectable microeconomics is synonymous with solving optimization problems"

(1990, 99). The sleaze, of course, is on the other foot. Nothing of a scientific, How-Big-Is-Big character is being accomplished by existence theorems or statistical significance.

The two characterizations I've claimed here of Barbara and me as confrontational and as interested in How Big Is Big are not separate. Someone who is confrontational and then listens, really listens, can be thought of as trying on the arguments for size. *Testing* means torturing the data to see how it works, though in actual economic rhetoric these days it has been reduced to the phony and easy standards of absolute Proof or conclusive Significance. (A test: another leader these past decades in calibrated simulation has been Irma Adelman, another confrontational female economist with whom I get along fine; ditto Cynthia Taft Morris, though Cynthia is sweet rather than confrontational.) A good, honest, Eastern, urban, Talmudic confrontation, with a lot of supportive interruptions, really trying to get to the bottom of disagreements and then trying to see How Big the facts have to be to support one side or the other is one way to have a scientific life. Existence theorem proving and significance testing, however California-polite in presentation, however masculine-pompous in pretension, is not.

We can do it, and get economics back to scientific work. By simulating Barbara.

Rule 15
Yet Don't Be Too Certain of Your "Expertise"

An Economic Uncertainty Principle

One of my columns for Scientific American *(November 1994).*

"If you're so smart, why ain't you rich?" It's a good question to keep in mind when listening to infomercials about easy money in real estate or to economists engaged in learned predictions of interest rates.

The most important discovery in economics science since 1970 is that this query, which I call the American Question, has no good answer. The early Latin poet Ennius sneered at forecasters "who don't know the path for themselves yet show the way for others." Only in recent decades have economists put principles and hard numbers behind this ancient jibe. It is rare that a scientific principle can make you money, but if I had learned the meaning of the American Question earlier and better I would be $10,000 richer—about $50,000 in present dollars including interest forgone. It turns out that you, too, can get rich by learning it (or at least you can avoid losing money, which in economic terms amounts to the same thing).

The American Question is a slayer of chutzpah. The Question is funny, but it's serious, too, and it cuts deep. It slays an economist who claims to predict next month's interest rate. Clearly, there is a fortune to be made with such knowledge. The price of interest-bearing securities such as bonds rises when rates fall, and vice versa. Knowing next month's interest rates is equivalent to knowing next month's bond prices. So why isn't the economist savant rich? Seriously, now. Keep quiet, get a second mortgage, buy bonds today, then sell them at a fat profit in a month. It's a sure thing. Why haven't you done it, oh smart economist?

Of course, a claim to know that the interest rate will fall next month is also a claim that the rest of the chumps in the market don't know. If they did, the interest rate would have fallen already, and there would be no profit to be made buying bonds today. There's no way around the conundrum, since orders to buy or sell bonds convey information about each trader's beliefs regarding next month's interest rate. An economist with perfect foreknowledge would soon inadvertently reveal it to everyone else in the market.

The notion that exclusive information is dissipated by the very act of using it goes beyond financial markets. Anyone who has watched the electronics industry during the 1980s and 1990s can recall a dozen or more brilliant new ideas that seemed like a license to print money when only one company had thought of them: memory chips, video games, IBM PC clones, word-processing software, ultralight portables. Then dozens of entrants jumped into the same niche, boldly assuming that forty could enjoy the same profit margins as one. Often even the original innovators lost their silk shirts.

You can tell the history of the American Question by looking at the Nobel Prizes in Economics that were awarded for asking it. Friedrich von Hayek (Nobel 1974) led the "Austrian" school of economics, which has been saying for a long time that if it were possible to outwit a society's judgment of what is profitable, social scientists would be rich. Merton M. Miller (Nobel 1990) observed that if, in fact, the hot tips your stockbroker sells you had any value, then running the broker's little formulas for picking "incorrectly valued" stocks should make you rich. Statistics show it ain't so (though I've been startled to see even Eugene Fama using *statistical significance* instead of financial significance as the standard). Robert Lucas (Nobel 1995) has pointed out that the American Question could also be asked of governments trying to fool some of the people some of the time. Lucas's work with Thomas Sargent and others is called rational expectations, a phrase with enough arrogance and mystery to be controversial, and is expressed in the toughest mathematics they could find (thus Newton: "To avoid being baited by little smatterers in mathematics, I designedly made the *Principia* abstruse"). But Lucas would agree that at bottom he is asking the same goofy old question: If the deep thinkers at the Federal Reserve Board can outguess the public, Lucas asks, why aren't they rich? Or, at the very least, why isn't the government solvent? Paul A. Samuelson (Nobel 1970)—who *is* rich, thank you—did not get the Nobel Prize for asking the Question. But he has held all along, as he put it in 1982, that "it's a mug's game for a dentist—or an associate professor of econometrics—to think that he can have an edge over those who count the cocoa pods in Africa and follow the minute-by-minute arrival of new information."

The Question is beginning to constrain economic argument the way Heisenberg constrains quantum mechanics or Gödel constrains mathematical logic. You can't understand a social fact and make money from it at the same time. If by chance you could, the market would adapt to render your understanding invalid. (The economic statistics that were once used to predict recessions, for example, now predict instead when the government will make policy changes intended to ward off the recessions.)

Here's the practical use of this deep scientific principle. Fire your stockbroker the instant he says that Fly-by-Nite Canadian Gold Mining Ltd. is "undervalued" or that "we're recommending" Whitewater Real Estate, Inc. Or, to take my own sad case, do not believe your brilliant former student at the University of Chicago when he comes up with a scheme, in which other economists have invested, to make money out of a glitch in the foreign exchange market. On that one I lost half my $10,000-before-inflation in one weekend, the other half more slowly.

So be smart and be rich. Do what I say, not what I did. Constrain economic science with the American Question, and, if someone offers you a tip, ask yourself why they are not using it themselves. As a Damon Runyon character put it: "Now, Herbie, I do not doubt your information, because I know you will not give out information unless it is well founded. But I seldom stand for a tip. . . . So I thank you, Herbie, just the same, but I must do without your tip."

"Modesty Is the
Best Policy,"
Says Herbert Stein

A review of Stein's book Washington Bedtime Stories *for the*
Washington Post *in 1986.*

We have about 100,000 self-described economists in the nation, 15,000 of them huddled in Washington. For a long time Herbert Stein led the Washington huddle. He ran part of the Committee for Economic Development for two decades, served on the Council of Economic Advisors under Nixon and was its chair, and sits now at the American Enterprise Institute. This makes him a "conservative" economist and a streetwise fellow, the street being Pennsylvania Avenue. He stands out among economists by writing well and by thinking more than most do about what he writes. *Washington Bedtime Stories* collects his thinking from recent columns in the *Wall Street Journal* and after-dinner speeches to conferences. He does a lot of dinners at conferences: "The Internal Revenue Services believes that a conference including a lecture by an economist cannot be for the purpose of pleasure and therefore must be a deductible expense."

Stein has watched the growth of the economics industry from the 1930s, up to a size about equal in employment to the motion picture industry. The big question is whether this is a Good Thing. Stein's answer is a cautious yes. Of course, economists disagree, though he points out that when they gather with lawyers and politicians "the economists are likely to agree with each other and to disagree with the consensus of the noneconomists." Most American economists agree on free trade against the consensus, and quite a few, including Stein, agree that the Japanese Invasion of the 1970s was exaggerated and harmless, a trade of Toyotas for pieces of paper costing pennies to engrave. Admittedly, the forecast by economists of next year's GNP is poor, but Stein points out that no one would have expected such an impossible feat of forecasting if the economists hadn't thought up the idea of GNP in the first place. And "if someone is going to talk about economics on TV it is probably better done by economists than by politicians, columnists, sociologists, or clergymen—who seem the most likely alternative."

Above all Stein thinks that economists have given useful advice to politicians: Mr. President, try voluntary exchange, which has made us rich; keep calm about the federal deficit, which has been big in other times; you're wrong to think that Alan Greenspan sets the interest rate. The politicians do not trust anyone who is not on their team, reasonably enough, so the immediate influence comes from advisors inside. Stein has sat inside and outside and can speak with authority. The outsiders, he argues, have their influence only in the long run, through conversation, by making conceivable the policies once thought inconceivable: the dirty float of the exchange rate, for example, or the moderate flattening of tax brackets; I remember back when advocating vouchers for schools would merely ruin a dinner party, even one mainly of economists.

The New York Times sneered in 1969 that the distinguishing feature of the Council of Economic Advisors when it first contained Stein was humility. The joke is on the Times, because since then the humble attitude toward the giving of economic advise has looked better and better, and even the Times has moderated its enthusiasm for fine-tuning. Stein was a pioneer in honest ignorance, a Socrates among the social engineers, arguing early and late that "1. Economists do not know very much. 2. Other people . . . know even less. . . . These beliefs do not provide a platform from which to make strong pronouncement about economics or public policy." Most people who pose as ignorant don't really believe they are. Stein believes that he and other economists really are.

Yet Stein would gladly learn and gladly teach. He can teach salient facts, such as that Japan's alarmingly fast growth rate until the 1990s would still have left it with a lower income than ours a century on; or that the deindustrialization of America has reduced jobs in manufacturing but not the share of manufacturing in output. And he can teach the bits of refined common sense that constitute the economic way of thinking, such as that foreign holding of American debt is no more destabilizing than American holding of the debt; or that jobs are lost for many reasons, few of them foreign, and that what matters are the net jobs found.

We economists, then, are useful people but not seers and "should be deciding what we will do if the initial assumption, whatever it is, turns out to be incorrect." Examine the loss function. Consult the properties of things. Ask How Big. You would expect no less of someone working on your teeth. Keynes said once that it would be splendid if economists could manage to get themselves thought of as humble, competent people on a level with dentists. When serving as economic advisor to the president, therefore, Stein was disappointed but not offended when he had to give up the last seat on *Air Force One* to Moscow for the president's dentist.

References

Adelman, Irma. 1978. "Simulation: Economic Processes." In William H. Kruskal and Judith M. Tanur, eds., *International Encyclopedia of Statistics,* 965–71. New York: Free Press.

Alchian, Armen, and William Allen. 1977. *Exchange and Production Theory in Use.* Belmont, California: Wadsworth.

Alchian, Armen, William Allen, and J. Hoel. 2000. *Universal Economics.* New York: Oxford University Press.

Ames, Edward, and Stanley Reiter. 1961. "Distribution of Correlation Coefficients in Economic Times Series." *Journal of the American Statistical Association* 56 (Sept.): 627–56.

Arrow, Kenneth. 1951. *Social Choice and Individual Values.* New York: Wiley.

———. 1959. "Decision Theory and the Choice of a Level of Significance for the t-Test." In *Contributions to Probability and Statistics: Essays in Honor of Harold Hotelling,* edited by Ingram Olkin and others. Stanford: Stanford University Press.

Austin, J. L. 1975. *How to Do Things with Words.* Cambridge, Mass.: Harvard University Press, 1962.

Bacon, Francis. 1620. *Novum Organum.* J. Gibson and P. Urbach, eds. Chicagos Open Court, 1994.

Ballard, C. L. 1988. "The Marginal Efficiency Cost of Redistribution." *American Economic Review* 78 (Dec.): 1019–33.

Barnes, Barry. 1996. *Elements of Social Theory.* Princeton: Princeton University Press.

Bauer, Peter. 1984. *Reality and Rhetoric: Studies in the Economics of Development.* Cambridge: Harvard University Press.

Becker, Howard. 1986. *Writing for Social Scientists.* Chicago: University of Chicago Press.

———. 1998. *Tricks of the Trade: How to Think about Your Research While Doing It.* Chicago: University of Chicago Press.

Bennett, R. L., and Barbara R. Bergmann. 1986. *A Micro-Simulated Transactions Model of the United States Economy.* Baltimore: Johns Hopkins University Press.

Bergmann, Barbara R. 1974. "A Microsimulation of the Macroeconomy with Explicitly Represented Money Flows." *Annals of Economic and Social Measurement* 3:475–89.

———. 1990. "Micro-to-Macro Simulations: A Primer with a Labor Market Example." *Journal of Economic Perspectives* 4 (winter): 99–116.

———. 1996. *Saving Our Children from Poverty: What the United States Can Learn from France.* New York: Russell Sage Foundation.

Bergmann, Barbara, Gunnar Eliasson, and Guy H. Orcutt, eds. 1980. *Micro-Simulation: Methods and Applications.* New York: Coronet Books.

Billig, Michael. *Arguing and Thinking,* 2d ed. Cambridge: Cambridge University Press, 1996.

Booth, Wayne C. 1974. *Modern Dogma and the Rhetoric of Assent.* Chicago and London: University of Chicago Press.

———. 1988. *The Company We Keep: An Ethics of Fiction.* Berkeley and Los Angeles: University of California Press.

Boring, Edwin G. 1919. "Mathematical versus Scientific Significance." *Psychological Bulletin* 16 (Oct.): 335–38.

Brock, W. A. 1988. "Introduction to Chaos and Other Aspects of Nonlinearity." In *Differential Equations, Stability, and Chaos in Dynamic Economics,* edited by W. A. Brock and A. G. Malliaris. New York: North Holland. (October 30, 1987, draft, Department of Economics, University of Wisconsin.)

Brooks, Peter. 1985. *Reading for the Plot: Design and Intention in Narrative.* New York: Vintage.

Brown, Vivienne. 1994. *Adam Smith's Discourse.* London: Routledge.

Bruner, Jerome. 1983. *In Search of Mind: Essays in Autobiography.* New York: Harper and Row.

Buchanan, James. 1992. *Better than Plowing: And Other Personal Essays.* Chicago: University of Chicago Press.

———. 1979. *What Should Economists Do?* Indianapolis: Liberty Press.

Campbell, J. Y. 1993. "Intertemporal Asset Pricing without Consumption Data." *American Economic Review* 83 (June): 487–512.

Card, David E., and William K. Krueger. 1997. *Myth and Measurement: The New Economics of the Minimum Wage.* Princeton: Princeton University Press.

Chamberlain, Edward. 1962. *The Theory of Monopolistic Competition.* Cambridge: Harvard University Press.

Chandrasekhar, S. 1987. *Truth and Beauty: Aesthetics and Motivations in Science.* Chicago: University of Chicago Press.

Christianson, Gale E. 1984. *In the Presence of the Creator: Isaac Newton and His Times.* New York: Free Press, 1984.

Clapham, John H. 1930. "Economic History as a Discipline." *Encyclopedia of the Social Sciences* (1930). Reprinted in *Enterprise and Secular Change,* edited by F. C. Lane and J. C. Riemersma. Homewood, Ill.: Irwin, 1953.

Collingwood, R. G. 1946. *The Idea of History.* Reprint. New York: Oxford University Press, 1956.

Collins, Harry. 1985. *Changing Order: Replication and Induction in Scientific Practice.* London and Beverly Hills: Sage.

Cooley, T. F., and S. F. LeRoy. 1981. "Identification and Estimation of Money Demand." *American Economic Review* 71 (Dec.): 825–44.

David, P. A. 1969. "Transportation Innovations and Economic Growth: Professor Fogel on and off the Rails." *Economic History Review,* 2d ser., 22 (Dec.): 506–25.

Debreu, Gerard. 1991. "The Mathematization of Economic Theory." *American Economic Review* 81 (Mar.): 1–7.

DeGroot, Morris H. 1989. *Probability and Statistics*. Reading, Mass.: Addison-Wesley.

Denton, Frank T. 1985. "Data Mining as an Industry." *Review of Economics and Statistics* 67 (Feb.): 124–27.

———. 1988. "The Significance of Significance: Rhetorical Aspects of Statistical Hypothesis Testing in Economics." In *The Consequences of Economic Rhetoric*, edited by A. Klamer, D. N. McCloskey, and R. M. Solow, 163–83. Cambridge: Cambridge University Press.

Depew, David, and Bruce Weber. 1996. *Darwinism Evolving: Systems Dynamics and the Genealogy of Natural Selection*. Cambridge: MIT Press.

Desmond, Adrian. 1976. *Hot-Blooded Dinosaurs: A Revolution in Paleontology*. New York: Dial Press.

Diamond, Arthur M. Jr., and David M. Levy. 1994. "The Metrics of Style: Adam Smith Teaches Efficient Rhetoric." *Economic Inquiry* 32 (Jan.): 138–47.

Dimand, Mary Ann, Robert W. Dimand, and Evelyn Forget, eds. 1996. *Women of Value: Feminist Essays on the History of Women in Economics*. Aldershot: Elgar.

Elster, Jon. 1978. *Logic and Society: Contradictions and Possible Worlds*. New York: Wiley.

Fama, Eugene, and Merton Miller. 1972. *The Theory of Finance*. New York: Holt, Rinehart.

Farley, John, and Gerald L. Geison. 1974. "Science, Politics and Spontaneous Generation in Nineteenth-Century France: The Pasteur-Pouchet Debate." *Bulletin of the History of Medicine* 48:161–98.

Feige, Edgar. 1975. "The Consequences of Journal Editorial Policies and a Suggestion for Revision." *Journal of Political Economy* 83 (Dec.): 1291–96.

Feyerabend, Paul. 1978. *Science in a Free Society*. London: NLB.

———. 1987. *Farewell to Reason*. New York: Verso.

Feynman, Richard, as told to R. Leighton. 1985. *"Surely You're Joking, Mr. Feynman!" Adventures of a Curious Character*. Edited by E. Hutchings. New York: W. W. Norton.

Fisher, Franklin M. 1989. "Games Economists Play: A Noncooperative View." *RAND Journal of Economics* 20 (spring): 113–24.

Fleck, Ludwig. [1935] 1979. *Genesis and Development of a Scientific Fact*. Edited by T. J. Trenn and R. K. Merton. Foreword by Thomas Kuhn. Chicago: University of Chicago Press.

Fogel, Robert W. 1964. *Railroads and American Economic Growth: Essays in Econometric History*. Baltimore: Johns Hopkins University Press.

———. 1979. "Notes on the Social Saving Controversy." *Journal of Economic History* 39 (Mar.): 1–54.

———. 1986. "Nutrition and the Decline in Mortality since 1700: Some Additional Preliminary Findings." National Bureau of Economic Research Working Paper no. 1802, Cambridge, Mass.

———. 1994. *Without Consent or Contract: The Rise and Fall of American Slavery*. New York: Norton.

Fogel, Robert W., and G. R. Elton. 1983. *Which Road to the Past? Two Views of History*. New Haven and London: Yale University Press.

Fogel, Robert W., and Stanley Engerman. 1974. *Time on the Cross: The Economics of American Negro Slavery.* Boston: Little, Brown.

Frank, Robert. *Passions within Reason: The Strategic Role of the Emotions.* New York: Norton.

Freedman, David, Robert Pisani, and Roger Purves. 1980. *Statistics.* New York: Norton.

Frey, Bruno S., Felix Oberholzer-Gee, and Reiner Eichenberger. 1996. "The Old Lady Visits Your Back Yard: A Tale of Morals and Markets." *Journal of Political Economy* 104, no. 6: 1297–1313.

Frey, Bruno S., Werner Pommerehne, and Friedrich Scheider. 1984. "Consensus and Dissension among Economists: An Empirical Inquiry. *American Economic Review* 74 (Dec.): 986–94.

Friedman, Milton. 1962. *Price Theory, A Provisional Text.* Chicago: Aldine.

———. "The Methodology of Positive Economics." 1953. In *Essays in Positive Economics.* Chicago: University of Chicago Press.

———. 1957. *A Theory of the Consumption Function.* NBER. Princeton: Princeton University Press.

Gerschenkron, Alexander. 1962. *Economic Backwardness in Historical Perspective: A Book of Essays.* Cambridge, Mass.: Harvard University Press.

———. 1970. *Europe in the Russian Mirror.* Cambridge, Mass.: Harvard University Press.

———. 1989. *Bread and Democracy in Germany.* Ithaca: Cornell University Press.

Gilman, Charlotte Perkins. 1898. *Women and Economics.* Boston: Small, Maynard.

Goldin, Claudia. 1992. *Understanding the Gender Gap: An Economic History of American Women.* New York: Oxford University Press.

———. 1998. "The Economist as Detective." In *Passion and Craft: Economists at Work,* edited by M. Szenberg. Ann Arbor: University of Michigan Press.

Goldin, Claudia, and Hugh Rockoff, eds. 1992. *Strategic Factors in Nineteenth-Century American Economic History.* Chicago: University of Chicago Press.

Gould, Stephen Jay. 1987. *Time's Arrow, Time's Cycle: Myth and Metaphor in the Discovery of Geological Time.* Cambridge, Mass.: Harvard University Press.

Granger, Clive. 1994. "A Review of Some Recent Textbooks of Econometrics." *Journal of Economic Literature* 32 (Mar.): 115–22.

Griliches, Zvi. 1976. "Automobile Prices Revisited: Extensions of the Hedonic Hypothesis." In *Household Production and Consumption,* edited by N. E. Terleckyj. Studies in Income and Wealth, vol. 40. New York: National Bureau of Economics Research.

Guthrie, W. K. C. *The Sophists.* Cambridge: Cambridge University Press, 1971.

Hahn, Frank. 1984. *Equilibrium and Macroeconomics.* Oxford: Basil Blackwell.

Halmos, Paul R. 1973. "How to Write Mathematics." In *How to Write Mathematics,* edited by Norman Steenrod and others, 19–48. Providence, R.I.: American Mathematical Society.

———. 1985. *I Want to Be a Mathematician: An Automathography.* New York: Springer Verlag.

Harding, Sandra. 1990. *The Science Question in Feminism.* Ithaca: Cornell University Press.

Harré, Rom. 1986. *Varieties of Realism: A Rationale for the Natural Sciences.* Oxford: Basil Blackwell.

Hayek, Friedrich. 1944. *The Road to Serfdom.* Chicago: University of Chicago Press.

Heilbroner, Robert. 1953. *The Worldly Philosophers.* New York: Simon and Schuster.

———. 1986 [1988]. "The Murky Economists." *New York Review of Books,* Apr. 24. Reprinted with revisions in *Consequences of Economic Rhetoric,* edited by Arjo Klamer and others, 38–43. New York: Cambridge University Press.

Hesse, Mary B. 1963. *Models and Analogies in Science.* London: Sheed and Ward.

Hoffer, Eric. 1979. *Before the Sabbath.* New York: Harper and Row.

———. 1983. *Truth Imagined.* New York: Harper and Row.

Hoyt, Elizabeth. 1938. *Consumption in Our Society.* New York: McGraw-Hill.

Johnson, Michael. 1990. *Business Buzzwords: The Tough New Jargon and Modern Business.* New York and Oxford: Basil Blackwood.

Judd, Kenneth L. 1998. *Numerical Methods in Economics.* Cambridge, Mass.: MIT Press.

Keller, Evelyn Fox. 1983. *A Feeling for the Organism: The Life and Work of Barbara McClintock.* New York: Free Press.

———. 1985. *Reflections on Gender and Science.* New Haven: Yale University Press.

Kendall, M. G., and A. Stuart. 1951. *Advanced Theory of Statistics,* vol. 2, 3d ed. London: Griffin.

Kerferd, G. B. 1981. *The Sophistic Movement.* Cambridge: Cambridge University Press.

Keynes, J. M. 1936. *The General Theory of Employment, Interest and Money.* London: Macmillan.

Kirzner, Israel. 1978. *Competition and Entrepreneurship.* Chicago: University of Chicago Press.

Klamer, Arjo. ed. 1996. *Value of Culture: On the Relationship between Economics and the Arts.* Ann Arbor: University of Michigan Press; Amsterdam: Amsterdam University Press.

———. 1984. *Conversations with Economists.* Savage, Md: Rowman and Littlefield.

Klamer, Arjo, and David C. Colander. 1990. *The Making of an Economist.* Boulder: Westview.

Klein, Lawrence. 1985. *Economic Theory and Econometrics.* Jaime Marquez, ed. London: Basil Blackwell.

Koopmans, Tjalling. 1957. *Three Essays on the State of Economic Science.* New York: McGraw-Hill.

Kregel, J. A., ed. 1989. *Recollections of Economists.* 2 vols. New York: New York University Press.

Kresge, Stephen, and Leif Wener, eds. 1994. *Hayek on Hayek.* Chicago: University of Chicago Press.

Kruskal, William H. 1978a. "Formulas, Numbers, Words: Statistics Is Prose."

American Scholar 47 (spring): 223–29. Reprinted in *New Directions for Methodology in Social and Behavioral Sciences,* edited by D. Fiske. San Francisco: Jossey-Bass, 1981.

———. 1978b. "Significance, Tests of." *International Encyclopedia of Statistics.* New York: Macmillan.

Kuhn, Thomas. 1970. *The Structure of Scientific Revolutions,* 2d ed. Chicago: University of Chicago Press.

———. 1977. *The Essential Tension: Selected Studies in Scientific Tradition and Change.* Chicago: University of Chicago Press.

Kurtz, A. K., and H. A. Edgerton. 1939. *Statistical Dictionary of Terms and Symbols.* New York: Wiley.

Kyrk, Hazel. 1933. *Economic Problems of the Family.* New York: Harpers.

Laband, David N., and Christopher N. Taylor. 1992. "The Impact of Bad Writing in Economics." *Economic Inquiry* 30 (Oct.): 673–99.

LaFolette, Marcel. 1993. *Stealing into Print.* Berkeley and Los Angeles: University of California Press.

Lakatos, Imre. 1976. *Proofs and Refutations: The Logic of Mathematical Discovery.* Cambridge: Cambridge University Press.

Landsburg, Stephen. 1997. *Fair Play: What Your Child Can Teach You about Economics, Values, and the Meaning of Life.* New York: Free Press.

Lanham, Richard A. 1993. *The Electronic Word: Democracy, Technology, and the Arts.* Chicago and London: University of Chicago Press.

Laslett, Barbara. 1990. "Unfeeling Knowledge: Emotion and Objectivity in the History of Sociology." *Sociological Forum* 5 (Sept.): 413–33.

Leamer, Edward. 1978. *Specification Searches: Ad Hoc Inferences with Nonexperimental Data.* New York: Wiley.

———. 1983. "Let's Take the Con Out of Econometrics." *American Economic Review* 73 (Mar.): 31–43.

Leontief, W. 1982. "Letter: Academic Economics." *Science* 217:104, 107.

Levi, Primo, and Tullio Regge. 1992. *Conversations.* Translated by R. Rosenthal. Harmondsworth: Penguin.

Levy, Steven. 1994. "Dr. Edelman's Brain." *New Yorker,* May 2, 62–73.

Lewis, C. S. 1942. *The Screwtape Letters.* London: Geoffrey Bles.

———. 1952. *Mere Christianity.* New York: Simon and Schuster.

———. 1956. *Surprised by Joy.* New York: Harcourt, Brace.

Lovell, Michael C. 1983. "Data Mining." *Review of Economics and Statistics* 45 (Feb.): 1–12.

Mallove, Eugene. 1991. *Fire from Ice: Searching for the Truth behind the Cold Fusion Furor.* New York: Wiley.

Mann, Thomas. [1901] 1994. *Buddenbrooks: The Decline of a Family.* Translated by John E. Woods. New York: Knopf..

Marks, Jonathan. 1992. "Scientific Misconduct: Where 'Just Say No' Fails." *American Scientist* 81 (July–Aug.): 380–82.

Marschall, Laurence A. 1988. *The Supernova Story.* New York: Plenum Press.

Marshall, Alfred. 1890. *Principles of Economics.* London: Macmillan.

Mayer, Thomas. 1975. "Selecting Economic Hypotheses by Goodness of Fit." *Economic Journal* 85 (Dec.): 877–83.

———. 1980. "Economics as a Hard Science: Realistic Goal or Wishful Thinking?" *Economic Inquiry* 18 (Apr.): 165–78.

McCawley, James D. 1981. *Everything That Linguists Have Always Wanted to Know about Logic (but Were Ashamed to Ask)*. Chicago: University of Chicago Press.

McCloskey, Deirdre N. 1973. *Economic Maturity and Entrepreneurial Decline: British Iron and Steel, 1870–1913*. Cambridge, Mass.: Harvard University Press.

———. 1983. "The Rhetoric of Economics." *Journal of Economic Literature* 31 (June): 482–517.

———. 1985a. "The Loss Function Has Been Mislaid: The Rhetoric of Significance Tests." *American Economic Review* 75 supp. (May): 201–5.

———. 1985b. *The Applied Theory of Price*, 2d ed. New York: Macmillan.

———. 1985c. *The Rhetoric of Economics*. Madison: University of Wisconsin; 2d rev. ed. 1998.

———. 1986. *The Writing of Economics*. New York: Macmillan; revised as *Economical Writing*. Prospect Heights, Ill.: Waveland Press, 1999.

———. 1989. "The Open Fields of England: Rent, Risk, and the Rate of Interest, 1300–1815." In *Markets in History: Economic Studies of the Past*, edited by David Galenson, 5–51. New York: Cambridge University Press.

———. 1990. *If You're So Smart: The Narrative of Economic Expertise*. Chicago: University of Chicago Press.

———. 1991. "Economic Science: A Search through the Hyperspace of Assumptions?" *Methodus* 3 (June): 6–16.

———. 1994a. *Knowledge and Persuasion in Economics*. Cambridge: Cambridge University Press.

———. 1994b. "Bourgeois Virtue." *American Scholar* 63, no. 2 (spring): 177–91.

———. 1996. *The Vices of Economists; The Virtues of the Bourgeoisie*. Ann Arbor: University of Michigan Press; Amsterdam: University of Amsterdam Press.

———. 1999a. *Crossing: A Memoir*. Chicago: University of Chicago Press.

———. 1999b. *Economical Writing*, 2d ed. Prospect Heights, Ill.: Waveland.

———, ed. 1971. *Essays on a Mature Economy: Britain after 1840*. London: Methuen.

McCloskey, Deirdre N., and Stephen Ziliak. 1996. "The Standard Error of Regression." *Journal of Economic Literature* 34 (Mar.): 97–114.

Meehl, Paul E. "Theory Testing in Psychology and Physics: A Methodological Paradox." *Philosophy of Science* (June 1967): 34, 103–15; reprinted in Morrison and Henkel 1970.

Mills, C. Wright. 1959. "On Intellectual Craftsmanship." In *The Sociological Imagination*. New York: Oxford University Press.

Morrison, Denton E., and Ramon E. Henkel. 1969. "Significance Tests Reconsidered." *American Sociologist* (May 1969): 4, 131–40; reprinted in Morrison and Henkel 1970.

———, eds. 1970. *The Significance Test Controversy—A Reader*. Chicago: Aldine.

Mulkay, Michael. 1985. *The Word and the World: Explorations in the Form of Sociological Analysis*. London: Allen and Unwin.

Myers, Gerald E. 1986. *William James: His Life and Thought.* New Haven: Yale University Press.

Nelson, John, Allan Megill, and D. N. McCloskey, eds. 1987. *The Rhetoric of the Human Sciences: Language and Argument in Scholarship and Public Affairs.* Rhetoric of the Human Sciences series. Madison: University of Wisconsin Press.

Nelson, Robert H. 1991. *Reaching for Heaven and Earth: The Theological Meanng of Economics.* Savage, Md.: Rowman and Littlefield.

Neyman, Jerzy, and E. S. Pearson. 1933. "On the Problem of the Most Efficient Tests of Statistical Hypotheses." *Philosophical Transactions of the Royal Society* A231:289–337.

Orcutt, Guy H., and others. 1961. *Microanalysis of Socioeconomic Systems: A Simulation Study.* New York: Harper Bros.

Pielou, E. C. 1992. *After the Ice Age: The Return of Life to Glaciated North America.* Chicago: University of Chicago Press.

Plimpton, George. 1997. *Women Writers at Work: The Paris Review Interviews.* New York: Random House.

Polanyi, Karl. 1944. *The Great Transformation.* Boston: Beacon.

Polanyi, Michael. 1946. *Science, Faith, and Society.* London: Geoffrey Cumberlege.

———. 1962. *Personal Knowledge: Towards a Post-Critical Philosophy.* Chicago: University of Chicago Press.

———. 1966b. *The Tacit Dimension.* Garden City, N.J.: Doubleday.

Pool, Robert. 1989. "Strange Bedfellows." *Science* 245 (Aug. 18): 700–703.

Prince, Gerald. 1973. *A Grammar of Stories.* Paris: Mouton.

Putnam, Hilary. 1990. *Realism with a Human Face.* Edited by James Conant. Cambridge, Mass.: Harvard University Press.

Rachels, James. 1993. *The Elements of Moral Philosophy,* 2d ed. New York: McGraw-Hill.

Reid, Constance. 1976. *Courant in Gottingen and New York: The Story of an Improbable Mathematician.* New York, Heidelberg, and Berlin: Springer.

Reid, Margaret. 1962. *Housing and Income.* Chicago: University of Chicago Press.

Root-Bernstein, Robert. 1983. "Mendel and Methodology." *History of Science* 21 (Sept.): 275–95.

Rorty, Amelie Oksenberg. 1983. "Experiments in Philosophic Genre: Descartes' Meditations." *Critical Inquiry* 9 (Mar.): 545–65.

Rorty, Richard. 1979. *Philosophy and the Mirror of Nature.* Princeton: Princeton University Press.

Rosovsky, Henry, ed. *Industrialization in Two Systems.* New York: Wiley.

Samuelson, Paul A. 1947. *Foundations of Economic Analysis.* Cambridge: Harvard University Press.

Sayre, Anne. 1975. *Rosalind Franklin and DNA.* New York: Norton.

Schelling, Thomas. 1978. *Micromotives and Macrobehavior.* New York: Norton.

Schopenhauer, Arthur. 1851 [1970]. *Essays and Aphorisms.* Translated by R. J. Hollingdale. Harmondsworth: Penguin.

Schultz, Theodore. 1988. "Are University Scholars and Scientists Free Agents?" *Southern Humanities Review* 22 (summer): 251–60.

Schumpeter, Joseph. 1942. *Capitalism, Socialism and Democracy.* New York: Harper Bros.

———. 1954. *History of Economic Analysis.* New York: Oxford University Press.

Selzer, John L., ed. 1993. *Understanding Scientific Prose.* Rhetoric of the Human Sciences series. Madison: University of Wisconsin Press.

Sen, Amartya. 1970a. "The Impossibility of a Paretian Liberal." *Journal of Political Economy* 72 (Jan.–Feb.): 152–57.

———. 1970b. *Collective Choice and Social Welfare.* Edinburgh: Oliver and Boyd.

———. 1987. *On Ethics and Economics.* Oxford: Basil Blackwell.

Siegfried, John, W. Lee Hansen, Robin Bartlett, Allen Kelley, D. N. McCloskey, and Thomas Tietenberg, "The Economics Major: Can and Should We Do Better than a B–?" *American Economic Review* 81 (May): 20–25.

Simon, Herbert. 1996. *Models of My Life.* Cambridge, Mass.: MIT Press.

Skidelsky, Robert. 1986. *Hopes Betrayed: 1883–1920.* London: Macmillan.

———. 1992. *Economist as Savior: 1920–1937.* London: Macmillan.

Smith, Adam. [1776] 1979. *An Inquiry into the Nature and Causes of the Wealth of Nations,* vol. 1. Glasgow Edition. Edited by R. H. Campbell and A. S. Skinner. Oxford: Clarendon Press.

———. *Theory of Moral Sentiments.* 1759 (6th ed. 1790). Glasgow Edition. Edited by D. D. Raphael and A. L. MacFie. Oxford: Clarendon Press.

Stein, Herbert. 1986. *Washington Bedtime Stories: The Politics of Money and Jobs.* New York: Free Press.

Stewart, Ian. 1990. *Does God Play Dice? The New Mathematics of Chaos.* Harmondsworth: Penguin.

Strunk, William, Jr., and E. B. White. 1959. *The Elements of Style.* New York: Macmillan.

Summerfield, Michael. 1991. *Global Geomorphology: An Introduction to the Study of Landforms.* London: Longman.

Sylla, Richard, and Gianni Toniolo, eds. 1991. *Patterns of European Industrialization.* New York: Routledge.

Tannen, Deborah. 1994. "Interpreting Interruption in Conversation." *Gender and Discourse,* 53–83. Oxford: Oxford University Press.

Thomas, Lewis. 1983. *Late Night Thoughts in Listening to Mahler's Ninth Symphony.* New York: Viking Press.

Thompson, William (Lord Kelvin). 1883. "Electrical Units of Measurement" (1883), reprinted in *Popular Lectures and Addresses,* vol. 1 (London, 1888–89).

Thurow, Lester. 1985. *The Zero-Sum Solution: Building a World-Class American Economy.* New York: Simon and Schuster.

Tinbergen, Jan. 1952. *On the Theory of Economic Policy.* Amsterdam: North-Holland.

Tukey, John. 1986. "Sunset Salvo." *The American Statistician.* 40 (Feb.): 72–76.

Tullock, Gordon. 1959. "Publication Decisions and Tests of Significance: A Comment." *Journal of the American Statistical Association* 54 (Sept.): 593.

Ulam, Stanislav. 1976. *Adventures of a Mathematician.* New York: Schribners.

Wald, Abraham. 1939. "Contributions to the Theory of Statistical Estimation and Testing Hypotheses." *Annals of Mathematical Statistics* 10 (Dec.): 299–326.

Weinberg, Stephen. 1982. "Beautiful Theories." MS.

White, Hayden. 1981. "The Value of Narrativity in the Representation of Reality." *On Narrative,* edited by W. J. T. Mitchell, 1–24. Chicago: University of Chicago Press.

Wilson, Edward O. 1994. *Naturalist.* Washington, D.C.: Island Press.

Woodruff, Jay. 1993. *A Piece of Work: Five Writers Discuss Their Revisions.* Iowa City: University of Iowa Press.

Zecher, J. R., and Deirdre N. McCloskey. 1984. "The Success of Purchasing Power Parity." In *Retrospective on the Classical Gold Standard,* edited by M. D. Bordo and A. J. Schwartz. Chicago: University of Chicago Press.

Index of Names

Abramowitz, Moses, 83
Adelman, Irma, 261, 264
Alchian, Armen, 15, 24, 28–31, 47, 60,
    131, 169, 178
Allais, Maurice, 59
Allen, William, 29
Allen, Woody, 182
Almon, Clopper, 47, 263
Amariglio, Jack, 112
Ames, Edward, 188
Anderson, Philip, 216
Arendt, Hannah, 67
Aristotle, 11, 12, 50, 118, 185
Ark, Bart van, 229
Arrow, Kenneth, 26, 61, 101, 143, 172,
    177, 188, 199, 201–2, 212, 216,
    220–25, 238–39, 242, 244, 251
Ashenfelter, Orly, 137
Atwood, Margaret, 132
Auden, W. H., 34, 168
Auerbach, Alan, 152
Austen, Jane, 51, 131, 169
Austin, J. L., 171
Ayittey, George, 119

Backhouse, Roger, 240, 244
Bacon, Francis, 104, 127, 233
Baker, Keith, 71
Balch, Emily Greene, 41
Baldwin, Richard, 229, 230
Ballard, C. L., 261
Baltimore, David, 55
Barnes, Barry, 54
Barro, Robert, 175
Bartlett, Robin, 5
Bates, Robert, 236
Batra, Ravi, 35
Bauer, P. T., 116–20, 174
Becker, Gary, 13, 25, 40, 129, 172, 178

Becker, Howard, 109
Bentham, Jeremy, 6, 13, 16, 36, 38, 129
Berg, Maxine, 40
Berger, John, 171
Bergmann, Barbara, 5, 29, 46, 47, 97,
    154, 220, 253–64
Bergmann, Gustav, 67
Billig, Michael, 127
Blau, Francine, 6
Blaug, Mark, 240, 244
Bloch, Marc, 87
Bloom, Allan, 75
Boltzmann, Ludwig, 250
Booth, Wayne, 34, 49–51, 123, 127,
    171, 182
Borcherding, Thomas, 131
Boring, Edwin, 202
Borts, George, 154
Bourbaki, Nicholas, 146, 216
Bower, Richard, 178–81
Brady, Dorothy, 39
Brenner, Reuven, 4
Broad, William, 52
Brock, William, 61, 212
Brolin, Brent, 171
Brooks, Peter, 123
Brown, Vivienne, 129
Bruner, Jerome, 110
Bruner, Karl, 117
Buchanan, James, 15, 22–27, 60, 109,
    143, 154, 240, 244
Burke, Edmund, 152
Burke, Kenneth, 170

Cagan, Phillip, 176
Campbell, J. Y., 261
Card, David, 207
Carter, Susan, 39
Cato the Elder, 119–20, 127